WHEN SAN FRANCISCO BURNED

A Photographic Memoir of the Great San Francisco
Earthquake and Fire of 1906

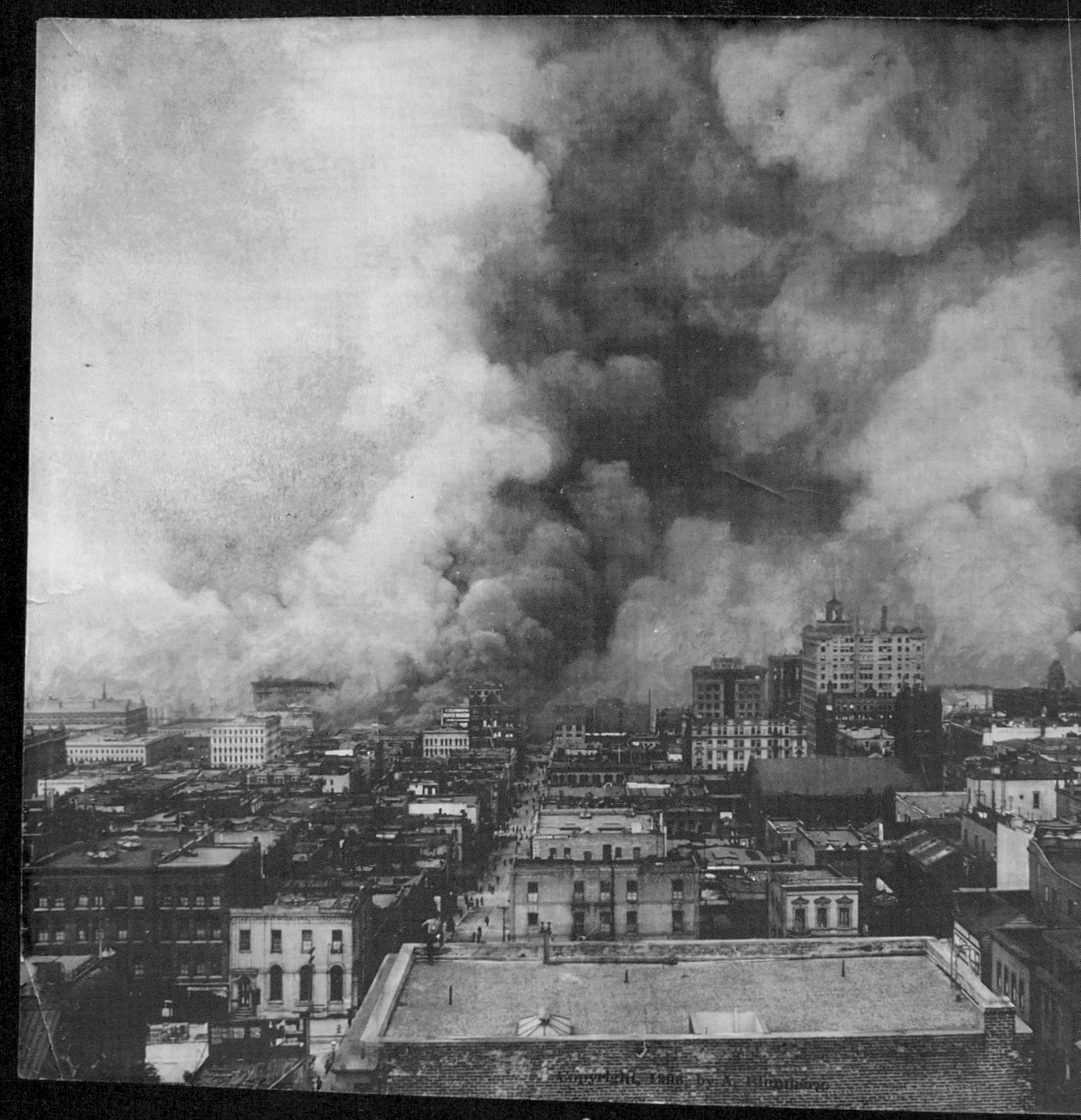

Copyright, 1906, by A. Blumberg

Burning of San Francisco - Wh

WHEN SAN FRANCISCO BURNED

A Photographic Memoir of the
Great San Francisco Earthquake
and Fire of 1906

by

Douglas L. Gist

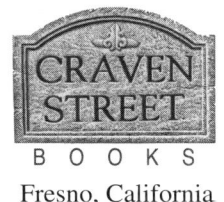

CRAVEN STREET BOOKS

B O O K S

Fresno, California

When San Francisco Burned:
A Photographic Memoir of the Great San Francisco Earthquake and Fire of 1906

Published by Craven Street Books
An imprint of Linden Publishing
2006 South Mary Street, Fresno, California 93721
(559) 233-6633 / (800) 345-4447
CravenStreetBooks.com

Craven Street Books and Colophon are trademarks of
Linden Publishing, Inc.

ISBN 978-1-61035-245-1

135798642

Printed in the United States of America
on acid-free paper.

Library of Congress Cataloging-in-Publication Data

Names: Gist, Douglas L.
Title: When San Francisco burned : a photographic memoir of the Great San
    Francisco Earthquake and Fire of 1906 / by Douglas L. Gist.
Description: Fresno, CA : Craven Street Books, 2016. | Based on the
    photographic album of Louis P. Selby. | Includes bibliographical
    references and index.
Identifiers: LCCN 2015049124 | ISBN 9781610352451 (paperback : acid-free
    paper)
Subjects: LCSH: San Francisco Earthquake and Fire, Calif., 1906--Pictorial
    works. | Selby, Louis P.--Photographic collections. |
    Disasters--California--San Francisco--History--20th century--Pictorial
    works. | Earthquakes--California--San Francisco--History--20th
    century--Pictorial works. | Fires--California--San
    Francisco--History--20th century--Pictorial works. | San Francisco
    (Calif.)--History--20th century--Pictorial works.
Classification: LCC F869.S357 G57 2016 | DDC 979.4/61051--dc23
LC record available at http://lccn.loc.gov/2015049124

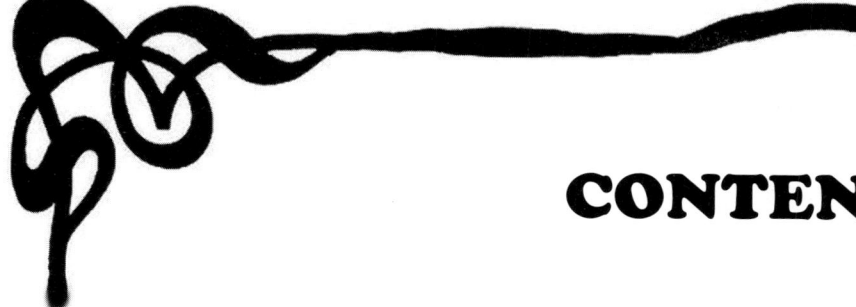
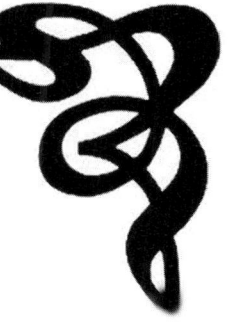

CONTENTS

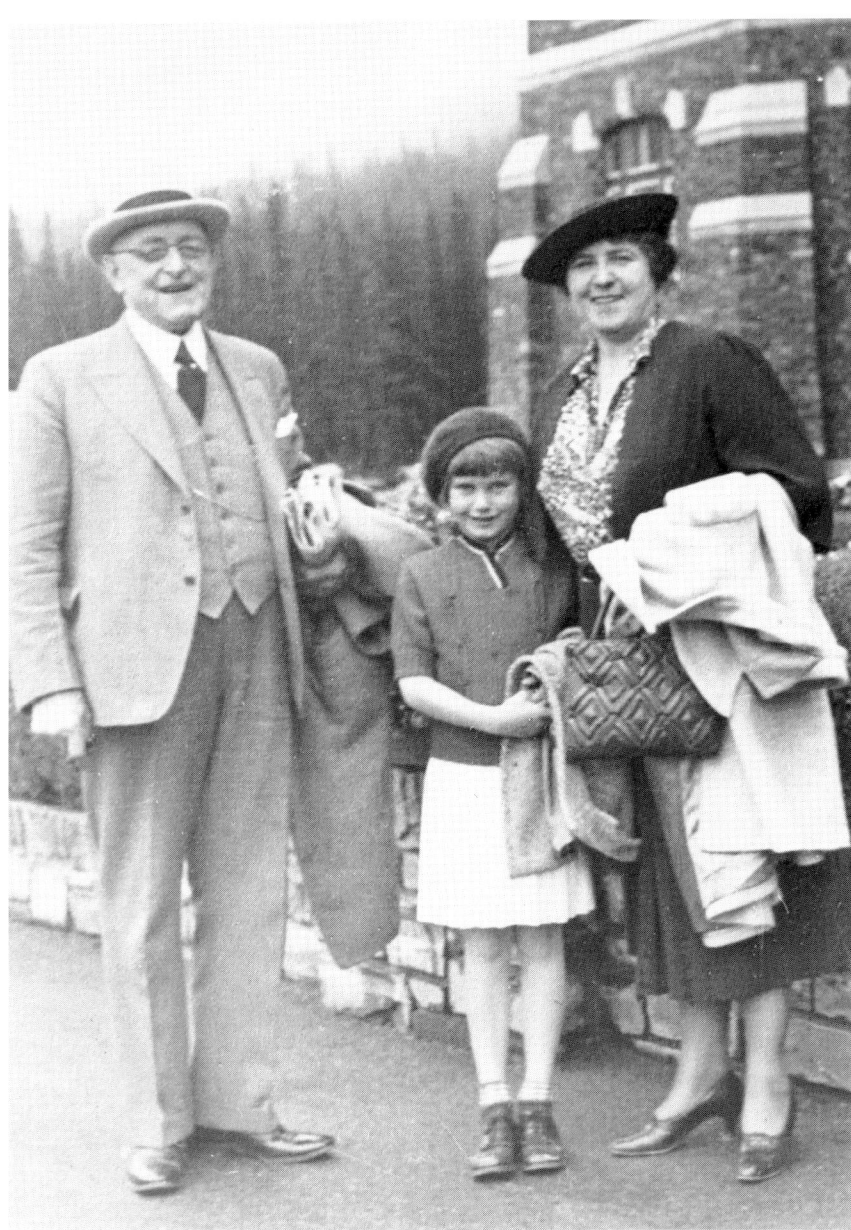

*Louis, Genevieve and Eleanor Selby
vacationing at Banff, 1930s.*

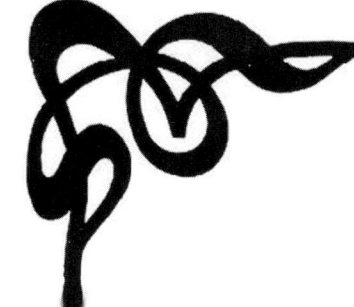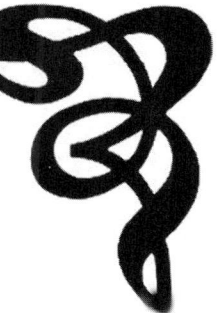

DEDICATION

This book was made possible by two people. I wish they were still here with us, and I must dedicate it to both of them.

The first is Louis P. Selby, my maternal grandfather, whom I never had the pleasure of knowing. Thanks to this project, I now feel quite close to him. Louis Selby was a businessman who operated in San Francisco and Oakland with his brothers. A substantial portion of the family's operations were destroyed by the 1906 earthquake and fire. The brothers ignored their losses long enough to wander the streets and photographically record the unfolding disaster. The resulting album created by Louis forms the basis of this book.

The second person is Eleanor Selby Gist, my dear mom. For many years, she was my motivation to complete this book. In her last months, I worked on this book while caring for her and spending time with her. Sadly, Mom passed away only a few weeks after Linden Publishing accepted this book for publication. Just days before her death, she asked me how long it would take for the book to appear, and was so discouraged when I said it would take at least a year. We lost Mom on June 14, 2011, a day I'll never forget. I wish she could have seen the completed book. However, I'm sure she's looking down now in approval.

When San
Francisco
Burned

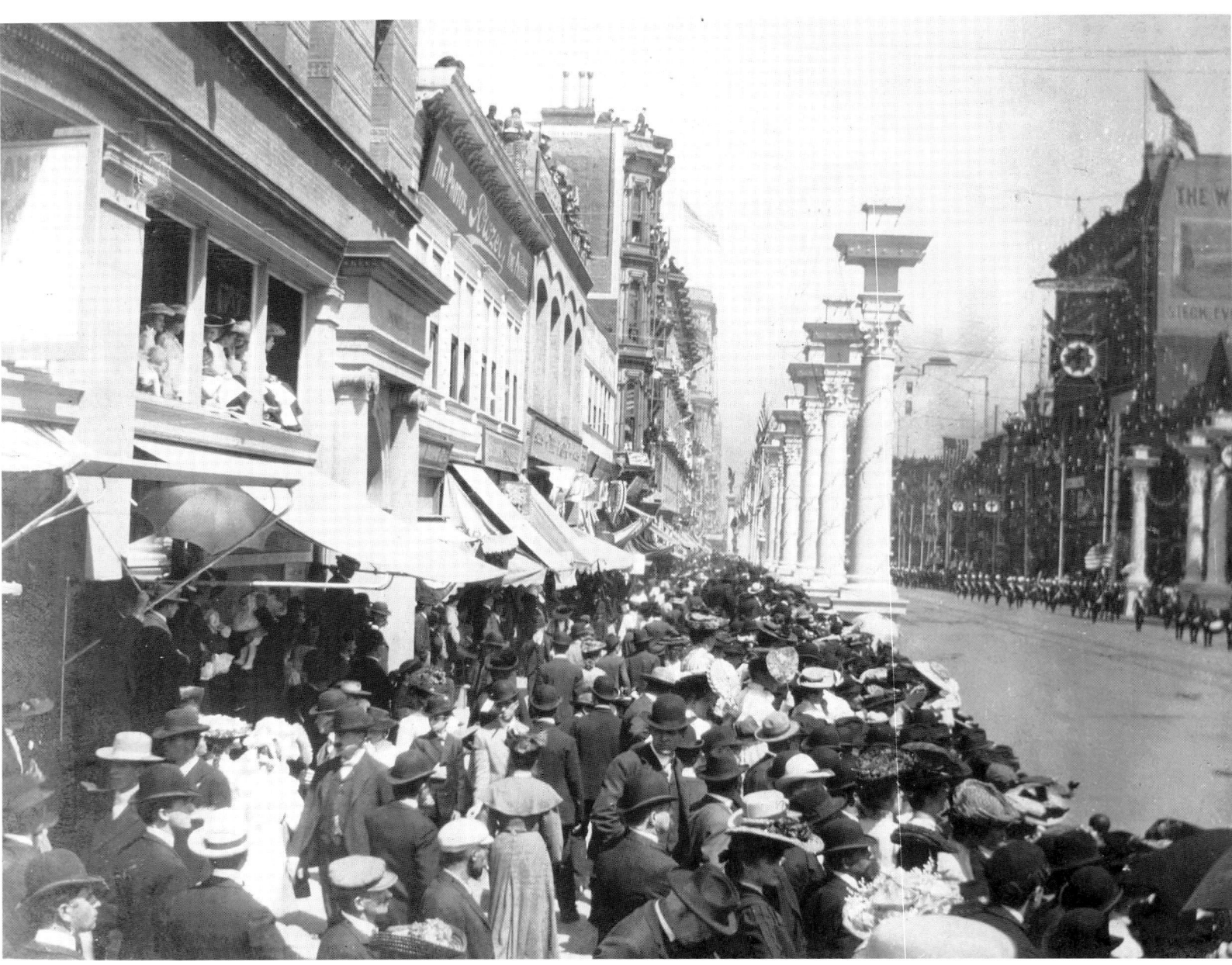

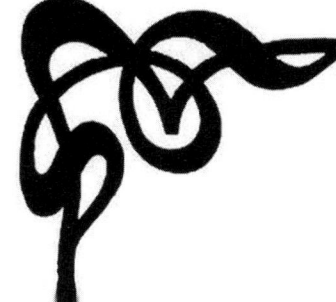
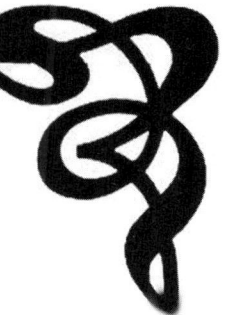

ACKNOWLEDGMENTS

A book such as this, with so many faded and damaged images, requires major work to bring its vintage content back to life for publication. I scanned and adjusted the photos back in 2004, when I first began creating this book, but technology has improved greatly since that time. It became necessary to rescan the album pages to achieve the best quality possible. I enlisted the help of my daughter, Megan Gist, in this undertaking. She has had a flair for photography for years and was familiar enough with the images to jump in where I left off and get the job done. She spent countless hours by my side as we made this book become a reality. Thank you for your help, Meg. It was fun working on this family project with you.

I would also like to mention my early conversations with Vicky Vaughn Shea, owner of Ponderosa Pine Design. Vicky, a skilled book designer and acquaintance from Reno, Nevada, was kind enough to meet with me and provide priceless suggestions on moving the book forward.

I want to acknowledge Linden Publishing's Kent Sorsky for his guidance and faith in this project as well. Thank you for taking our project out to the world so that others may enjoy it.

Opposite: Pre-earthquake and fire view of San Francisco on Parade Day; from the Selby album—see page 55.

FOREWORD

When San Francisco Burned is a valuable new view of the San Francisco earthquake and fire of 1906. Many of the images contained within were sent to me a few years ago by my publisher with a query regarding whether they should pursue this book. Looking at the photos, I was surprised by the fact that I had not seen most of them before. There were only so many photographs taken during those first few days of the disaster, and most are rehashed and have been republished over and over again. This was new. My response was to move forward with it as quickly as possible. I'm delighted to see that the project has been realized.

This photo album is an absolute treasure for those of us who had family in the city on April 18, 1906. My paternal grandfather, a second generation native, was there, as was his extended family. He lost family members in the event. My paternal grandmother and her mother were across the bay in Melrose (now part of Oakland). When I asked my grandfather about it in the 1950s, he just shook his head and said it was bad.

He would say no more. My maternal grandparents had a farm in Hilmar, California, just south of Turlock. My grandmother stated that at night they could see the glow of the fire from their porch.

Given their shared experience, seeing the city through the eyes of Louis Selby and his brothers was to see it through my own family's eyes. These are not "professional" photographs—and that is all the better. Selby had no preconceptions about taking images that would or would not sell. He was simply creating a visual diary of his experience and of what was happening around him to his city.

Much more than a documentation of the disaster's massive property destruction, these photographs vividly portray the impact to people: There are shots of dead people, of dead horses and cows, of people stunned by what was happening to them, people pulling themselves up by their bootstraps, and people pitching in wherever they could.

The Selby brothers roamed all over the city, getting shots of the spreading fire, of the migration of people as the fire encroached on their neighborhoods, and of places where they huddled when they thought they were safe. The resilience and generosity of San Franciscans is depicted in photographs of kitchens, stores, and housing which sprung up to assist the afflicted—much sponsored by the U.S. Army & Navy. The shots of the homeless in line for clothing and bread are priceless, as is the image of Mrs. Crocker's free lunch on Union Square. Women cooked on stoves out in the street, the indoor chimneys not being reliable enough to risk another fire. Images of men digging out the survivors and the dead illustrate the determination to rise above the chaos. Human decency was much in evidence, and all—rich or poor—pitched in to do something.

By staying just ahead of the fire, the Selbys produced evocative images that captured the sense of urgency as the flames methodically devoured the city. The photo album's block-by-block views, enhanced by the inclusion of professional or "copyright" photos to fill in the gaps, lend tremendous detail to the overall experience. Looking into the destroyed Emporium or seeing the injured being removed from the back of the Mechanics' Pavilion Hospital while the front was on fire are never to be forgotten images.

In addition to its historic images, this book's "Then and Now" chapter offers an additional treat: a unique photographic comparison of vintage San Francisco with the modern city. Rather than side-by-side images, the author overlays the 1906 photos with recent ones he took on an excursion to the city. This lends an interesting perspective, showing how some vistas have changed but little while others no longer bear much resemblance to what had been. The "Time Line" at the end of the book is an excellent refresher for those of us who may already be familiar with the story of the 1906 disaster, and offers a great introduction for those who are learning. *When San Francisco Burned* is a rare treasure that belongs on the bookshelf of anyone who loves this great city.

—James R. Smith, author of
San Francisco's Lost Landmarks

When San Francisco Burned

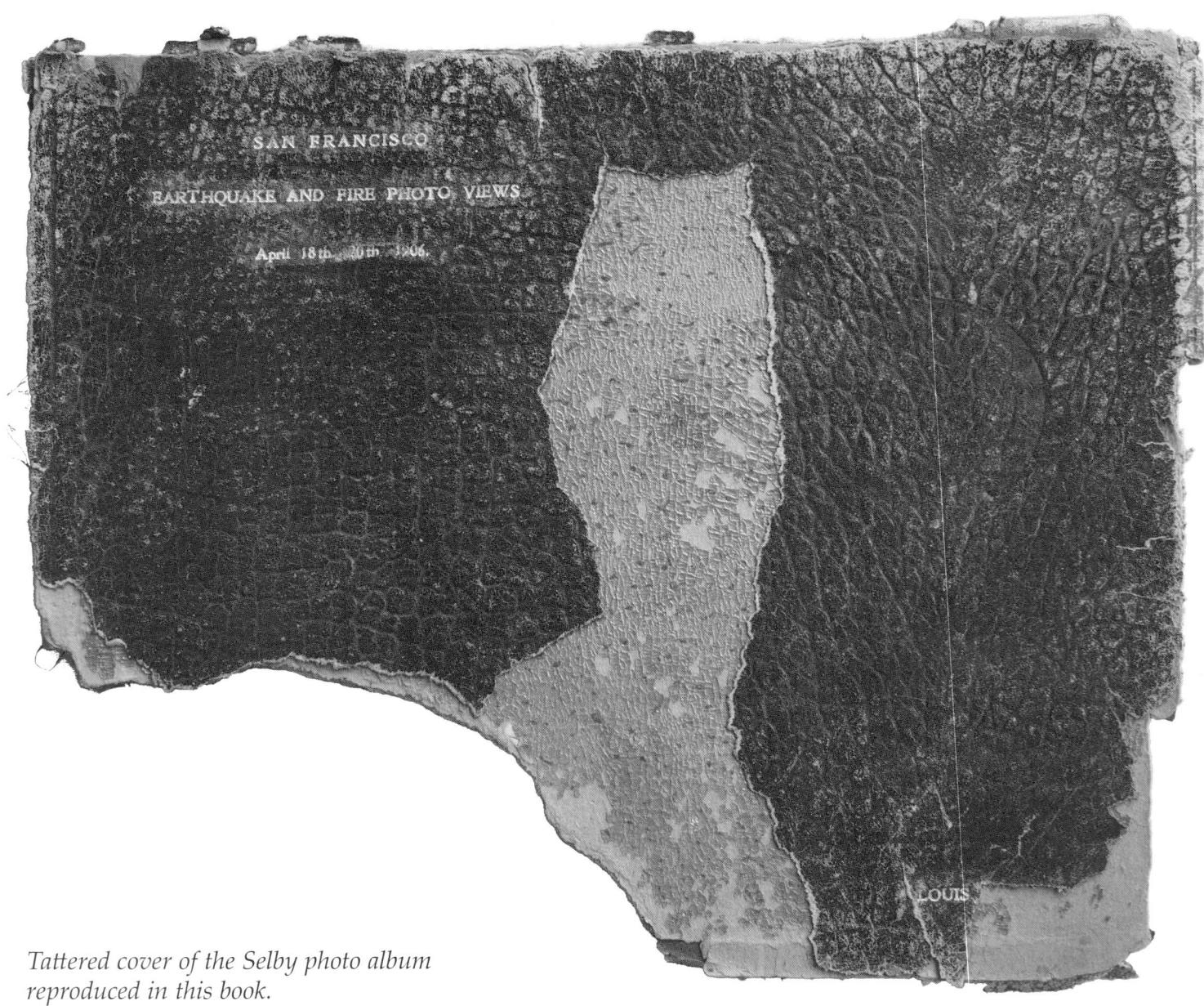

Tattered cover of the Selby photo album reproduced in this book.

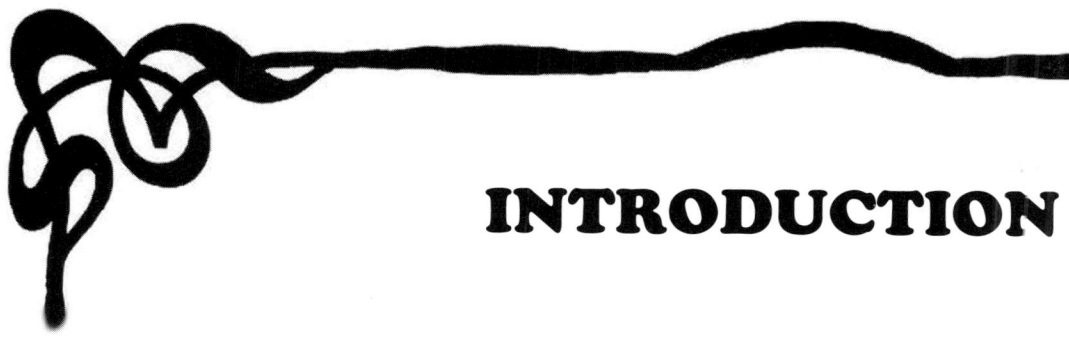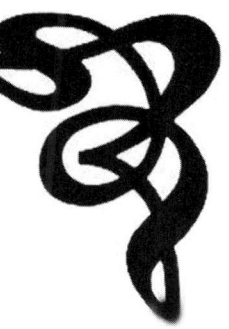

INTRODUCTION

What if you had a treasure to share with the world, a treasure now more than one hundred years old? I have that treasure, and I am about to share it with you.

The 1906 San Francisco earthquake and fire is one of the most notable disasters in history. Photographs and memories of it have surfaced throughout the years, found in locked steamer trunks and home basements, silently forgotten in time.

I am fortunate enough to come from one of those early Bay Area families that kept a record of its 1906 experiences. Along with a few stories passed on from those days, my maternal grandfather, Louis P. Selby, assembled a magnificent album of several hundred photographs documenting this massive tragedy.

Although some of this album's photos were taken by others and copyrighted for commercial sale, many more were taken by Louis Selby, or by his brothers David, Albert, and Walter. Louis took the time to painstakingly paste in the photos and, in his own handwriting, provide captions for most of the images.

My mother, Eleanor Selby Gist, preserved this album in the hope it would be published so others would enjoy and appreciate her father's efforts to document the memories of those fateful days. While growing up, I was long conscious of the animated conversations and amazement that ensued whenever we leafed through the album. We all felt it deserved a larger audience, which it will now achieve.

As I assembled this book from the family archives, I was kept company by several items connected closely to its subject matter. I sat at an oak roll top desk, handmade by San Francisco's George H. Fuller Desk Company and owned by my grandfather, Louis Selby Jr., and later passed on to my father, Walt Gist. It's accompanied by two other items also owned by the men—a matching oak file cabinet and a panoramic photo of the earthquake and fire, showing what San Francisco looked like at 10 a.m. on April 18, 1906, just four hours after the first shock hit. These items now have a place of honor in my den. Could there be any more appropriate memorabilia to have at hand as I created this volume?

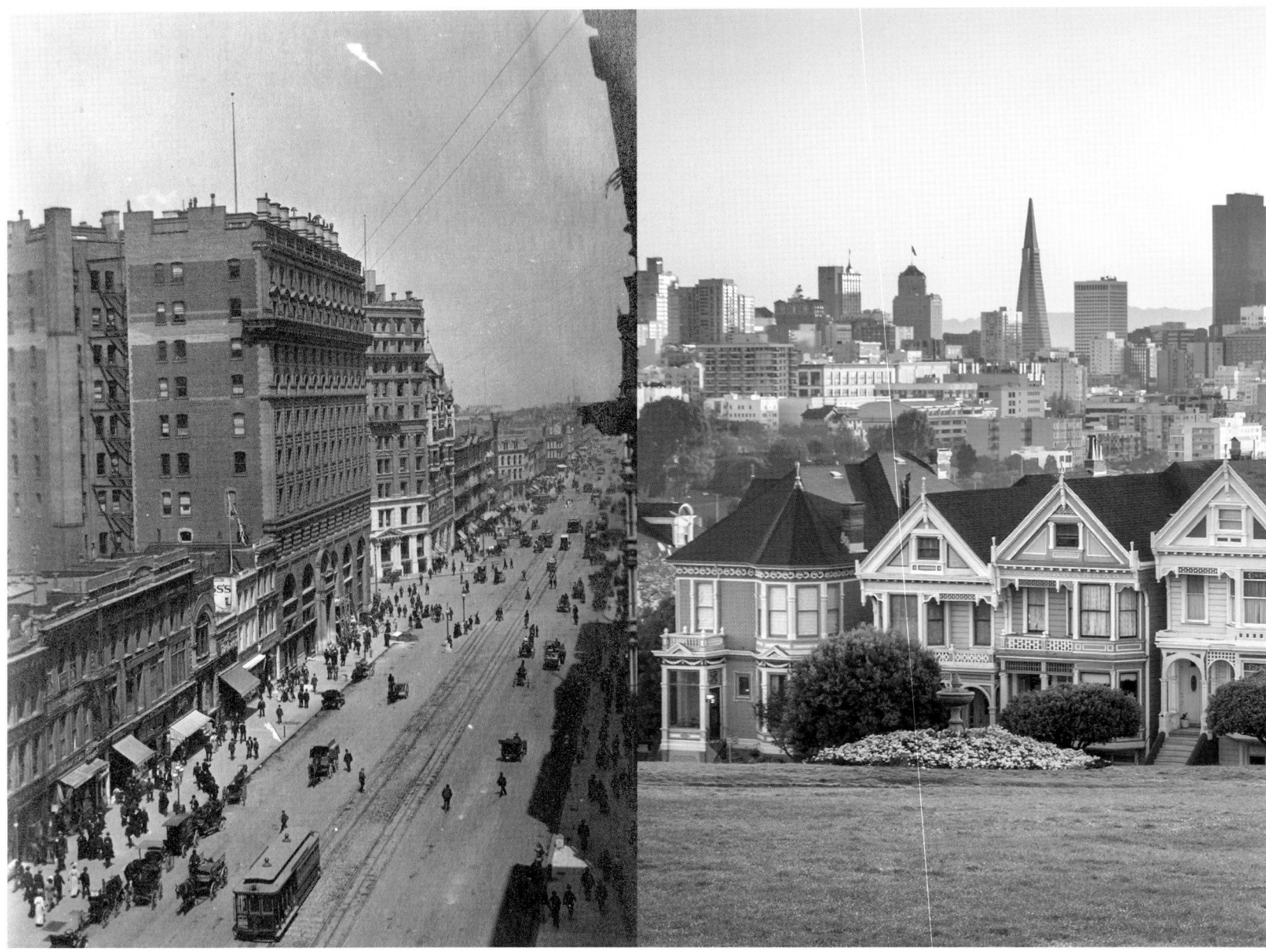

Even more appropriately, as I wrote this introduction on June 22, 2012, at 8:50 p.m., the earth shook beneath my feet. A quake measuring 4.2 on the Richter Scale struck Reno, where I live. There was no damage and no one was hurt, but for a moment, I was taken to that time when San Franciscans had the earth pulled out from under them. For a split second, I was living what my ancestors lived, surrounded by their personal property!

I hope you enjoy what you encounter in the following pages. I'm very pleased to make good on my promise of publishing my grandfather's work. It's been saved all these years just for you.

San Francisco: Then and Now

Just close your eyes for a moment and let San Francisco flow into your imagination. From the moment the first nail was hammered and the first bricks were fired to construct San Francisco, she has been one of the most famous cities in the world. The city is just waking up to the start of a new day. Do you see the steep hills, the cable cars rolling along with bells ringing? Do you smell the aroma of seafood at Fisherman's Wharf? Are you watching the effects of the sunrise on the magnificent Golden Gate Bridge? Perhaps you see the sun as it rises over the East Bay hills. You might be hearing The Animals' 1967 song "San Franciscan Nights" wafting through your speakers, or maybe Tony Bennett's 1962 "I Left My Heart in San Francisco" playing on your radio. Can you hear the ships' horns blow as they pass through the bay?

Today, San Francisco is known across the world as an artsy and progressive city, having been the center of the 1960s flower child movement. It is the city of "coloring outside of the lines" and "the city of acceptance."

Now, let your thoughts of San Francisco drift back in time. Can you hear the sounds of horse hooves and carriage wheels rolling down Market Street, over brick and dirt roadways? Dogs are barking, a young man is selling newspapers on the corner, and shopkeepers are opening their doors for a new day's business. Can you smell the odor of coal burning, as smoke rises from the chimneys, warming homes in the cold morning?

It was this San Francisco, as lively and alluring as today's city, which came to an abrupt end in late April 1906. Of all the severe earthquakes which have hit the Bay Area during recorded history, the Great Earthquake and Fire became the most famous of them all, and the disaster has never had a serious competitor. It marked the end of the old city and the beginning of the new one we all know and love.

I would guess that if you were to ask anyone, anywhere, what San Francisco is known for, his answer would be the Golden Gate Bridge, cable cars, and the 1906 San Francisco Earthquake.

Now, let us take a walk through the city considering how it was before the earthquake, what it became as a result of the earthquake, and how those very locations destroyed then look today.

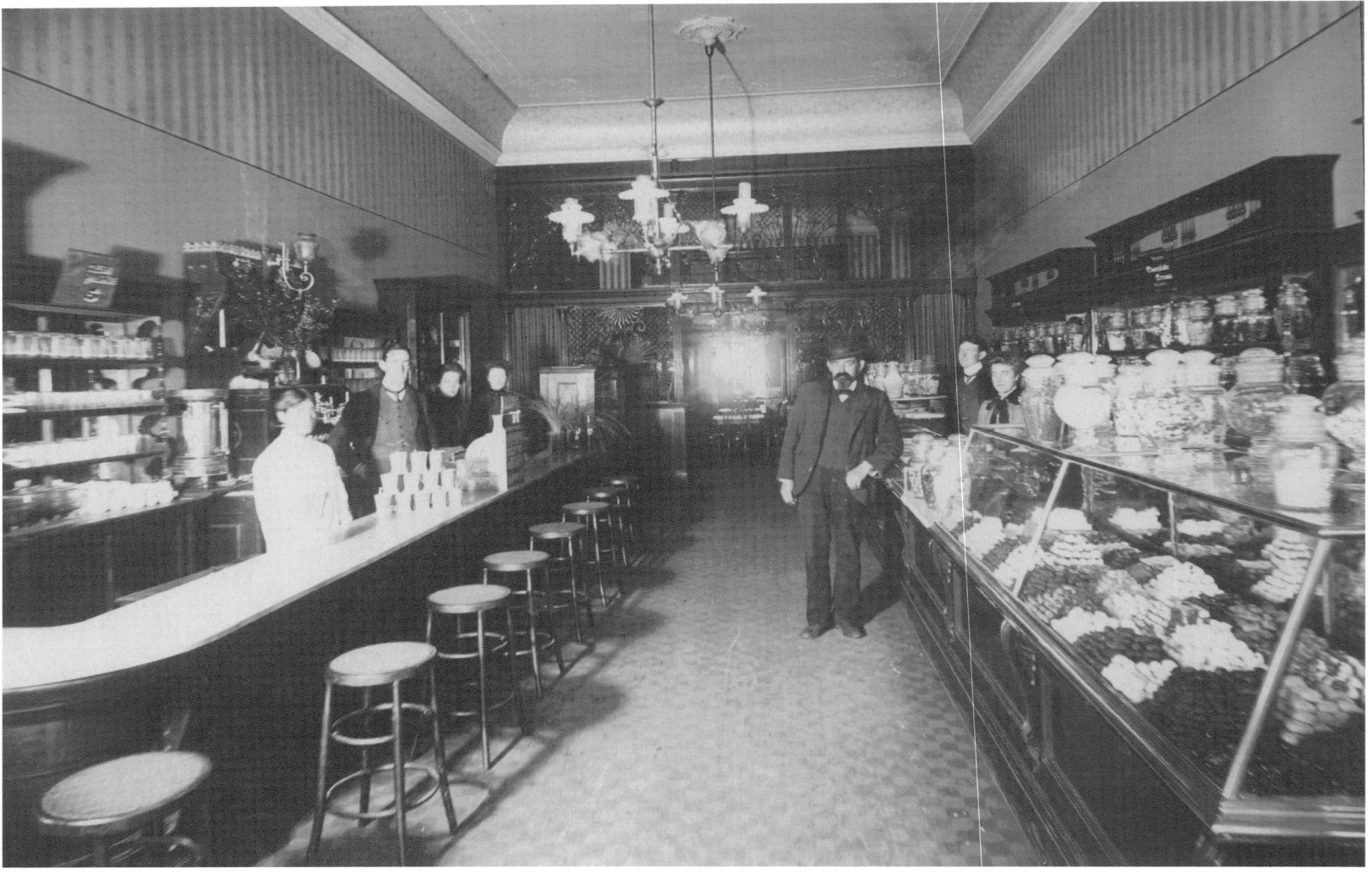

The elder Louis Selby inside one of the family candy stores. The date is before 1906, as he passed away that year.

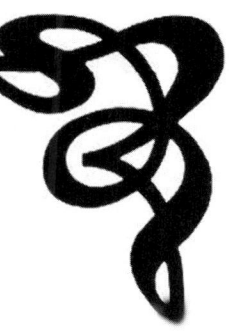

THE SELBY STORY

Louis P. Selby Jr. was born in Chicago, Illinois, in 1873. He was the son of Louis Selby Sr., who immigrated from Portugal to America in 1860 to realize his dreams and find new opportunities. I was told by my mother that when the family arrived, the family name was changed from Da Silva or some similar name to Selby in order to stem any anti-Portuguese discrimination. The name has stayed with the family ever since.

The elder Selby met Delia McCann, the love of his life and future bride, in Chicago. She was a native of Armagh County, Northern Ireland, born in 1848, the daughter of Neal and Delia McCann. The family, now including five children, left Illinois for California in 1876 and settled in Oakland, adding seven more children to the family.

The Selby children included John, Margaret, Charles Joseph, Louis P. Sr., David, May, Grace, Theresa, Walter, Albert, Florence, and Clarence. The Selby Twelve's era ended in 1970 when Clarence, the baby of the family, passed away.

Louis Jr. sold newspapers as a young man, saving every penny to invest in stocks and businesses. He amassed a tremendous amount of cash by the time the Panic of 1896 struck. When the stock market bottomed out and nobody had money to spend, he did. He invested in products he knew would rebound and experienced astounding success.

His own father was a confectioner by trade and entered into several businesses during his lifetime. He passed away in November of 1906, leaving his sons with a tremendous business sense that would support them well throughout their lives. Delia, his mother, followed in death nearly ten years later, in 1916.

In 1895, the Selby brothers started a small confectionery store in Oakland. This business grew into manufacturing candies and ice cream, and soon became a first-class attraction for satisfying a sweet tooth. Situated at 1057 Washington Street, the operation was called "a dream of elegance" in the July 29, 1905, *Oakland Tribune*.

At the same time, the Selby brothers operated a second store at 1150 Market Street in San Francisco, offering not just their wonderful candies but a soda fountain as well. They could not have been better located, right in the middle of Market Street's hustle and bustle. This location was ruined by the earthquake and fire. Today, the site is home to the UN Plaza, and not a sign of its former use is apparent.

The Selby brothers' business interests were broad. They also owned the National Pepsin Gum Company, with offices located at 703 Market Street (near the candy shop) and plant facilities at 1138 Mission Street. This business produced the Hilo Licorice and Mayberry gums sold by the Selbys, among other items.

Another family business was the Brown Phosphate Company, producer of the Brown's Celery & Phosphate beverage, located in Oakland. This bottled drink, containing syrup, water, and five percent alcohol, was touted as a fountain of youth. Newspapers of the day testify its distribution was widespread throughout the western United States.

Just how far the renown of Selby products traveled is indicated by the following story: In 1958, having been abroad for a year, family member Ruth Selby Shepardson was returning to the United States. She was traveling on the Italian liner *Christoforo Columbo*. One evening she was dancing with an older gentleman as they discussed luxury liners of past years. Ruth mentioned one of the liners, *Empress of Britain*, and her dancing partner said he once traveled on that ship. She said: "Maybe you met my uncles. They were in the gum business. Their name was Selby." He said: "Oh, I remember a short, jolly man who used to whip out a pack of gum and say, 'Here, have a piece of the best gum in the world, Selby Gum.'"

The Marlowe Theater, an early movie house located on Broadway between Tenth and Eleventh streets in Oakland, was still another commercial venture of the Selby brothers. A 1909 advertisement states: "The Marlowe caters to ladies, gentlemen, and children. It has polite attendants, is kept scrupulously cleaned, and its pictures are strictly moral and entertaining."

My maternal grandmother, Genevieve O'Neill, was born in Vallejo, California, in 1888. She was the daughter of Patrick O'Neill and Bridget Kelley O'Neill, both emigrants from Moycullen, Ireland.

The O'Neills crossed the Atlantic Ocean, with their cattle aboard ship, intended to be their path to wealth and success in America. An unfortunate incident happened at sea, and all was lost. The family did, fortunately, escape with their lives.

They arrived in the United States and settled in Philadelphia, remaining there through the Civil War and afterward. From there they brought their family of nine girls and one boy to the Golden State in the 1880s, settling in Vallejo. The family moved to Oakland in 1891.

Genevieve, at the young age of eighteen, had left her family in Oakland and was living in San Francisco on that fateful day of April 18, 1906. She worked on the waterfront now occupied by Fisherman's Wharf.

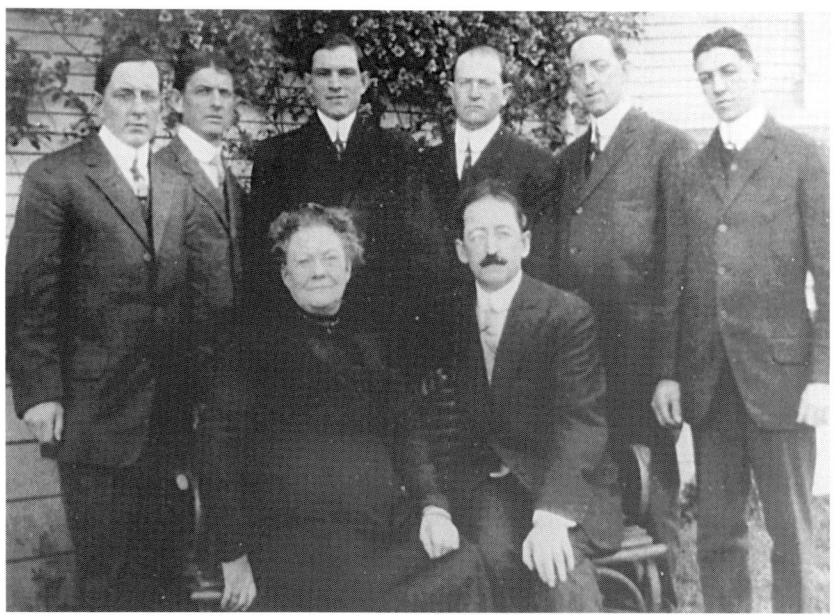

The Selby brothers and their mother. Front, left to right: Delia and John. Rear, left to right: Walter, Charles, Albert, David, Louis and Clarence.

Stock certificate from one of the Selby companies, along with a stick of the celebrated Selby chewing gum.

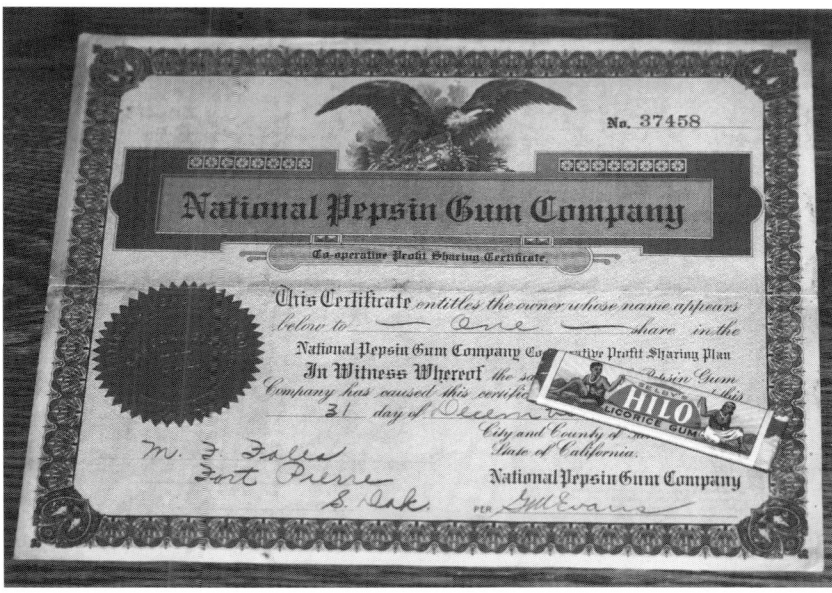

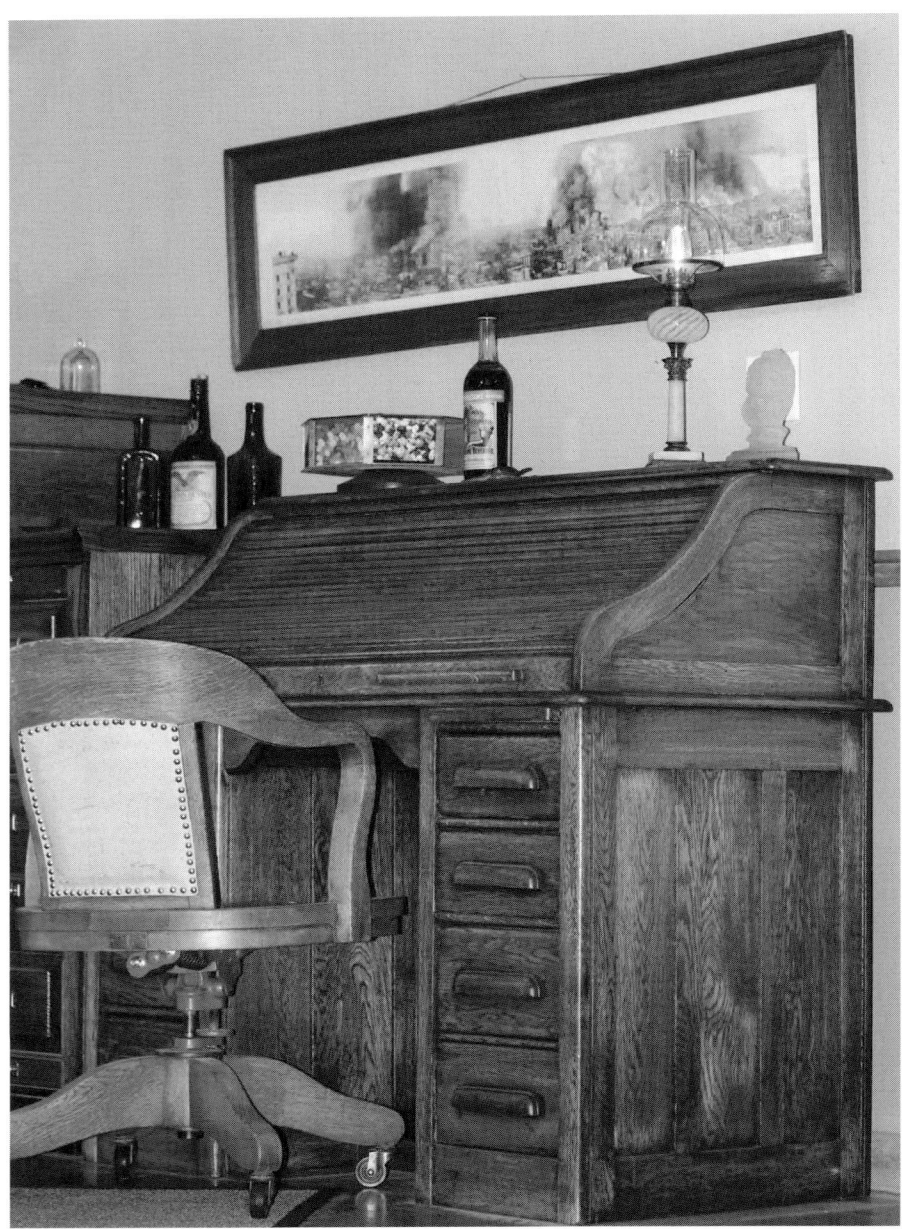

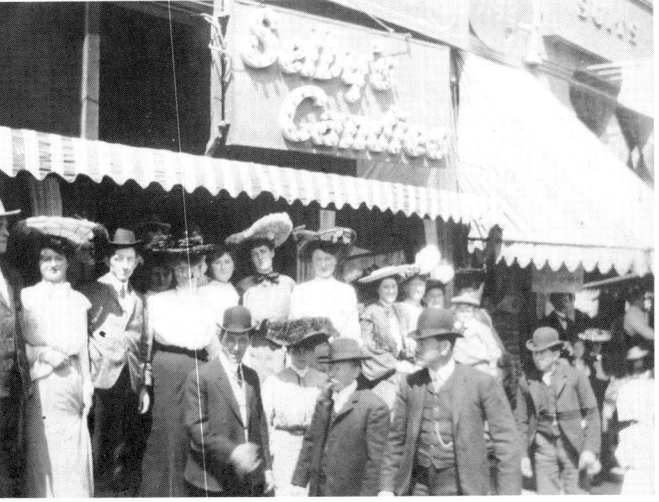

Above: Exterior of the San Francisco Selby candy store on Parade Day, with family members standing in foreground. Left: The desk owned by Louis Selby Jr., still in family hands. Atop the desk is a bottle of Brown's Celery Phosphate Soda, a Selby product. Above it is a framed panorama of the San Francisco earthquake and fire, another family heirloom.

There were some eighteen fruit packing facilities in San Francisco in that day, and Genevieve ran a day care facility for plant employees' children.

As the day's disasters unfolded, Genevieve soon realized she had to leave the city immediately. She grabbed what belongings she could, including her dog Tootsie, and prepared for a journey through hell in order to reach the Oakland ferry. She picked her way through rubble, fires, and crowds of frantic people, at last reaching the Ferry Building to wait for the next vessel outgoing.

As no Bay Bridge was yet available, a hastily assembled fleet began moving survivors to the East Bay. Already Genevieve knew that pet dogs were being shot on site and residents were forbidden from removing pets from the city by way of the ferry boats. So she put Tootsie under a blanket to pose as a baby and carried the dog through the long lines at the shore. After waiting for her turn, she boarded a boat with her little dog hidden from sight and traveled to Oakland without detection.

As the vessel made its way across the bay, Genevieve watched as her beloved San Francisco burned behind her. Luckily, scared little Tootsie never made a sound during the voyage. Genevieve went to stay with one of her sisters in Oakland, and later Tootsie had a litter of puppies. One was named Quake in honor of the disaster. My mom later named one of her dogs Flame to commemorate the fire.

Louis Patrick Selby Jr. would go on to marry Genevieve Elizabeth O'Neill in the late 1920s. They settled in the East Bay community of Kensington and had only one child, my mother. Eleanor Marie Selby. She grew up with a view of the glorious Golden Gate Bridge and always loved San Francisco. I now sit in amazement at the fact we often dined and wandered along the waterfront where her mother once lived and worked. Back then, I was too small to realize the family history involved in this story. If only we could all sit down and share those stories now!

Louis Jr. passed away in 1952 at age 79. As the varied family investments proved, he was a man with magnificent business sense. I was told by other relatives that they often asked his advice on financial matters, which they employed to great reward. What a wonderful legacy he left! Genevieve lived on until 1970, in the same house where she had lived for more than five decades and raised her loving daughter.

While Mom was born too late to experience the 1906 disaster, she was around to witness the Loma Prieta earthquake of October 17, 1989. Centered in Santa Cruz County, the 6.9 magnitude temblor caused extensive damage and loss of life in San Francisco and Oakland. Although she was living in Reno at the time, Mom was visiting a cousin in Oakland when the shocks hit. Mindful of stories passed down from 1906, she was frightened that more shaking would occur and harm her. To ease her fears and my own, that evening after work I left Reno for the East Bay, scooped her up, and headed back to Nevada.

What is it about earthquakes and this family?

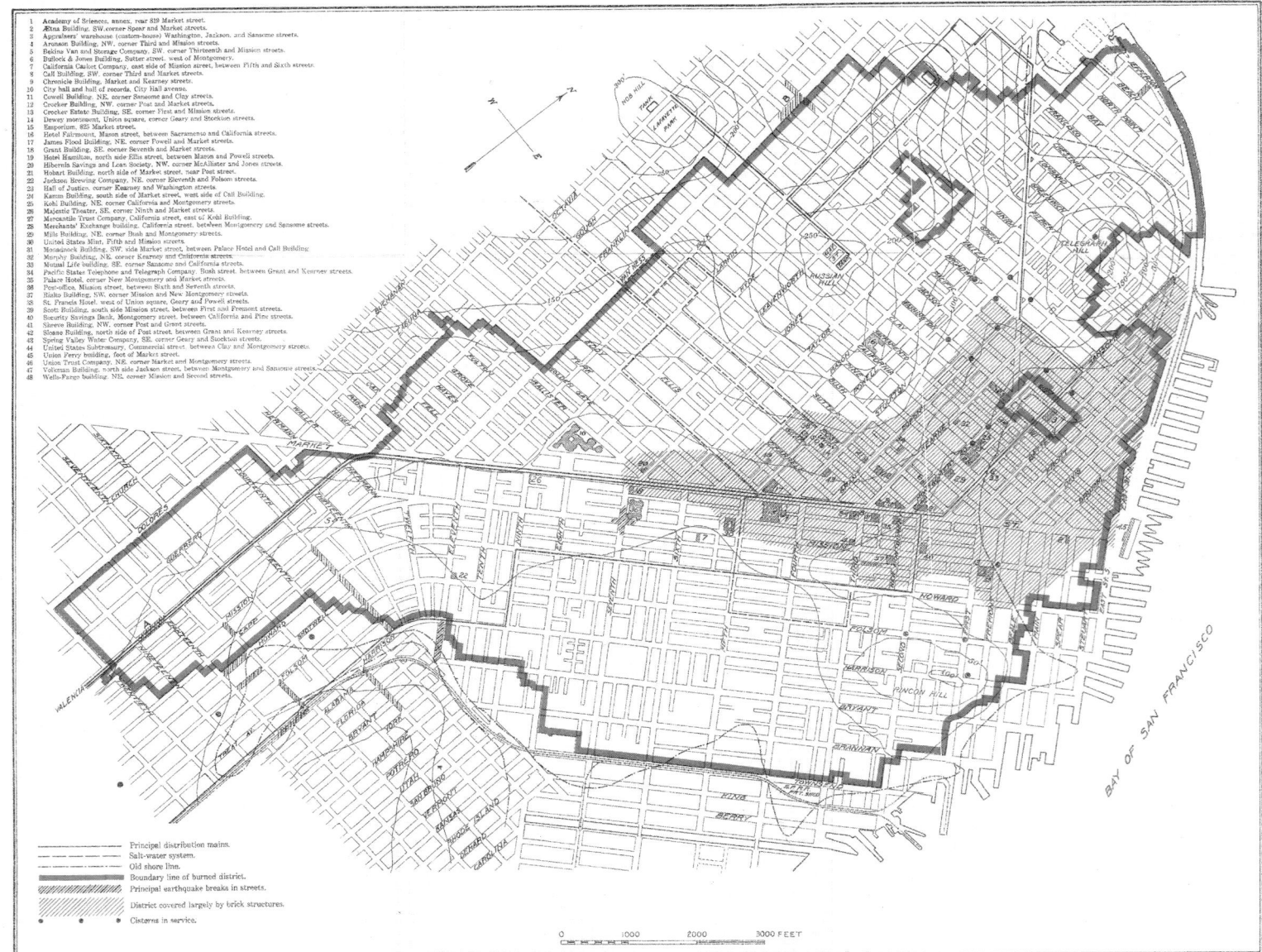

1 Academy of Sciences, annex, rear 819 Market street.
2 Ætna Building, SW.corner Spear and Market streets.
3 Appraisers' warehouse (custom-house) Washington, Jackson, and Sansome streets.
4 Aronson Building, NW. corner Third and Mission streets.
5 Bekins Van and Storage Company, SW. corner Thirteenth and Mission streets.
6 Butlock & Jones Building, Sutter street, west of Montgomery.
7 California Casket Company, east side of Mission street, between Fifth and Sixth streets.
8 Call Building, SW. corner Third and Market streets.
9 Chronicle Building, Market and Kearney streets.
10 City hall and hall of records, City Hall avenue.
11 Cowell Building, NE. corner Sansome and Clay streets.
12 Crocker Building, NW. corner Post and Market streets.
13 Crocker Estate Building, SE. corner First and Market streets.
14 Dewey monument, Union square, corner Geary and Stockton streets.
15 Emporium, 825 Market street.
16 Hotel Fairmont, Mason street, between Sacramento and California streets.
17 James Flood Building, NE. corner Powell and Market streets.
18 Grant Building, SE. corner Seventh and Market streets.
19 Hotel Hamilton, north side Ellis street, between Mason and Powell streets.
20 Hibernia Savings and Loan Society, NW. corner McAllister and Jones streets.
21 Hobart Building, north side of Market street, near Post street.
22 Jackson Brewing Company, NE. corner Eleventh and Folsom streets.
23 Hall of Justice, corner Kearney and Washington streets.
24 Kamm Building, south side of Market street, west side of Call Building.
25 Kohl Building, NE. corner California and Montgomery streets.
26 Majestic Theater, SE. corner Ninth and Market streets.
27 Mercantile Trust Company, California street, east of Kohl Building.
28 Merchants' Exchange building, California street, between Montgomery and Sansome streets.
29 Mills Building, NE. corner Bush and Montgomery streets.
30 United States Mint, Fifth and Mission streets.
31 Monadnock Building, SW. side Market street, between Palace Hotel and Call Building.
32 Murphy Building, NE. corner Kearney and California streets.
33 Mutual Life building, SE. corner Sansome and California streets.
34 Pacific States Telephone and Telegraph Company, Bush street, between Grant and Kearney streets.
35 Palace Hotel, corner New Montgomery and Market streets.
36 Post-office, Mission street, between Sixth and Seventh streets.
37 Rialto Building, SW. corner Mission and New Montgomery streets.
38 St. Francis Hotel, west of Union square, Geary and Powell streets.
39 Scott Building, south side Mission street, between First and Fremont streets.
40 Security Savings Bank, Montgomery street, between California and Pine streets.
41 Shreve Building, NW. corner Post and Grant streets.
42 Sloane Building, north side of Post street, between Grant and Kearney streets.
43 Spring Valley Water Company, SE. corner Geary and Stockton streets.
44 United States Subtreasury, Commercial street, between Clay and Montgomery streets.
45 Union Ferry building, foot of Market street.
46 Union Trust Company, NE. corner Market and Montgomery streets.
47 Volkman Building, north side Jackson street, between Montgomery and Sansome streets.
48 Wells-Fargo building, NE. corner Mission and Second streets.

——————— Principal distribution mains.
– – – – – – Salt-water system.
– · – · – · Old shore line.
▬▬▬▬▬ Boundary line of burned district.
▨▨▨▨▨ Principal earthquake breaks in streets.
▨▨▨▨▨ District covered largely by brick structures.
• · • · • Cisterns in service.

0   1000   2000   3000 FEET

MAP OF SAN FRANCISCO SHOWING BURNED DISTRICT; ACCOMPANYING REPORT OF RICHARD L. HUMPHREY.
1907

EARTHQUAKE AND FIRE

On Wednesday, April 18, 1906, at 5:12 in the morning, just as sleeping San Francisco awoke for a new day, animals stirred strangely as an unbelievable rumbling shook the populous city. Buildings swayed, ceilings fell, and floors dropped out from under foot. Helpless souls ran for protection under doorways, window frames, and furniture. Others flew into the streets, dressed in night clothes only, as terror swept the city.

The ground had broken open for a length of 270 miles along the San Andreas Fault. Many other communities besides San Francisco were damaged badly, including Oakland, the East Bay communities, Santa Rosa to the north, and Santa Cruz to the south. Tremors were felt as far away as southern Oregon, Los Angeles, and even in the high deserts of central Nevada.

Many must have thought the world was coming to a horrible end. For some, it did. Thousands died and, later, numerous survivors found they had lost all their worldly goods. Estimated at 8.25 on the modern Richter Scale, this earthquake turned the ground to jelly, crumbled brick buildings into dust, and jerked wooden structures off their foundations, leaving what looked like a pile of toothpicks. Streets became impassable due to fresh holes in the ground and debris strewn everywhere.

Much of San Francisco had been developed atop fill dirt, brought in along the waterfront years before to expand the city's buildable space. Placed over water and wetlands, the ground was highly unstable. When the earthquake hit, the earth collapsed, taking buildings, roadways, and lives with it.

Gas lines were severed, and overturned stoves provided all that was necessary to start the fires that almost leveled the beautiful city by the bay. By 6:30 a.m., only a little more than an hour after the quake, the first fires of note broke out near Market Street's Palace Hotel and at the base of Telegraph Hill. The Market Street fire first ravaged an area to the south, but soon spread north, into the business district. The blaze continued through the Mission District and Hayes Valley, fueled by the many dry wood structures in those neighborhoods.

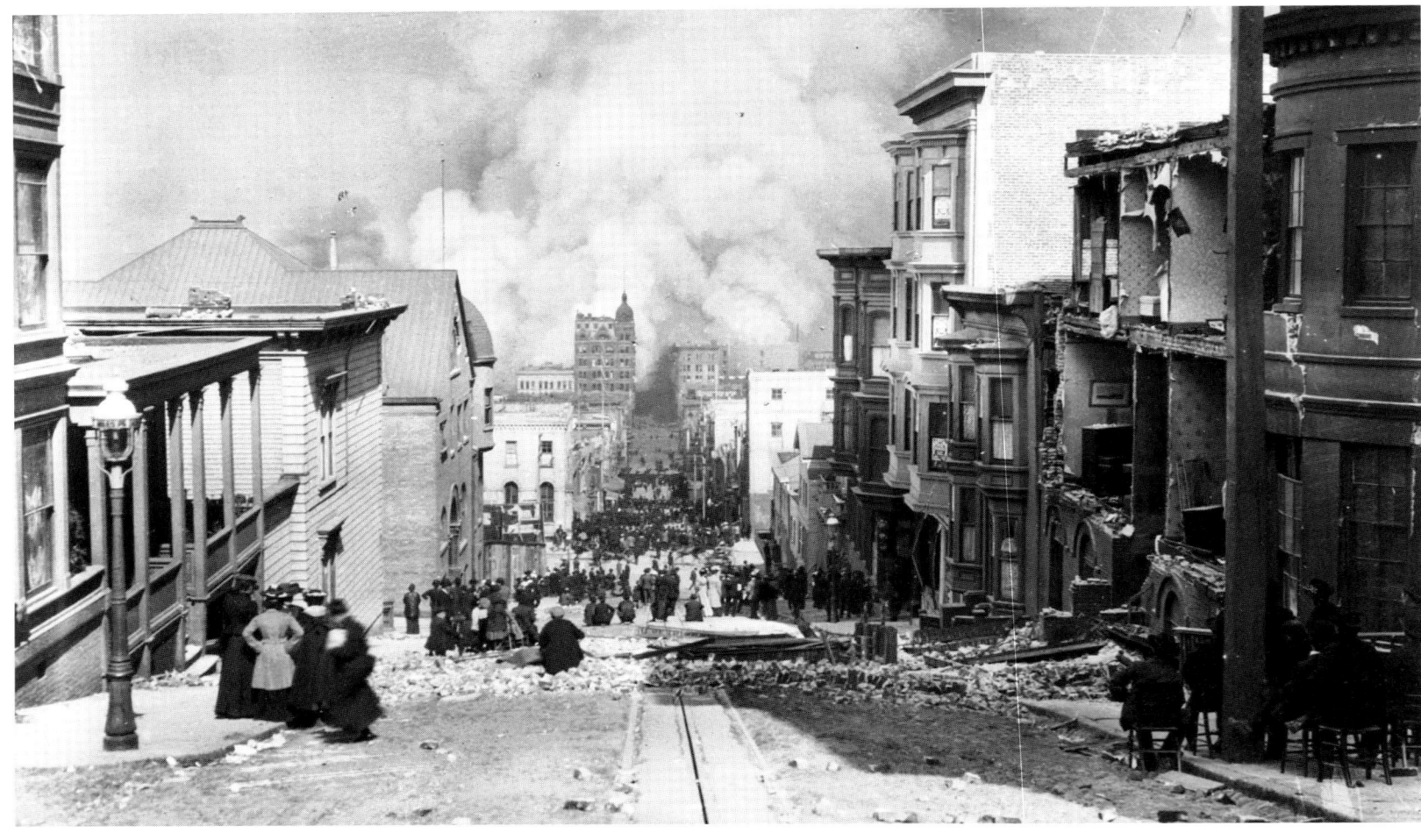

Perhaps the most famous photograph of the twin disasters—"Looking Down Sacramento Street, San Francisco, April 18, 1906," by Arnold Genthe. Shot with a borrowed camera, as Genthe's studio had perished minutes earlier.

Waterlines and cisterns had split, disrupting water access and making it impossible to fight the flames. Firefighters were unable to move their equipment about the city due to the destruction. Their efforts to attack the fires where thwarted by rubble-blocked roadways and dry hydrants. By 10 a.m., dozens of fires were burning throughout the city.

Explosives were utilized to destroy structures and head off the fast-moving walls of flame. At first, government officials withheld permission to dynamite buildings in order to create fire breaks, instead restricting explosive use to structures already on fire. As a result, the fire simply skirted around those buildings brought down intentionally and burned on with a destructive force. It took three days before the blazes petered out.

Control of the city had been lost. Thieves looted damaged and abandoned stores and homes while police officers were busy with other tasks, such as moving the wounded to temporary hospitals.

In an effort to stem the lawlessness, Mayor Eugene Schmitz announced: "As it has come to my attention that thieves are taking advantage of the present deplorable conditions and are plying their nefarious vocations among the ruins in our city, all peace officers are ordered to instantly kill anyone caught looting or committing any other serious crimes."

City Hall was in ruins and municipal jails were now unsafe. Mayor Schmitz ordered all petty offenders released, while those charged with more serious crimes were sent to San Quentin State Prison by boat.

By mid-morning, the military placed troops at the disposal of the mayor until such time that conditions should return to normal. Soldiers worked in conjunction with police in preserving order and distributing provisions to those in need.

One looter was caught burglarizing Shreve's Jewelry Store at Post and Grant. He was turned over to a soldier who killed him and left his body to be consumed by the fire. The man's corpse became a subject of many photographs from the disaster, including one in this very book.

The city morgue, designed only for the usual amount of deaths, was filled to the brim with disaster victims. The central police station's target range was turned into an emergency morgue, but when fire threatened that building, dozens of bodies stored there were taken to Portsmouth Square for temporary burial.

As in all disasters, the good of humankind emerged as neighbors helped neighbors, and public safety officers performed without regard for their own safety.

Patrolman Max Fenner was the only San Francisco police officer known to have lost his life as a result of the disaster. He was standing across from the Essex Lodging House, a tall brick building on Mason near Ellis streets when the earthquake occurred. Fenner saw that the front wall of the building was about to collapse and simultaneously saw a woman running out of the building. He rushed to protect her, only to have the building fall on him. The woman raced to safety. Officer Fenner was killed.

In another incident, a man was found under a collapsed building on Third near Mission. The man was pinned under rubble in such a way that rescuers could not free him. As the fire approached, the man, knowing what he was about to endure, begged a potential rescuer to kill him before the fire reached him. With that, the bystander pulled a revolver and shot the man to death. The shooter, along with a witness, reported his "good deed" to Mayor Schmitz.

As fires continued to rage and the Hall of Justice's destruction became imminent, officers took police records to Portsmouth Square for safekeeping. As they had no water to protect the documents from the flames, tremendous heat, and flying embers, officers seized a nearby saloon and poured beer onto the boxes to prevent their destruction.

Finally, on the evening of April 19th, Captain LeVert Coleman received permission to begin dynamiting buildings ahead of the fire as it approached Van Ness Avenue. This provided the opportunity to take down buildings far ahead of the flames, which had the desired effect on the fire, stopping forward progress at Van Ness and at the intersections of Broadway, Franklin, and Gough streets.

Captain Coleman wrote that the work of setting the explosives and related tasks was done by volunteers in order to save lives and property. They encountered very difficult conditions, having to set charges inside actively burning buildings and carry explosives past fires and sparking electrical wires.

All use of cooking stoves was moved to the streets, and homeless camps were set up in city parks as well as in cemeteries. The military and San Francisco police stood guard of the city while rescuing, feeding, and clothing the citizens.

In 1906, San Francisco was a large city of approximately 400,000 residents. Some 265,000 of them suddenly became homeless in the course of this disaster. More than $500 million in property damage was sustained, not taking into account lost business revenues or wages.

The human losses were much greater than any statistician could measure. Lives were lost, lives were ruined, and a once vibrant city was left destroyed by an unimaginable event. Although 3,000 deaths were attributed to the earthquake and fire, many more were never documented due to the extreme confusion of the times.

As the fires were gradually snuffed out, the totality of the damage was assessed. It quickly became clear that the three days of intense fire caused substantially greater damage than what the earthquake wrought. In all, 28,000 buildings were destroyed. Some 342 city blocks were destroyed north of Market Street and 111 more to the south. Five square miles were incinerated.

Following the tragedy, many residents left the city and never returned. The population of the East Bay increased while that of San Francisco decreased.

THE ALBUM

The Selby album is here reproduced in its approximate order; many of the pages became separated from the binding over years of use, and their precise order is now uncertain. Information that expands on the album captioning has been included in the margins.

A large number of the photographs presented here represent Selby work; several are explicitly labeled as such, but most are not. In addition, a number of supplementary views were obtained by the Selbys from other sources and used to help make the album more comprehensive. Unsurprisingly, many of these added images came from the Pillsbury Picture Company of Oakland, which operated fairly close to the Selby home base.

The following is a descriptive list of those who contributed the non-Selby images:

Bailey, Charles Z. (Los Angeles). Well-known California photographer of the early twentieth century, whose work featured locales scattered throughout the state.

Blumberg, A(braham). (Alameda). He was advertising earthquake and fire views in the May 1906 issue of *Camera Craft*, priced between 50 cents and $2.50. Note that his discreet rubber stamp is found well within the image area, perhaps as a dodge against would-be photo copyists.

Cohen, Edgar A. (Alameda). East Bay-based, like Blumberg, his career began in 1898 and his subject material ranged over much of northern California. He was especially noted for his images of Monterey Bay and its vicinity.

Moller, J. B. (San Francisco). Had a photographic studio on Eighteenth Street and is known to have sold earthquake and fire views commercially.

Noel, S. D. Details unknown.

Pillsbury Picture Company (Oakland). Beginning as a staff photographer for the *San Francisco Examiner*, Arthur C. Pillsbury fortuitously began an independent business in "wholesale photography" a month before the earthquake and fire, and thus he was well-poised to document the disasters. Much of his work was used in early twentieth-century postcards and, interestingly, he was a pioneer in stop-motion filming and microphotography.

"Stoddard" (San Francisco). Known to have operated at 835 Octavia Street. Oddly, the immediate pre- and post-earthquake/fire Crocker-Langley directories for San Francisco carry no listings for this photographer, and the University of California, Berkeley's Bancroft Library appears to have no substantive information about him/her either.

Stone, F. L. Details unknown. He appears to have had a studio and produced commercial images that found their way into other albums and archives of California subjects.

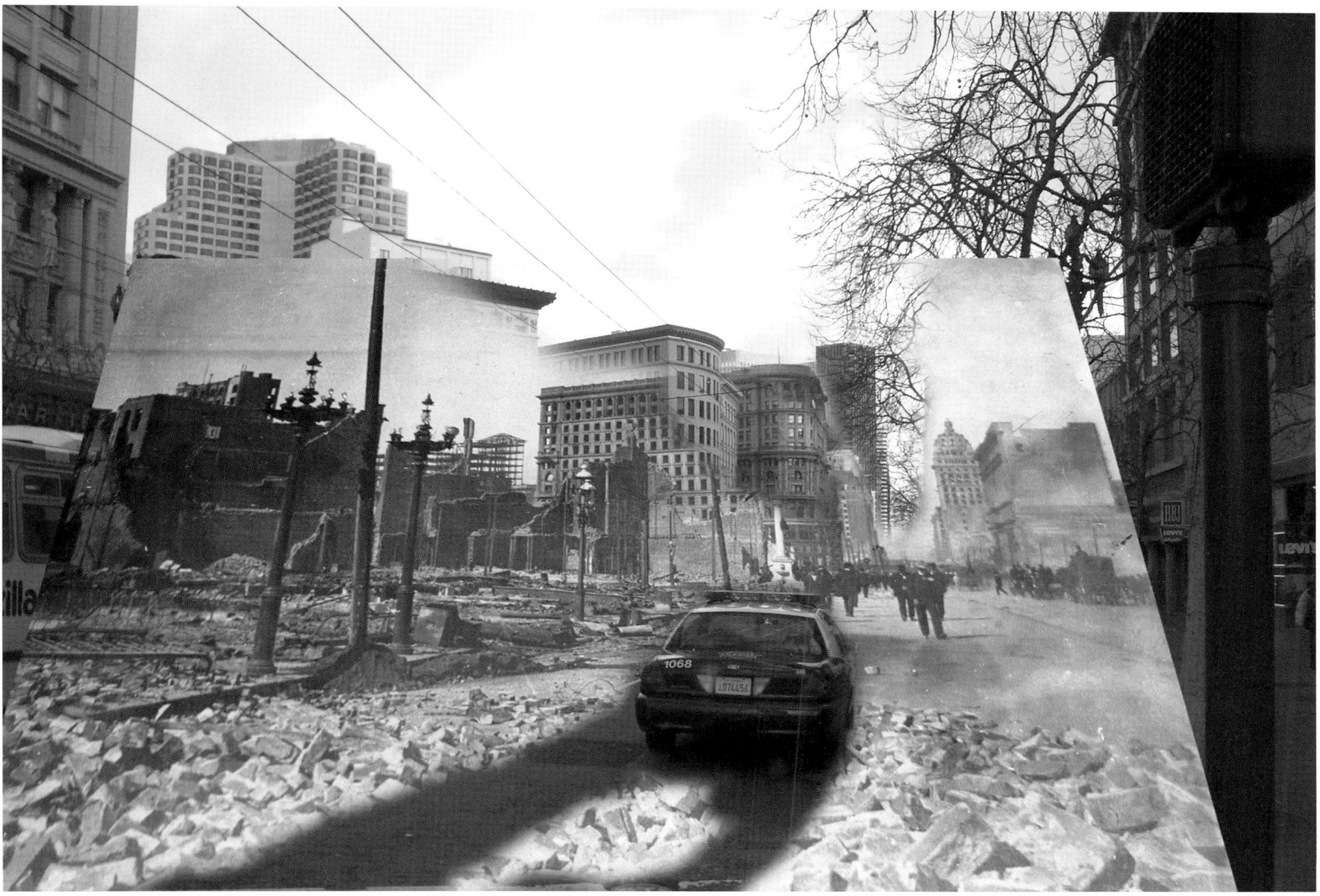

Market Street looking east from Taylor: a composite view splicing a 1906 image with a contemporary view. See also page 88. More of these images may be found in the "Then and Now" section, beginning on page 105.

Street, William J. (San Francisco). His studio was based at 1535 Bush before the disasters and relocated subsequently to 165 Belvedere. He was a founding member of the Professional Photographer's Association of California.

Whigham, Richard P. (San Francisco). An immigrant from Northern Ireland, he had a studio on Market Street that was destroyed in the earthquake and fire. Amazingly, he recovered fast enough to document the disasters and soon relocated to 1615 Fillmore, west of downtown.

Worden, Willard E. (San Francisco). Noted commercial photographer, especially of the 1906 events. He was prosperous enough to operate two pre-disaster studios (at 26 Montgomery and 2830 Baker streets). He appears to have lost both facilities and was based at 1141 Turk in 1907. Much of his work is preserved in the Wells Fargo Corporate Archives.

Right: Image inserted loosely in the Selby album depicting an unidentified policeman, apparently at the corner of Market and Fifth, with vast billowing smoke clouds in the distance.

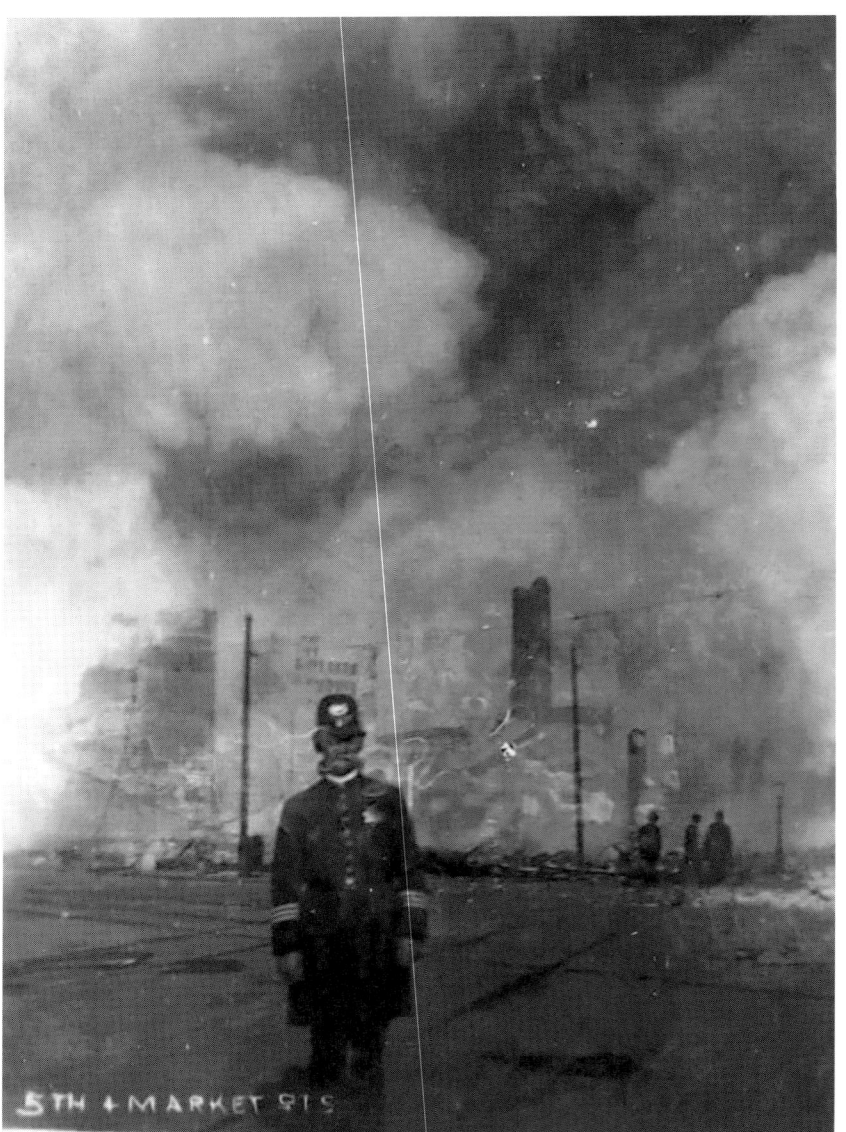

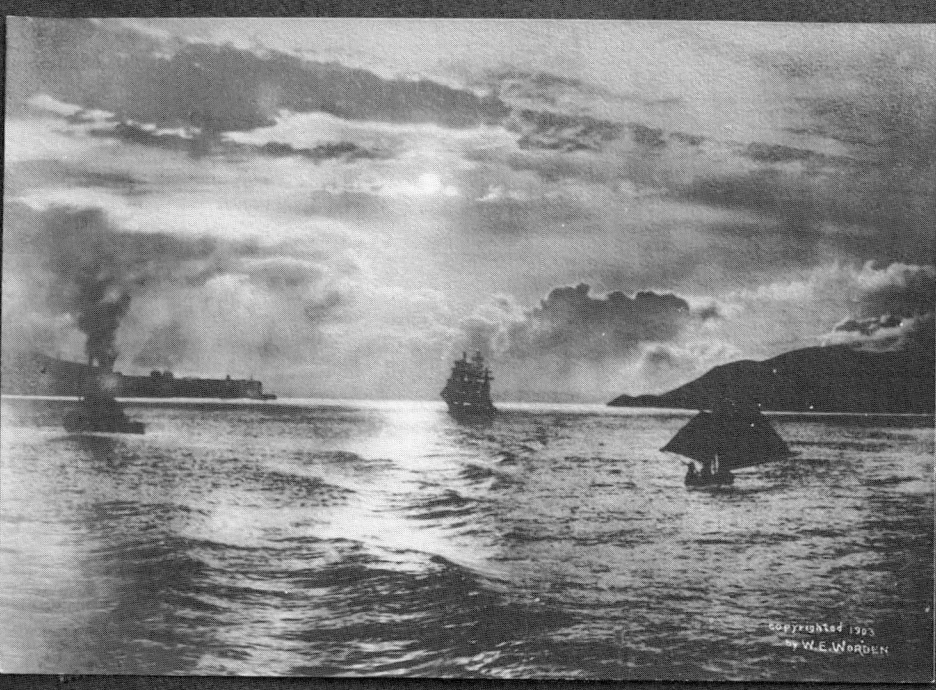

*"The Golden Gate"
Entrance to San Francisco*

Copyrighted 1903
by W.E. Worden

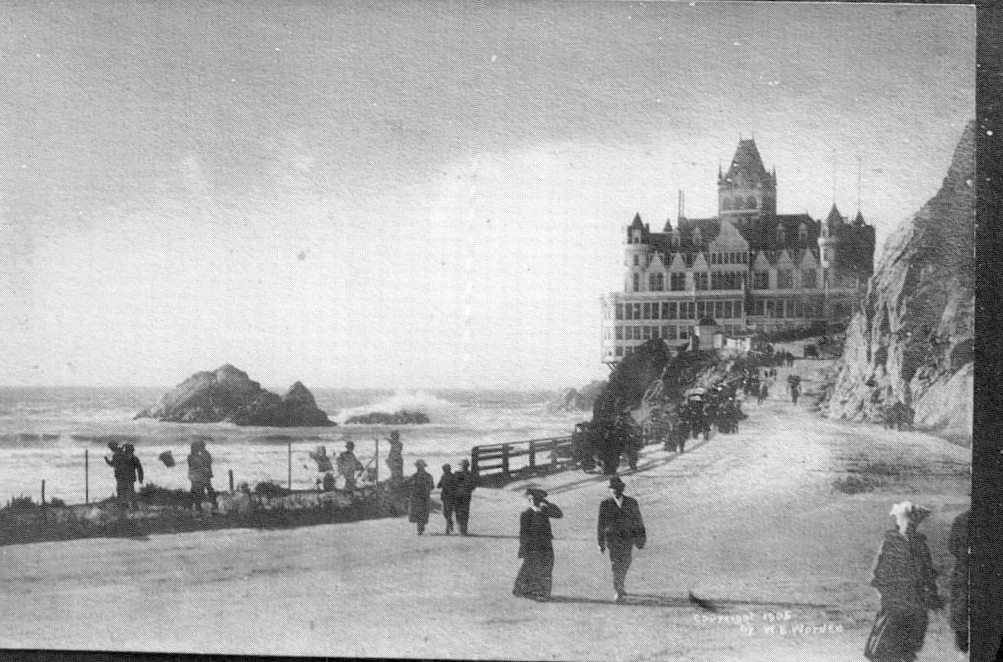

*"Cliff House"
Seal Rocks
San Francisco*

*destroyed by fire
September 7-07.*

COPYRIGHT 1905
BY W.E. WORDEN

The Album

"The Golden Gate"—San Francisco's famed entrance by sea, circa 1906 and long before construction of the bridge. (Worden)

"Cliff House" Perched above the Pacific, this is perhaps San Francisco's best-known restaurant. First built in 1858, it was remodeled in 1863. This photo shows the elegant third version, built in 1896 by San Francisco financier Adolph Sutro. While it somehow managed to survive the earthquake, as the caption notes, it was destroyed by fire in 1907. The current Cliff House is styled to look like the replacement originally built in 1909. (Worden)

When San Francisco Burned

"'The Ruins'"
A view likely taken near Mission and Fremont streets, with the Ferry Building in the distance. In some areas, one could hardly walk down the streets, much less move a vehicle through them.

"Ruins of Poodle Dog Restaurant"
Located at the corner of Eddy and Mason streets, this elegant six-story San Francisco institution (visible in left of image) was badly damged.

"Call Building on fire"
Barely visible at extreme left of image.

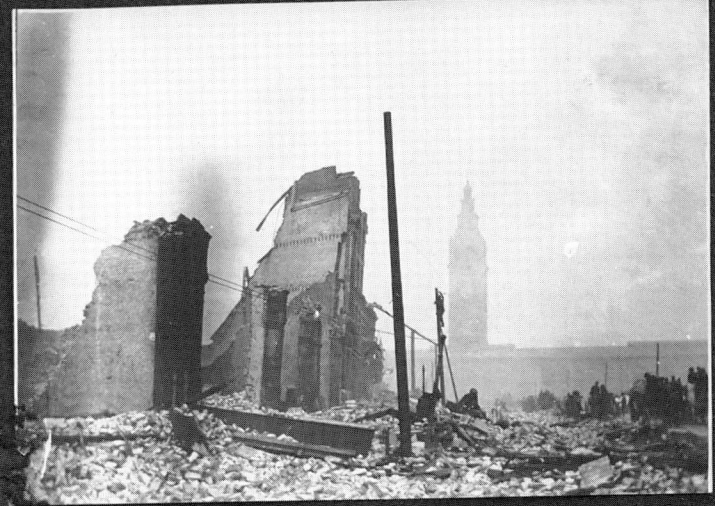

"The Ruins"

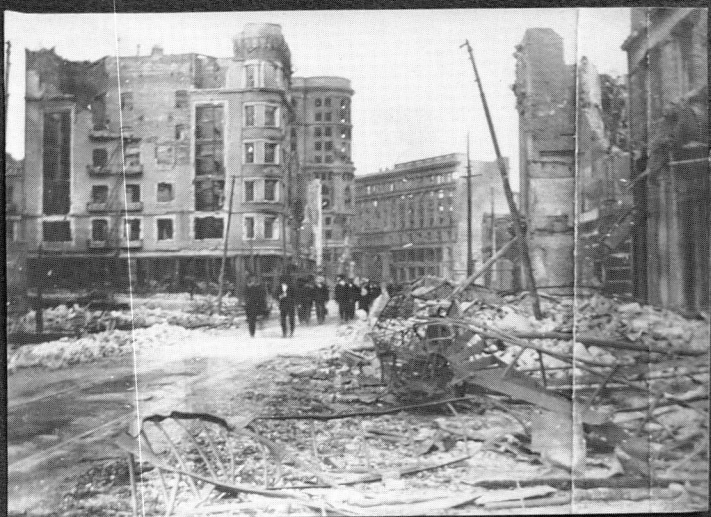

Ruins of Poodle Dog Restaurant

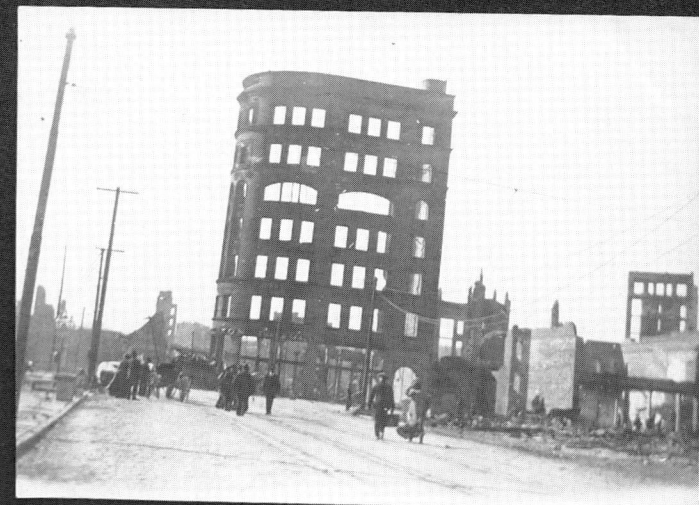

Ruins Taylor & Market Sts

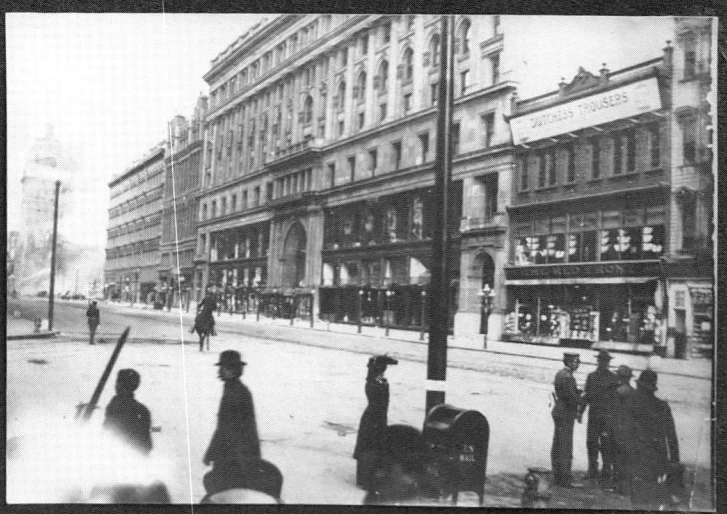

Call Building on fire

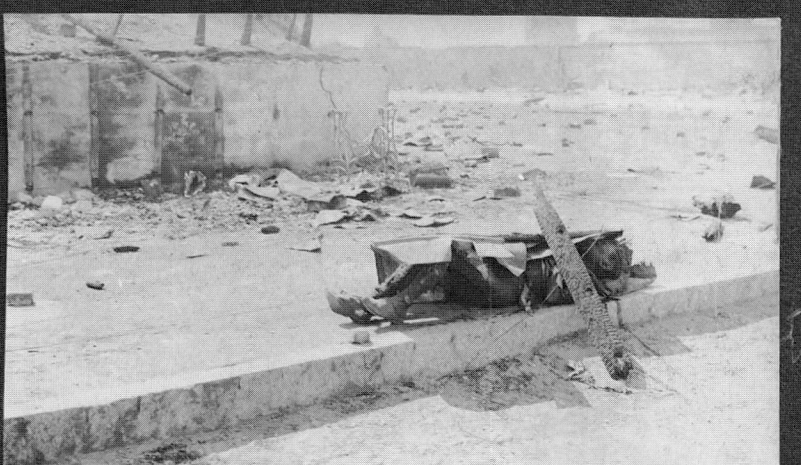

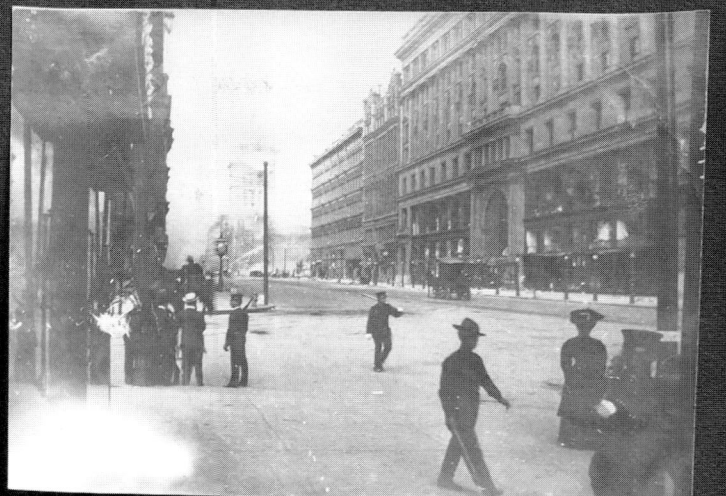

Remains of a victim.

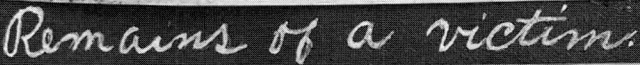

*U. S. Post Office
Mission St.
View*

COR 7TH AND MISSION ST.

"Remains of a victim"
Said to have been a looter, this man's body was left on the street as a grim deterrent to would-be thieves.

[Unidentified photo]
Another dim view of the burning Call Building, similar to the image on the previous page but shifted more to the left.

"U.S. Post Office, Mission St. View"
The displaced iron lamppost and sidewalk testify to the earthquake's brute force. (Pillsbury?)

When San Francisco Burned

"As San Francisco appeared 3 hours after Earthquake" A view, apparently taken from a watercraft, showing the large area ablaze behind the shoreline. The Ferry Building is seen at extreme right.

"Cattle killed on Mission St. by Earthquake" Zoning regulations being different than today, livestock were kept within 1906 San Francisco. Many were killed when buildings and materials collapsed and dropped on them. Carcasses were often left to rot in the street. (Stoddard)

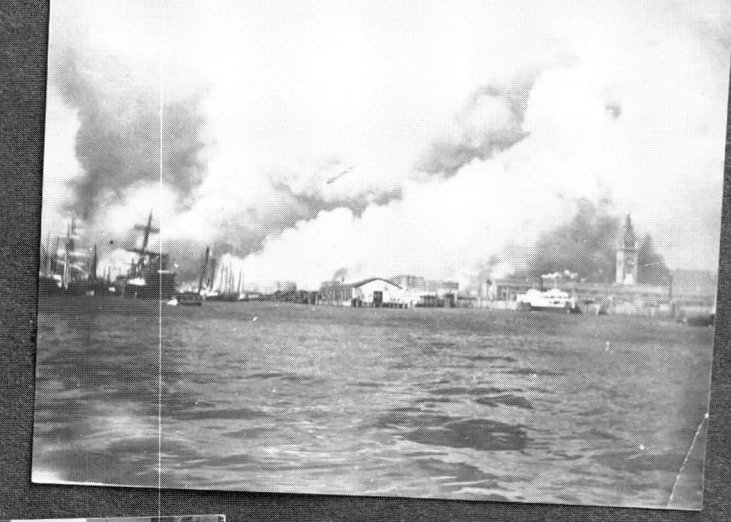

As San Francisco appeared 3 hours after Earthquake

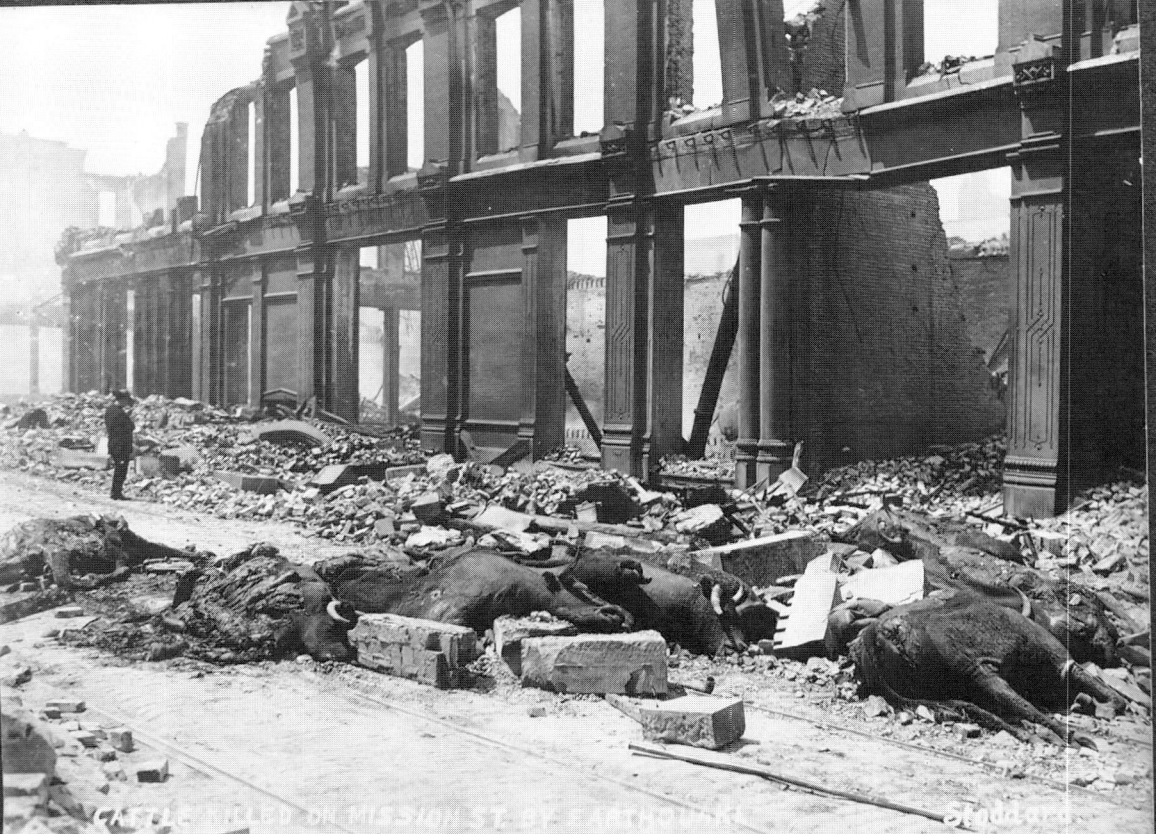

Cattle Killed on Mission St. by Earthquake

"*Federal troops arriving on Market St…*"
Hit badly by flames some hou[rs] later, this major thoroughfare appears relative[ly] intact as soldiers arrive to keep the peace.

"*Market St., looking west*"
In this view, the fire has obvious[ly] hit the street har[d.] Bystanders are few, and it appe[ars] no effort is being made to fight the fire.

"*Refugees out in the cold*"
Two ladies in their finery hov[er] near what migh[t] be their only remaining perso[n]al possessions. [The] ruins are visible [in] the background.

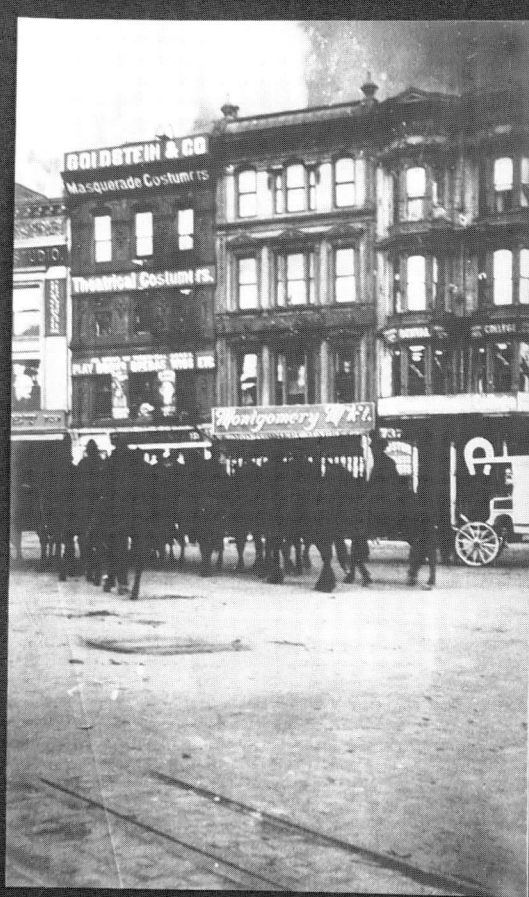

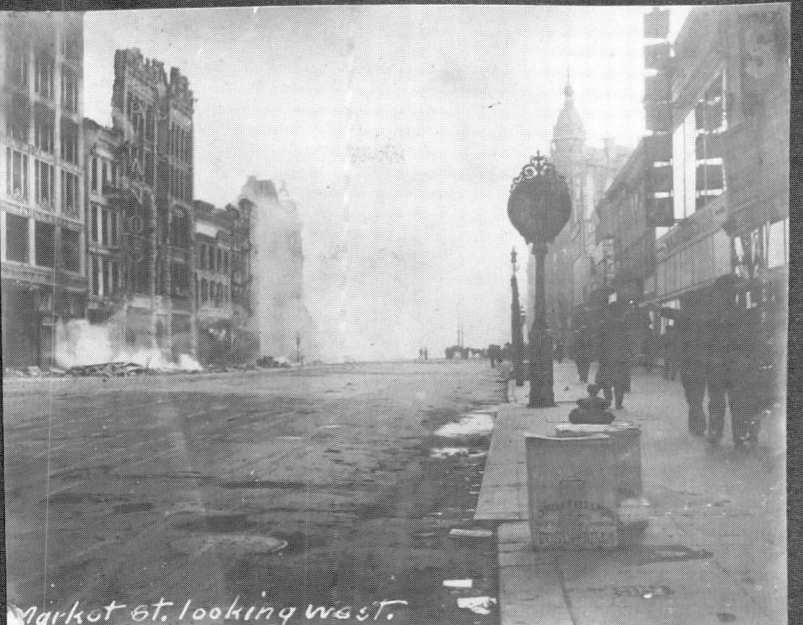

Market st. looking west.

Market St., looking west

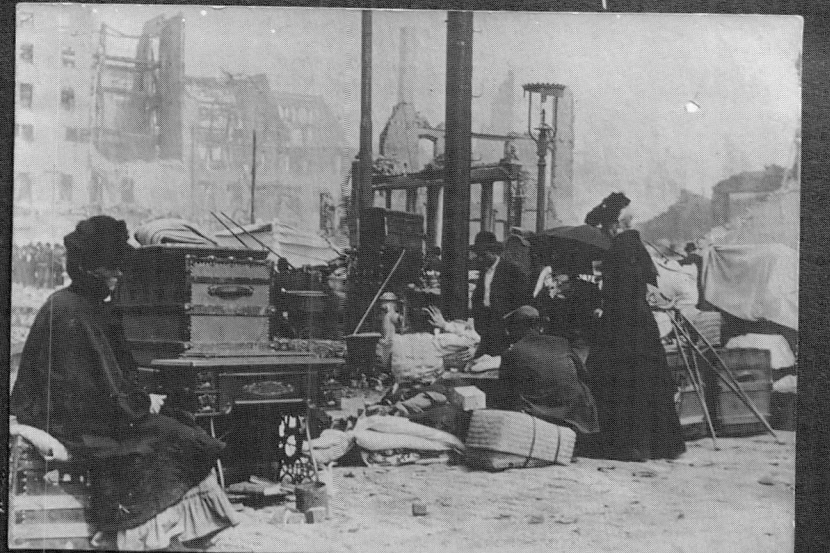

Federal troops arriving on Market St before the fire

Refugees out in the cold

When San Francisco Burned

"St Ignatius Church on fire…" Founded in 1855, the church and school complex seen here from the back was built in 1880 and became one of San Francisco's leading cultural institutions. After its 1906 destruction, operations were moved to a temporary building near Golden Gate Park known as the Shirt Factory.

"Earthquake damage 3rd Street" Here a large façade has crumbled into the street sideways, one illustration of how streets became impassable following the earthquake.

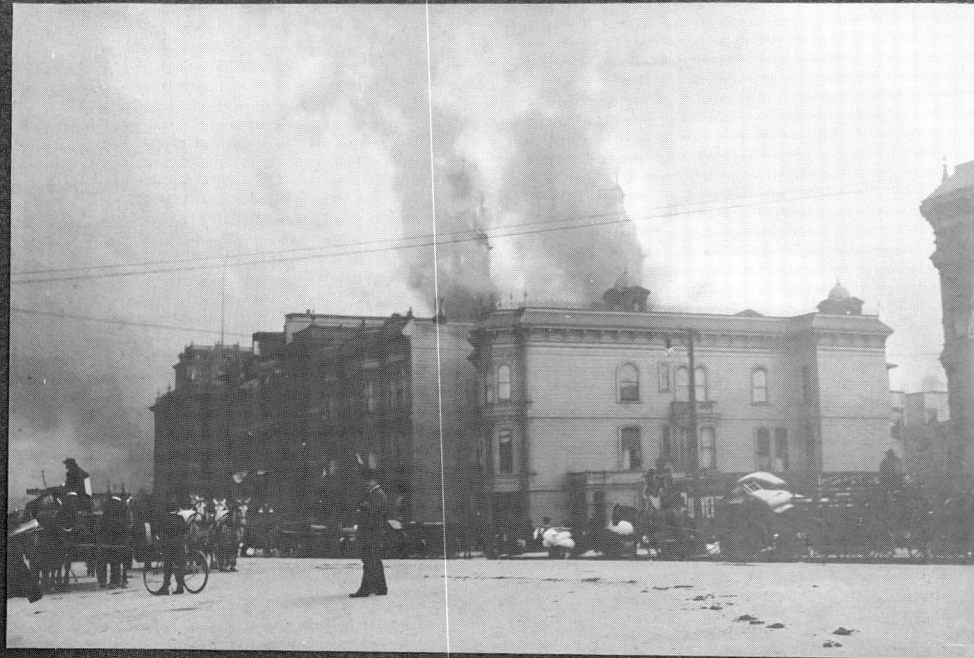

St Ignatius Church on fire, view from Van Ness Ave.

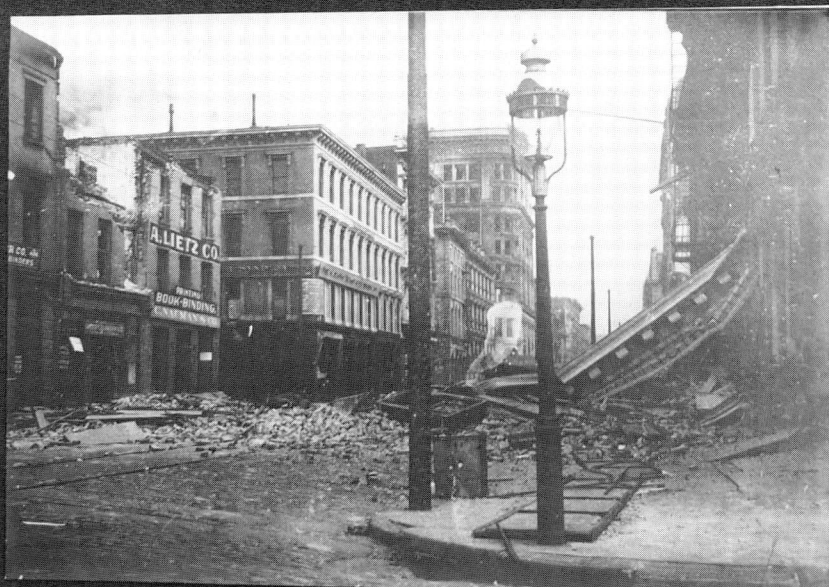

Earthquake damage 3rd Street

St Ignatius
Church & College
Hayes St.

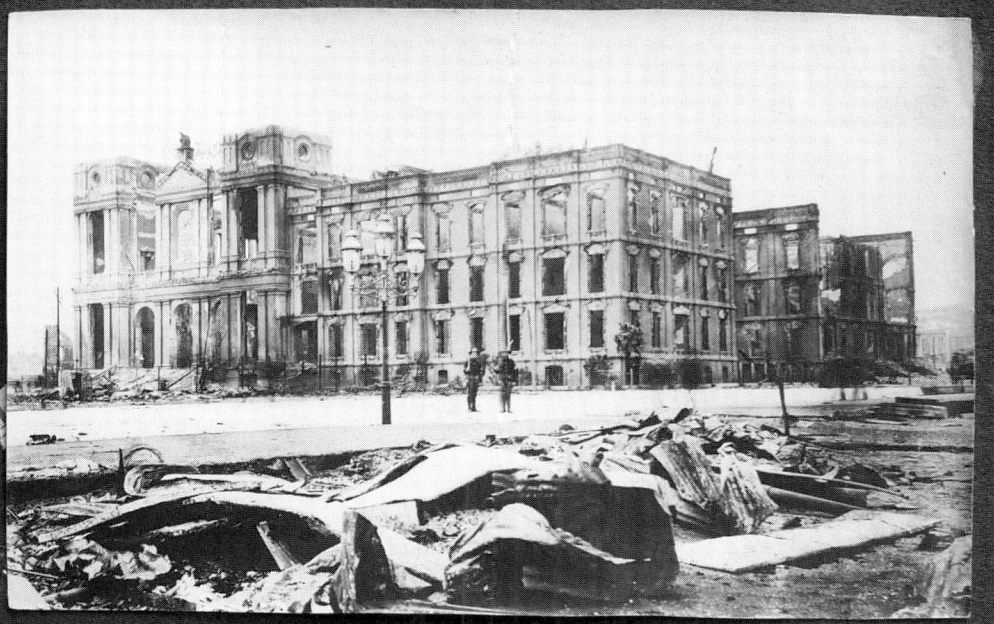

"St Ignatius
Church & College
Hayes St."
A better view of
the devastated
complex seen on
the previous page.

"Tired and weary,
they rest…"
With the fire busily
consuming most
of San Francisco's
downtown, there
was little for
survivors to do but
pause and watch
their city succumb
to the flames.

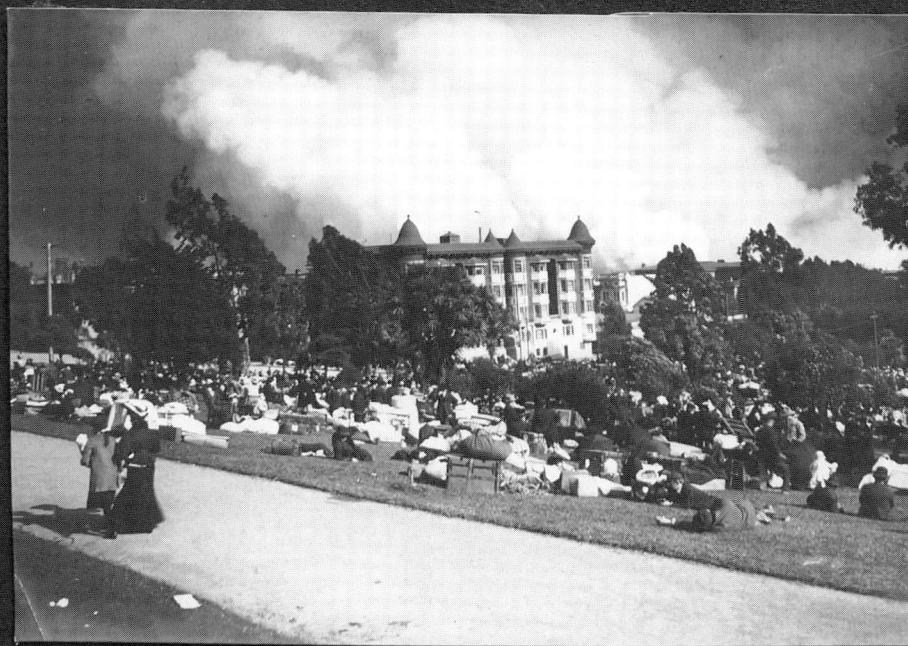

Tired & weary, they
rest while
the city burns

When San Francisco Burned

"Restaurant and Children's play grounds at Golden Gate Park"
While none of Golden Gate Park was damaged by fire, structures such as these sustained major earthquake damage.

"Earthquake damage to Street Railway" The twisted earth seen here bears mute witness to the earthquake's tremendous force.

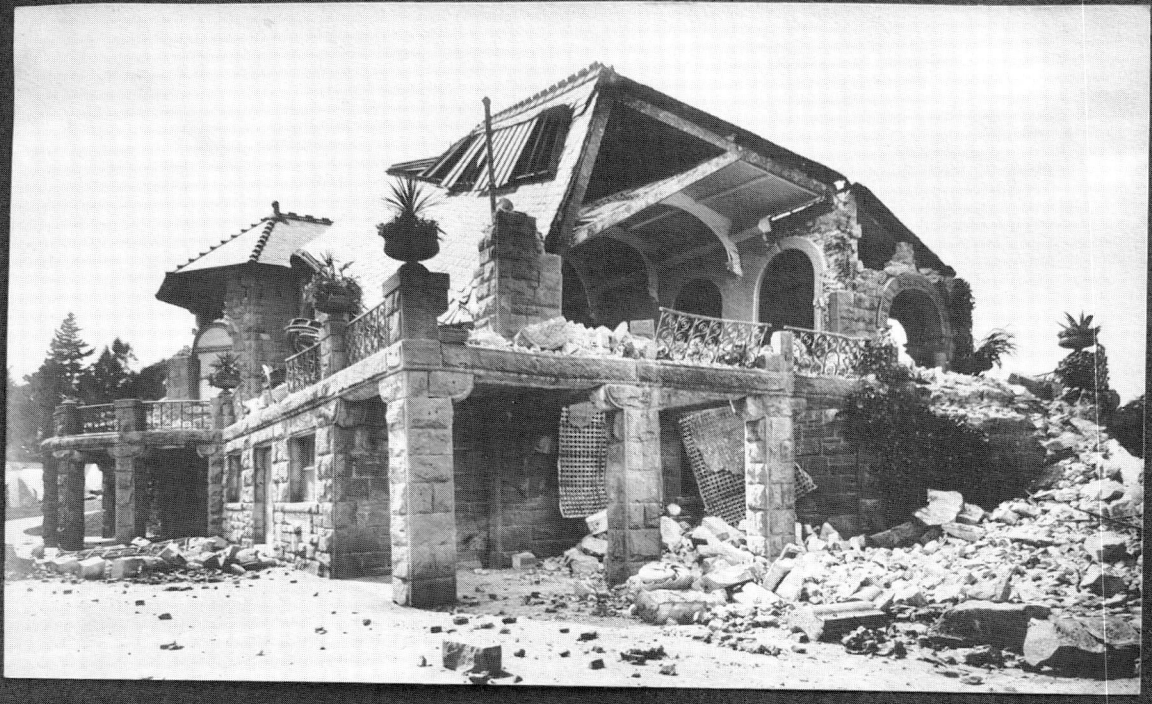

Restaurant + Children's play grounds at Golden Gate Park

Earthquake damage to Street Railway

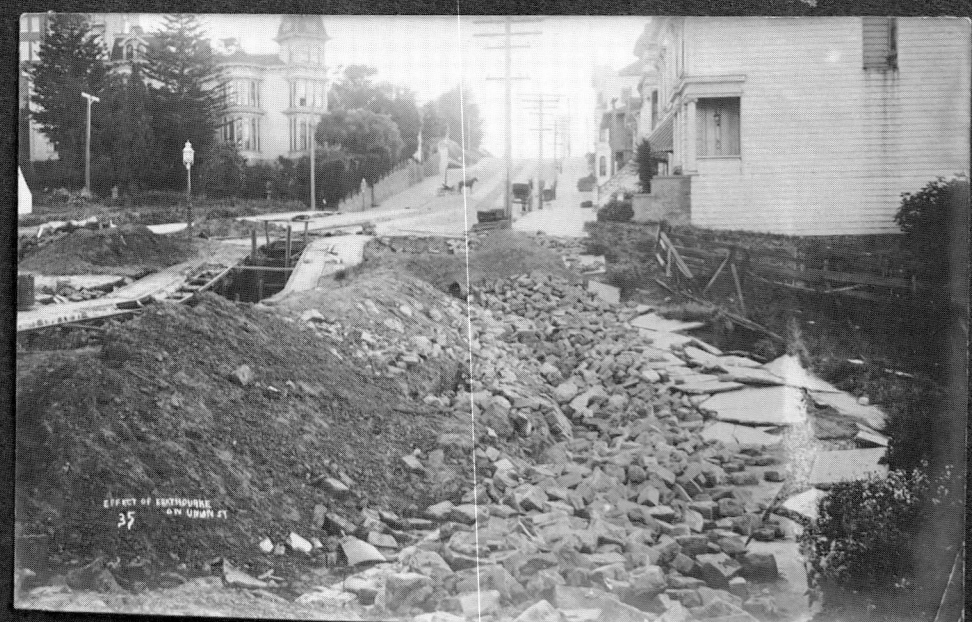

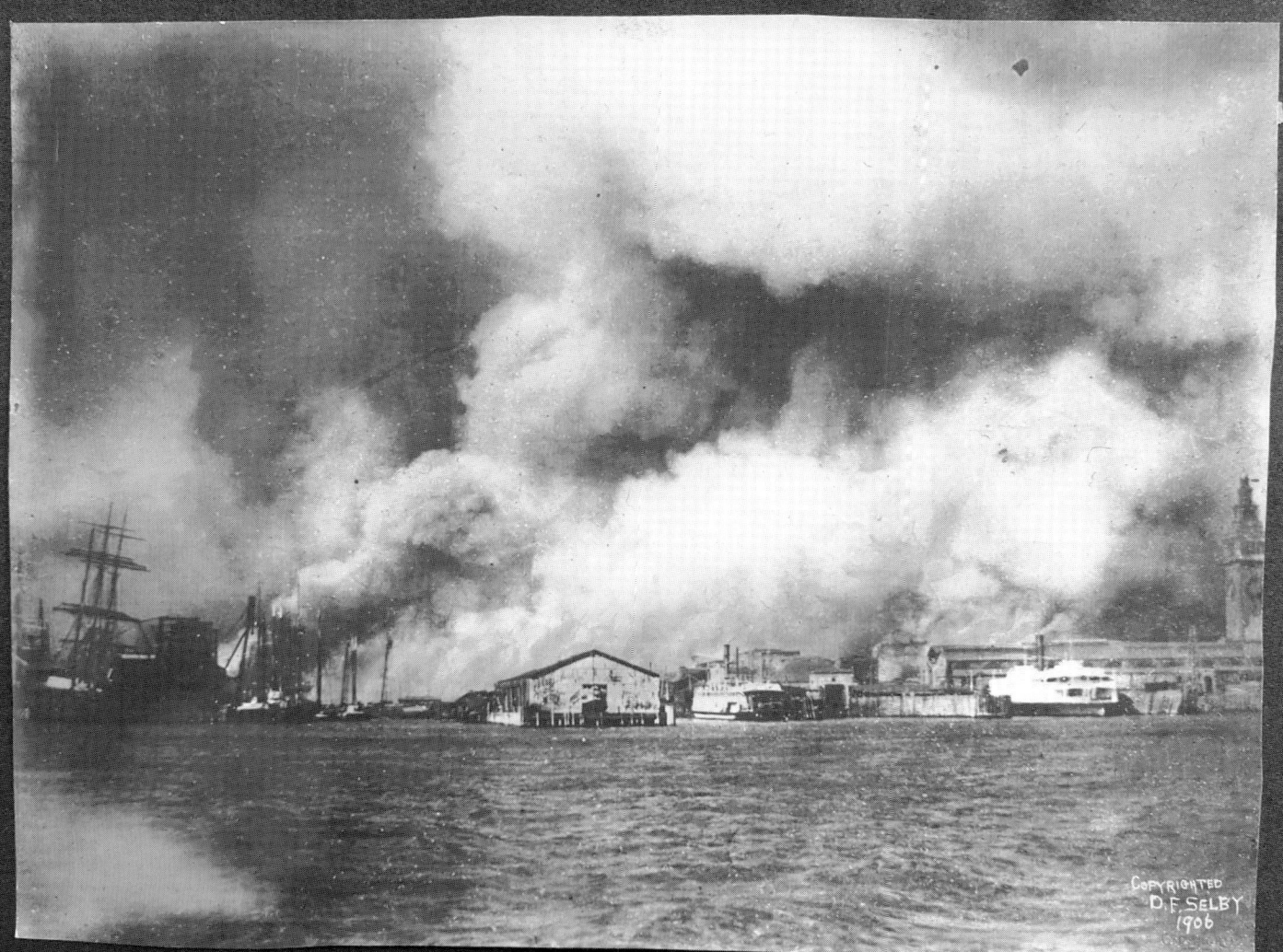

"View of fire from San Francisco Bay… A slightly differe[nt] view of the scene shown on page 8[?] showing the fire[s] at a fairly early stage of their evolution. This photo was copy-righted and poss[i]bly taken by Da[vid] F. Selby.

COPYRIGHTED
D.F. SELBY
1906

*View of fire from San Francisco Bay
3 hours after Earthquake*

When San Francisco Burned

"The city burning..."
This photograph was taken from an unidentified hilltop, apparently close to San Francisco's center and looking roughly east. The fire is bearing down rapidly on the wooden buildings in the foreground and, as the caption states, all were later destroyed by the fire.

"Earthquake results in a graveyard"
Post-earthquake, tumbled tombstones and markers were a common sight in cemeteries around the Bay Area.

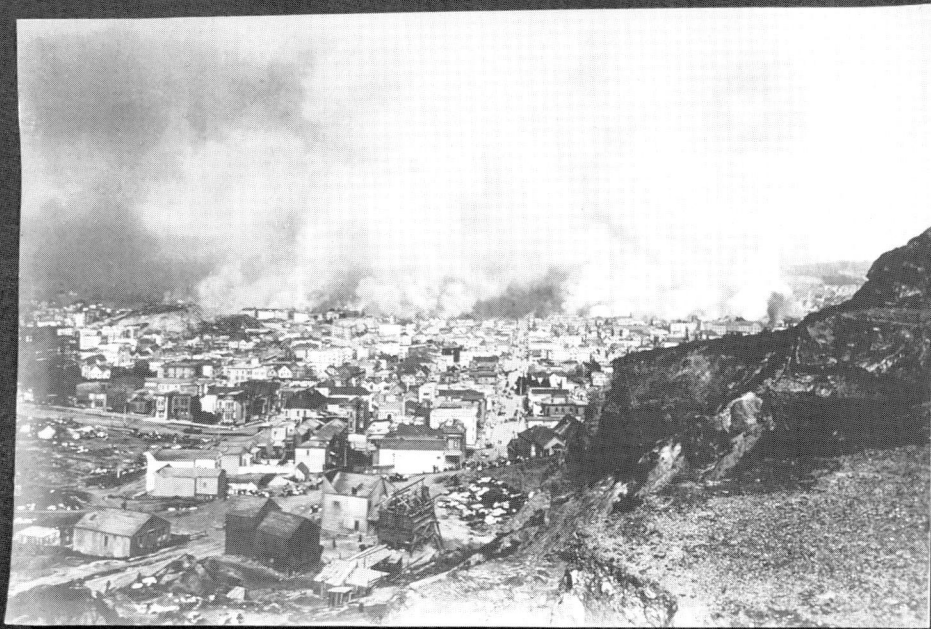

The city burning all these buildings were afterwards distroyed

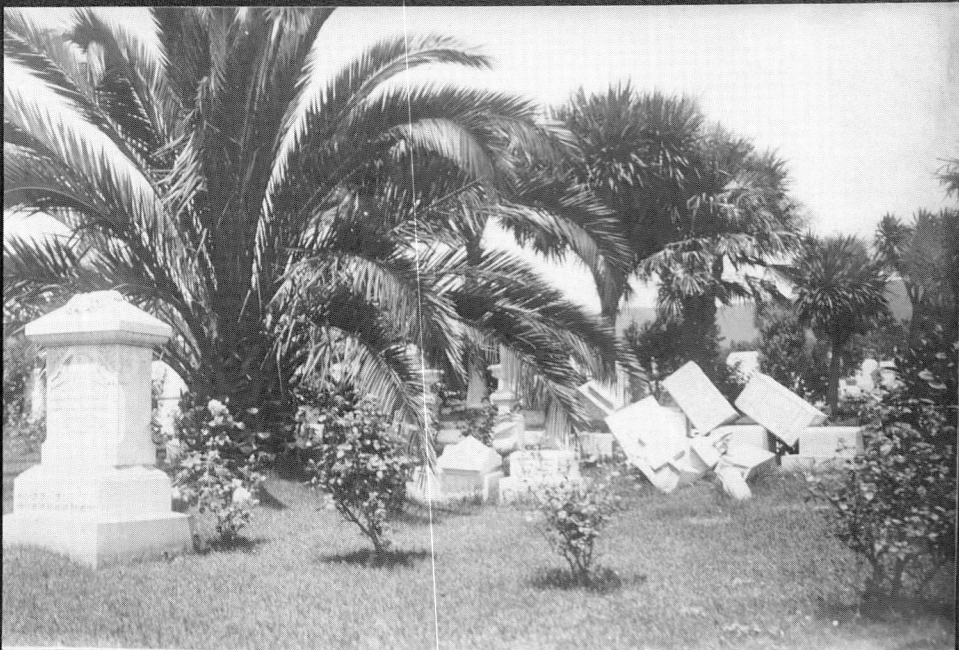

Earthquake results in a Grave yard.

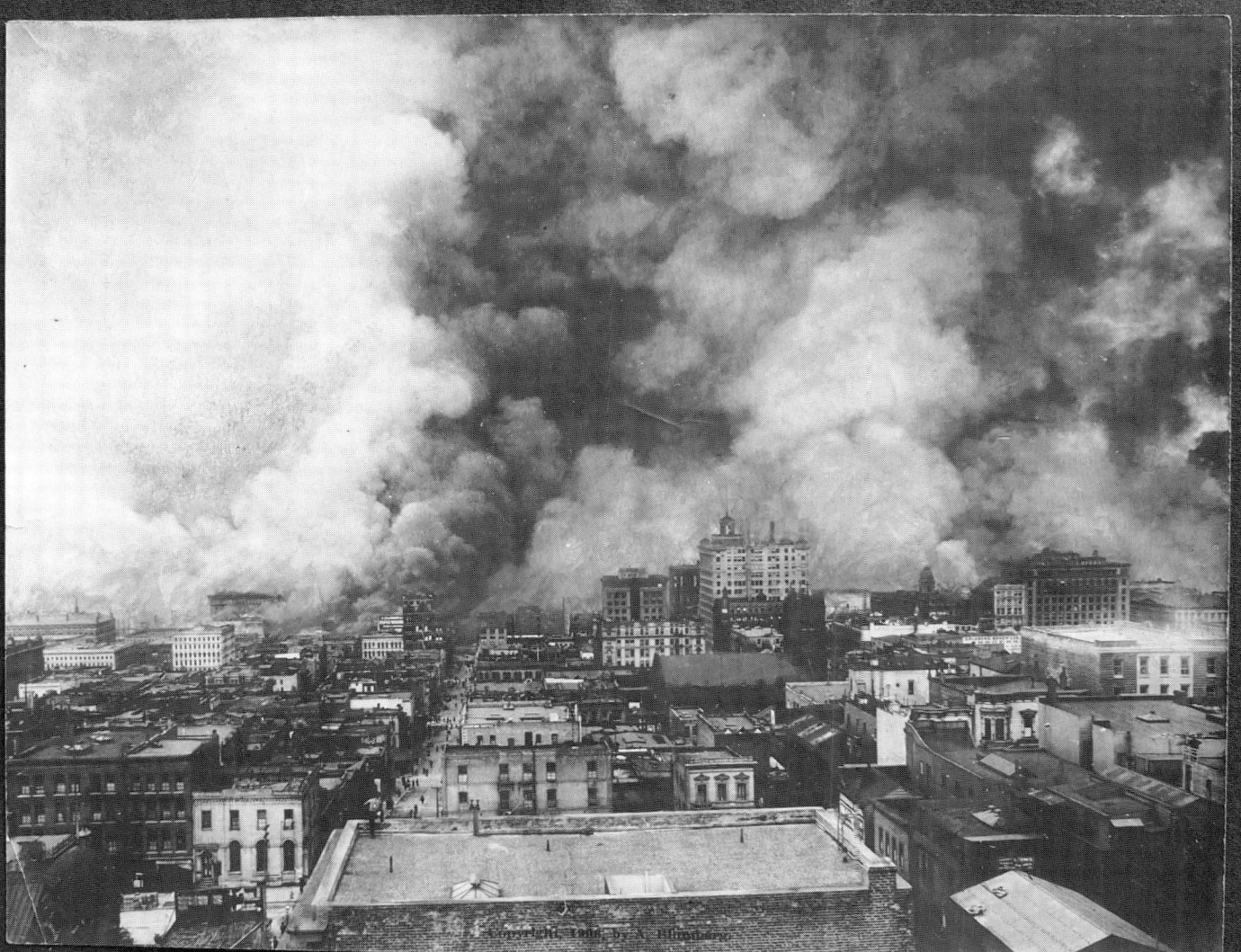

Burning of San Francisco - Wholesale district

"Burning of San Francisco— Wholesale district"
Another photo of the area, this one taken from a higher perspective (precise location unknown), showing people watching as the fire advances.

15

When San Francisco Burned

"The City Ablaze View down Grove St."
This view looks down from Alamo Square. As the fire nears, activity is intensive. A lone man at right stands on a rooftop, possibly taking photos to capture the scene. (Blumberg)

"San Francisco Burning April 18th–06"
The upper view shows post-fire devastation, looking east from Van Ness. At extreme left the Fairmont Hotel is visible, with the burned-out Call Building near the right. (Pillsbury?) City Hall is visible in the lower shot.

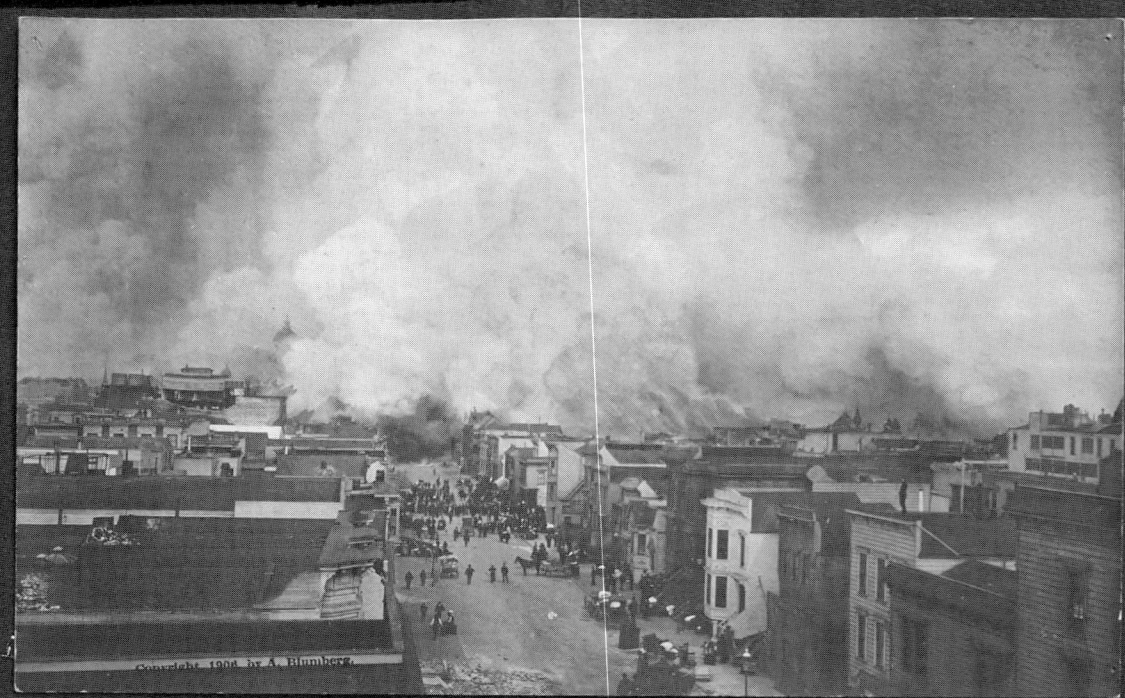

The City Ablaze
View down
Grove St.

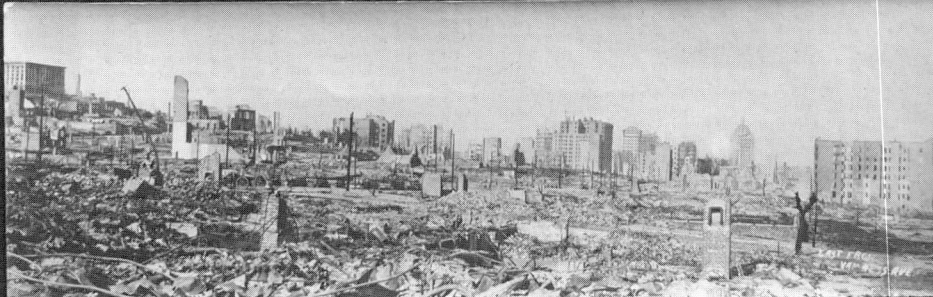

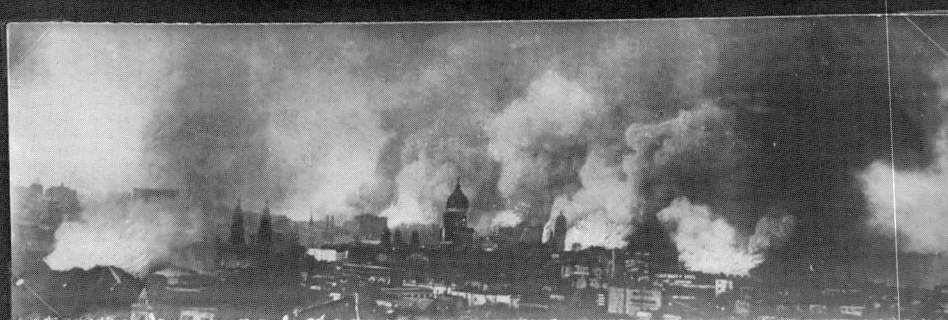

San Francisco
Burning
April 18th – '06.

16

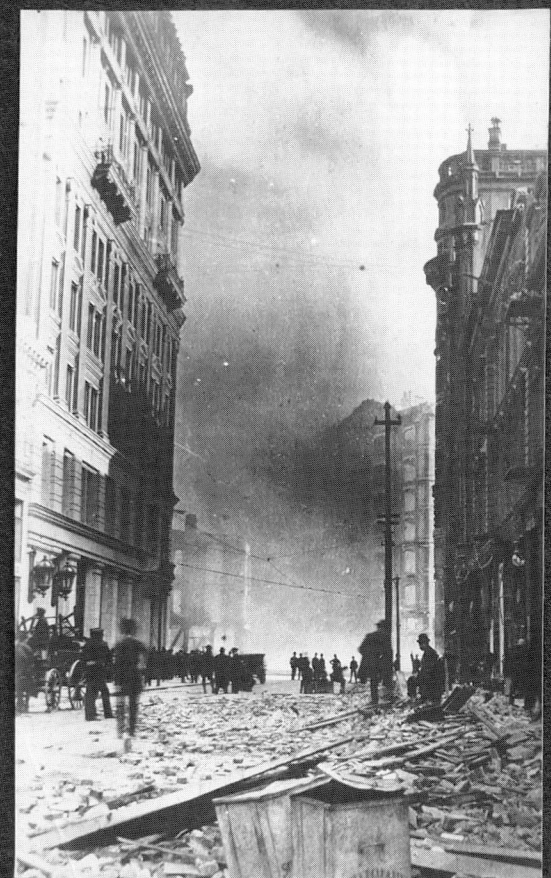

Montgomery St cor Market & Post

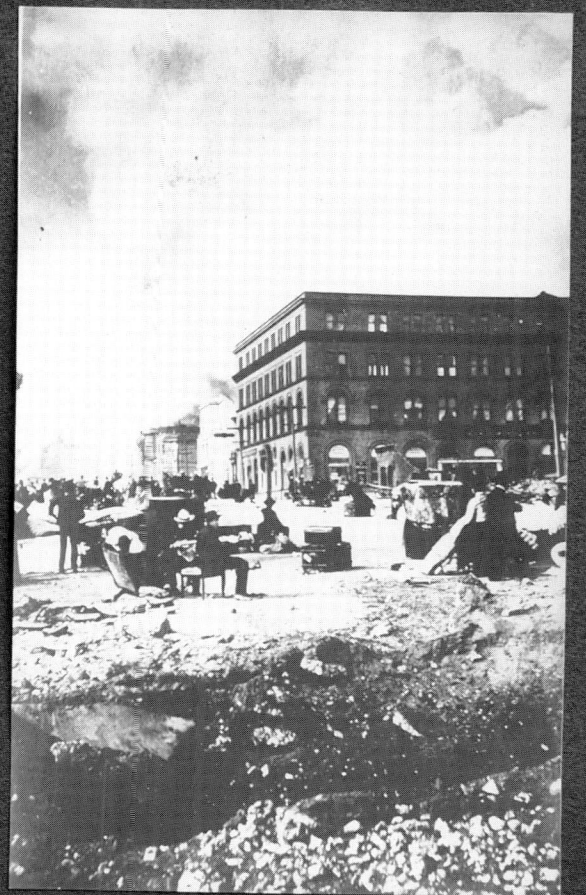

Van Ness Ave before the fire

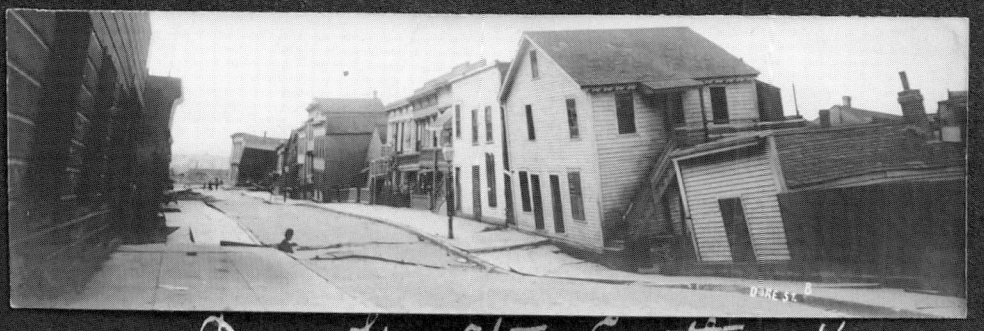

Dore St after Earthquake

"Montgomery St cor Market & Post" Wood and brick lay scattered in the roadway, and the blurred figures testify to the moment's urgency.

"Van Ness Ave before the fire" Refugees are visible beyond the large fissure in the foreground, and billowing smoke clouds hover far above the street.

"Dore St after Earthquake" Built on loose fill dirt, the structures seen here were located on what was once shoreline. They shifted, thrusted and sank with the earthquake's waves. A man is visible inside one of the street cracks—one wonders why he was there, or whether he was looking for water. (Pillsbury?)

When San Francisco Burned

"What the Earthquake did to a Wagon Factory" Note the wagon wheels scattered among the building's remnants.

"Earthquake damage on Mission St." The U.S. Post Office can be seen to the left.

"The city ablaze" In this bayside view, showing docked ships and little else, fires are so intense that the cityscape has almost vanished.

"Residence on Nob Hill burning" Note what appears to be a rifle-toting soldier near the lower right corner. (Unidentified photographer)

18

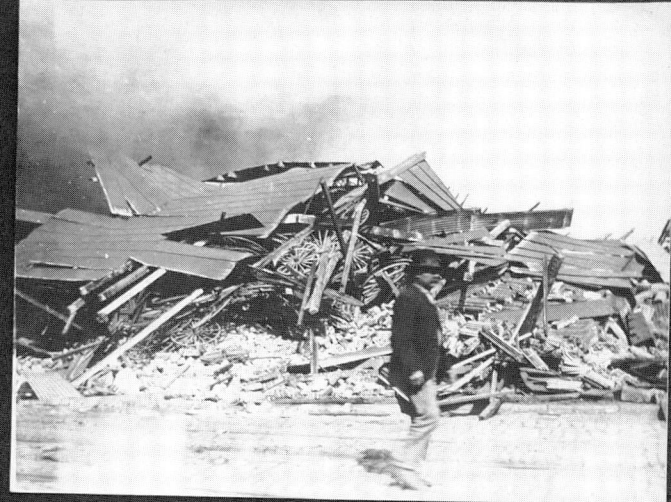

What the Earthquake did to a Wagon Factory

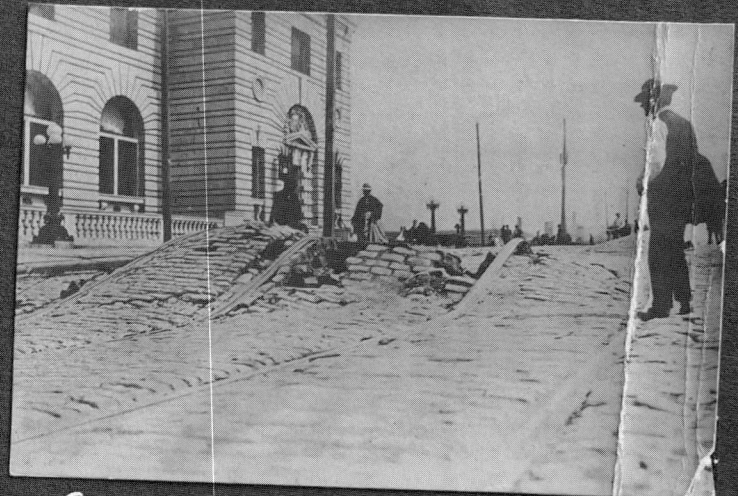

Earthquake damage on Mission St.

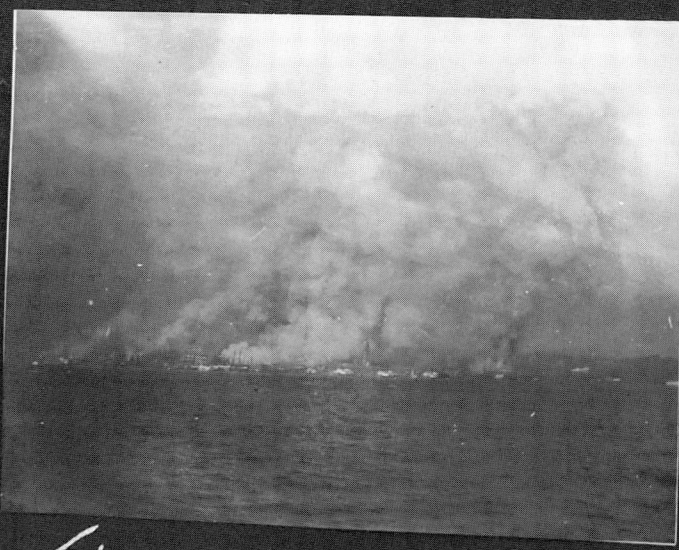

The city ablaze

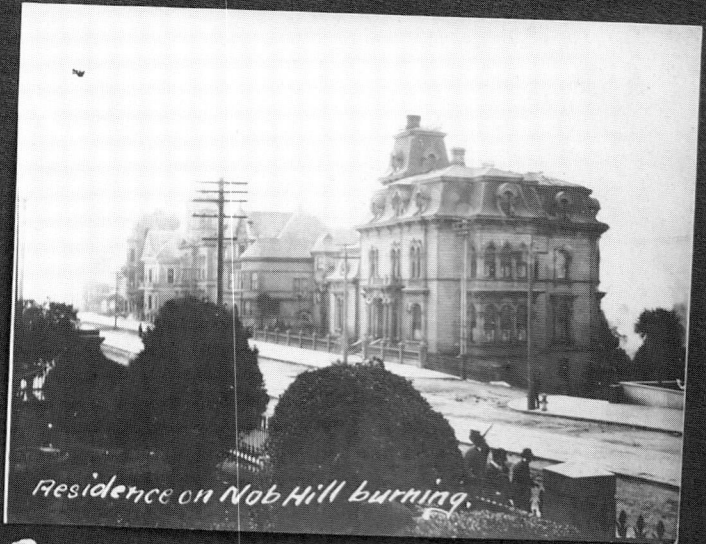

Residence on Nob Hill burning.

Residence on Nob Hill burning

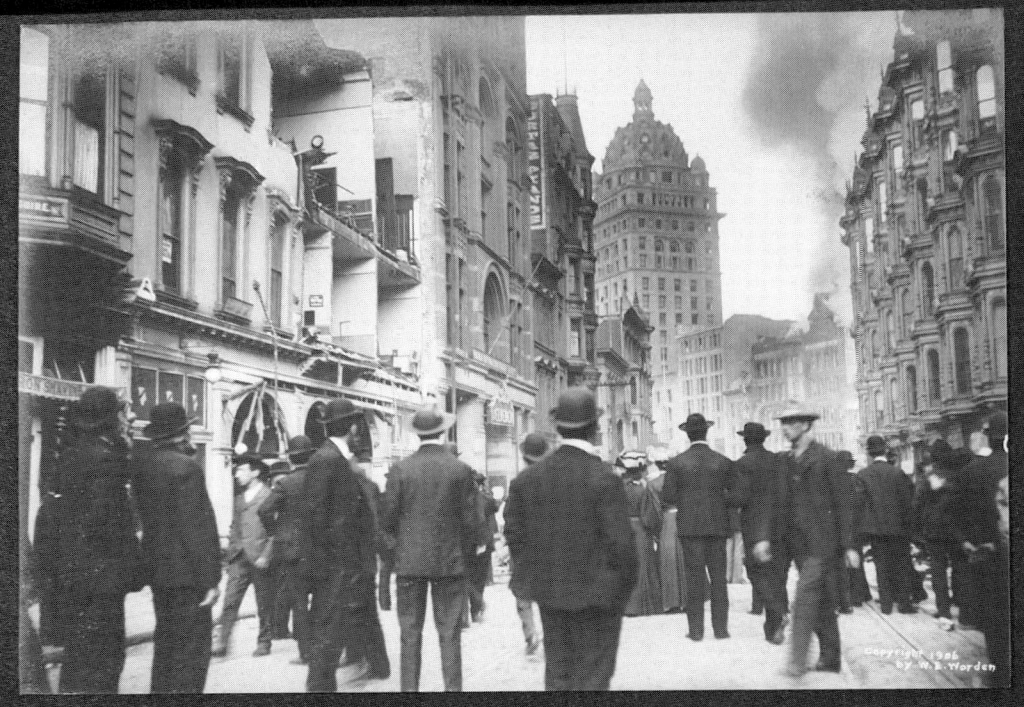

O'Farrell St showing front of building shaken down by Earthquake

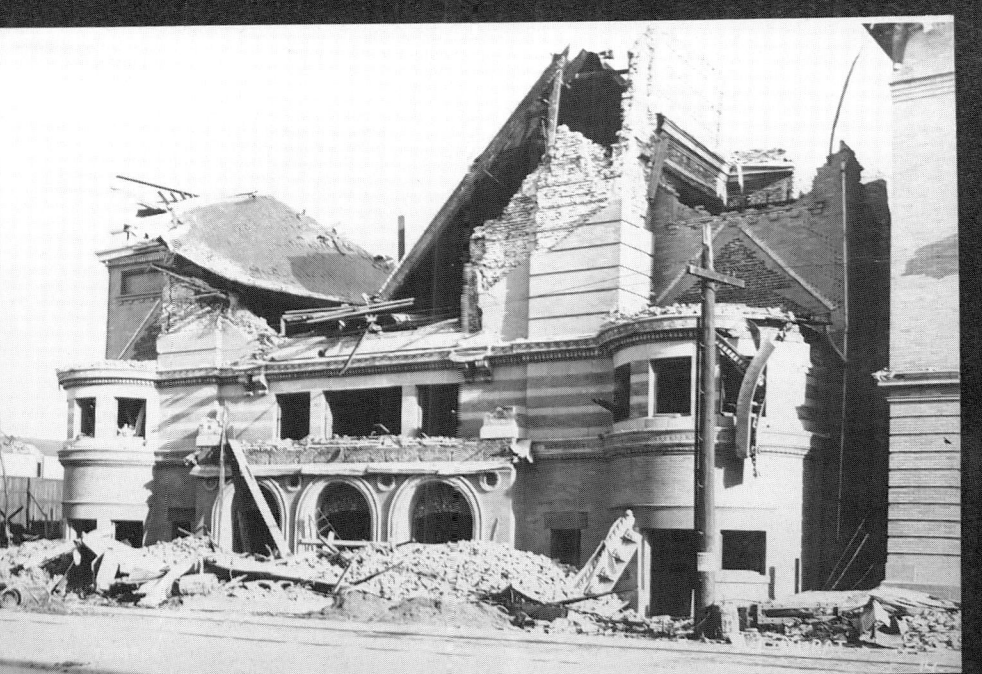

Earthquake damage showing Jewish Synagogue

The Album

"O'Farrell St showing…" The scene here looks almost normal, except for the missing façade at left and the ominous smoke plume at right. The Call Building stands, as yet unscathed, near the center. (Worden)

"Earthquake damage showing Jewish Synagogue" Temple Beth Israel, on Geary between Steiner and Fillmore streets, was nearing completion when the earthquake struck. It became one of San Francisco's more spectacular ruins. See also pages 50 and 103.

19

When San Francisco Burned

"Earthquake damage—St. [Dom]inic's Church" While the iron [fr]ameworks seen [ ]here withstood [ ]the earthquake, [t]he surrounding [mas]onry fell apart.

"Market St. ablaze" [Th]e couple in the [for]eground sports [an] almost-carefree appearance.

"Palace Hotel on fire" [T]he grand dame [of] San Francisco's [ ]hotels, built in [18]75 by financier [W]illiam Ralston, [b]urns at the end of the corridor. Rebuilt, it still presides over [S]an Francisco's busiest street.

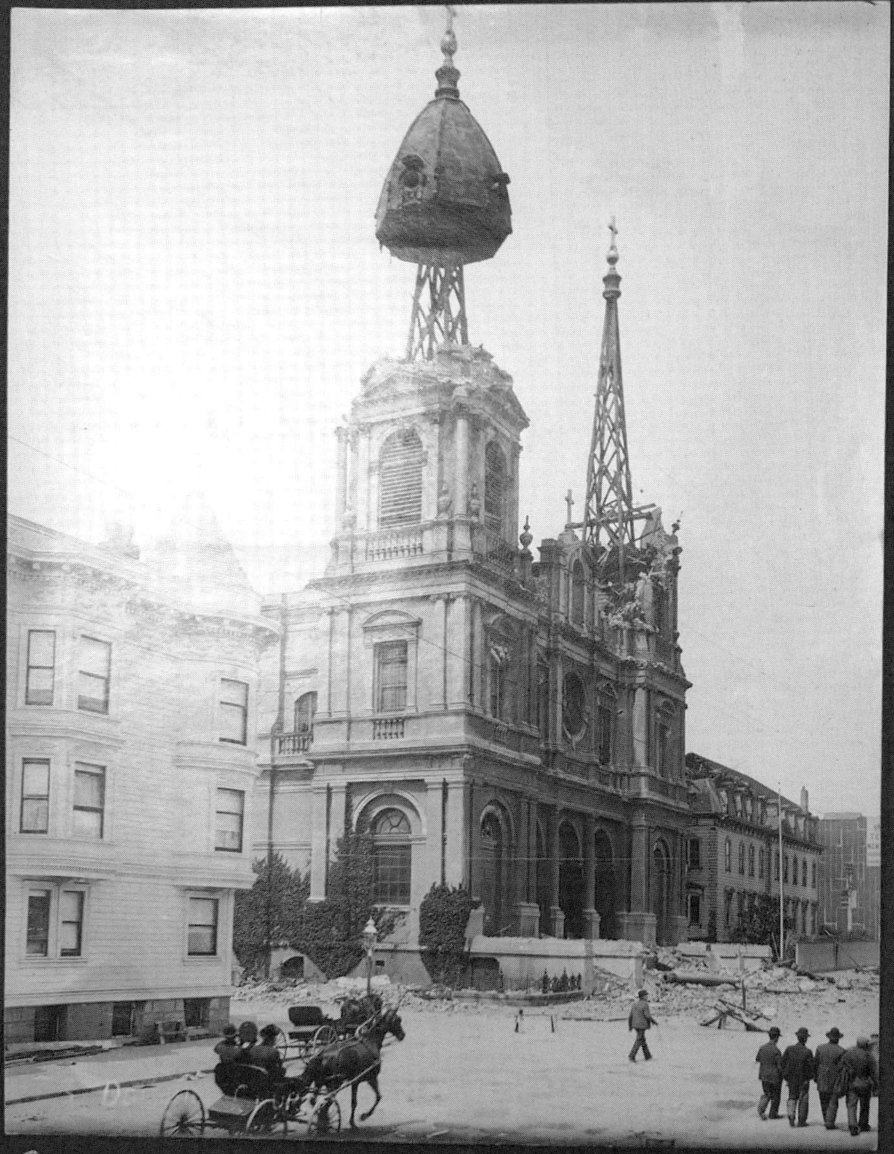

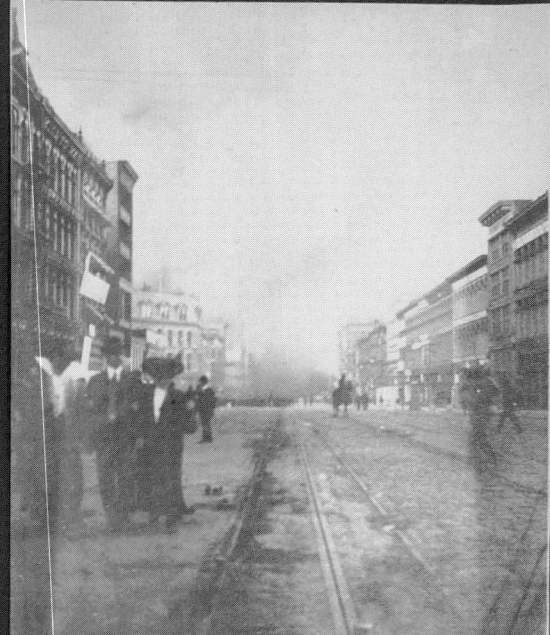

Market St. ablaze

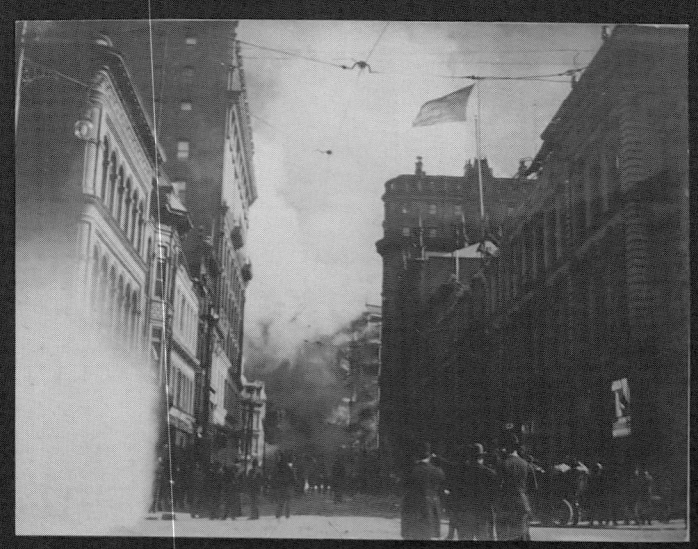

Earthquake damage—St. Dominic's Church

Palace Hotel on fire

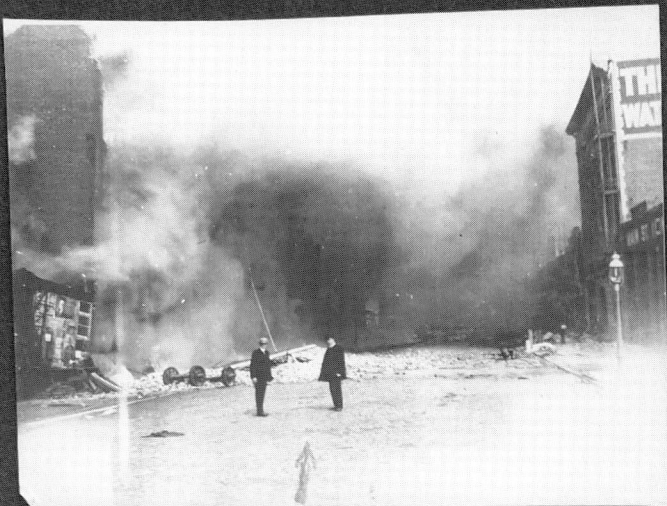

Main St. – ablaze –

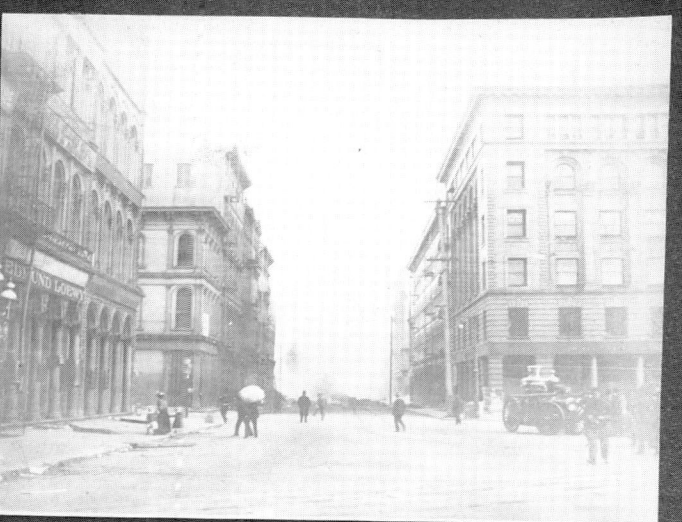

Battery St. before fire reached it

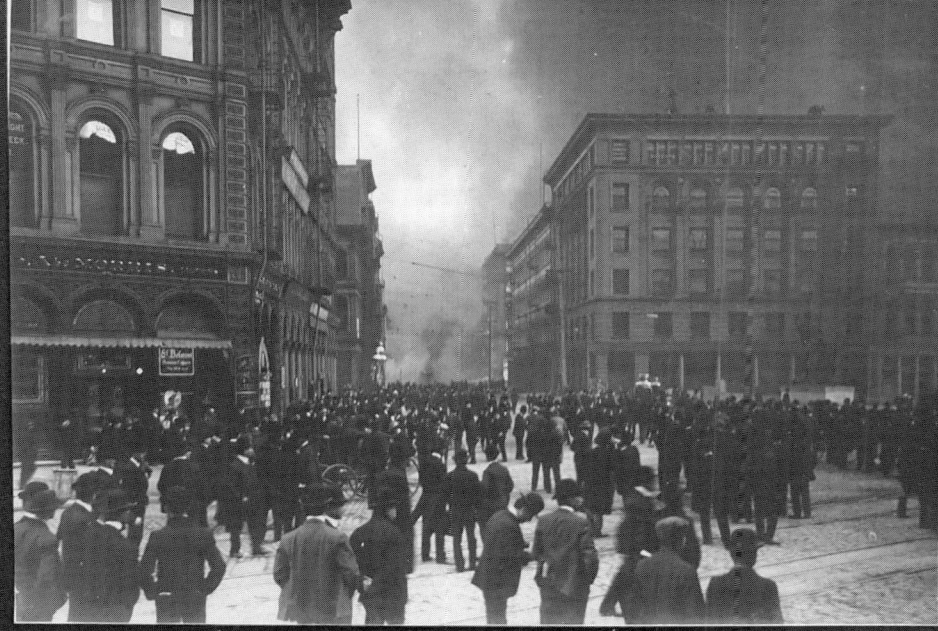

Wholesale district burning, from Sansome & Market Sts

"Main St.—ablaze—" This photograph shows the fire burning only two blocks from the Ferry Building and just off Market. I believe the two men in the shot are my grandfather, Louis Selby, and his brother, Albert.

"Battery St. before fire reached it" This scene is north of Market. A wall of fire looms in the distance. Edmund Loewy's clothing business is visible on the left, while the fire engine at right is likely useless—no hoses are in the street, suggesting no water was available.

"Wholesale district burning…" In this all-too-common scene, a crowd has gathered to watch as flames approach.

When San Francisco Burned

"Moving from advancing fire" Two men and a woman move a small wagon or baby carriage, loaded with what might be all their remaining possessions. The woman and small children on the sidewalk are in no apparent hurry—perhaps they have nowhere left to run. (Cohen)

"A corner of Jefferson Square" Located in the Western Addition, Jefferson Square marked one of the fire zone's edges.

"Ruins Sansome & Market Sts." Typical view. Note askew mailbox in center of the street.

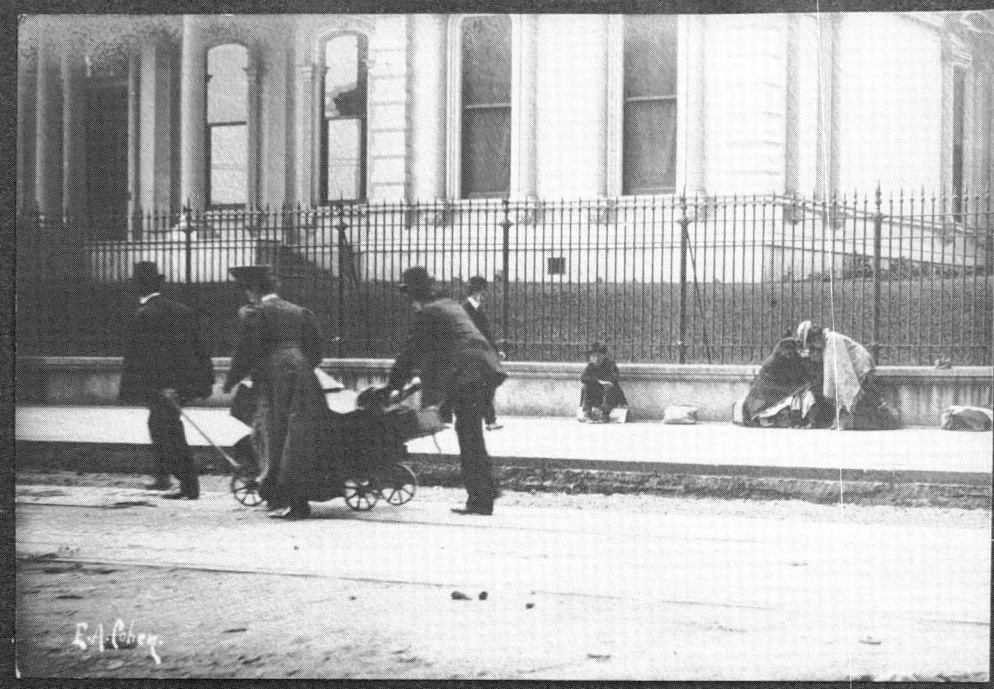

Moving from advancing fire

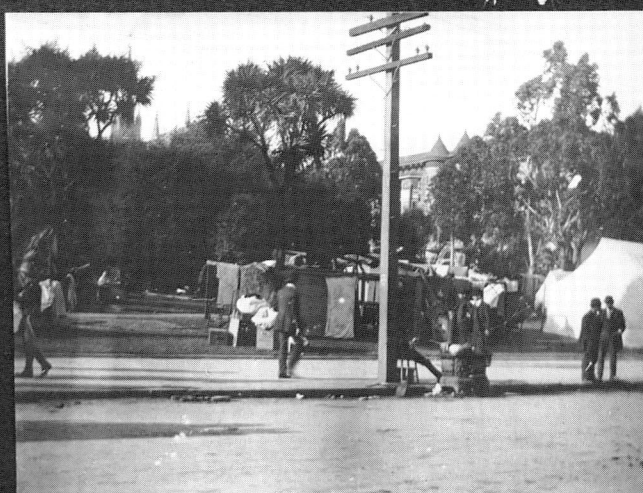

A corner of Jefferson Square

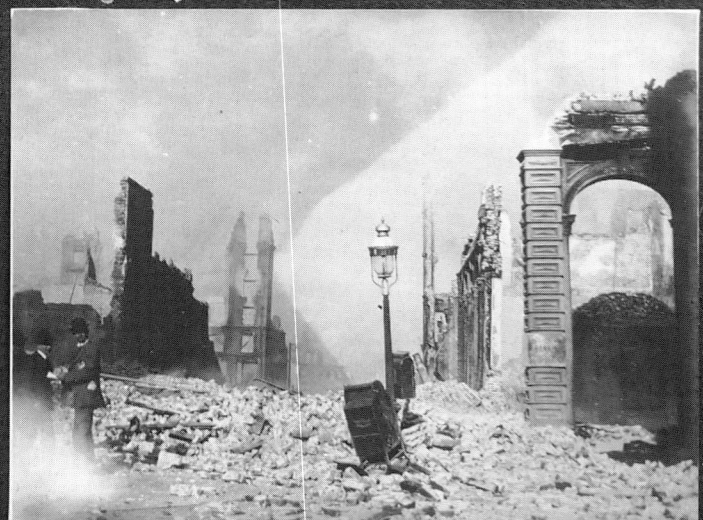

Ruins Sansome + Market Sts

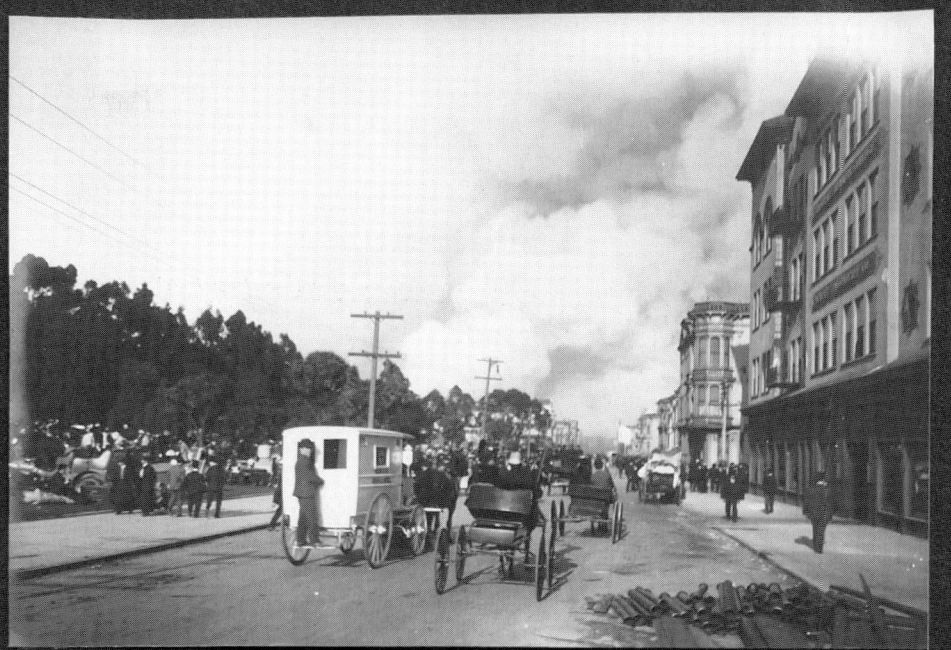

Golden Gate Ave opposite Jefferson Square

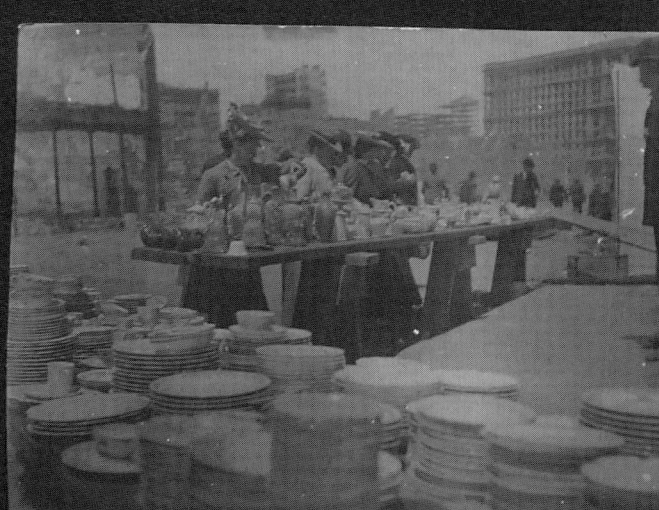

Buying relics of the fire.

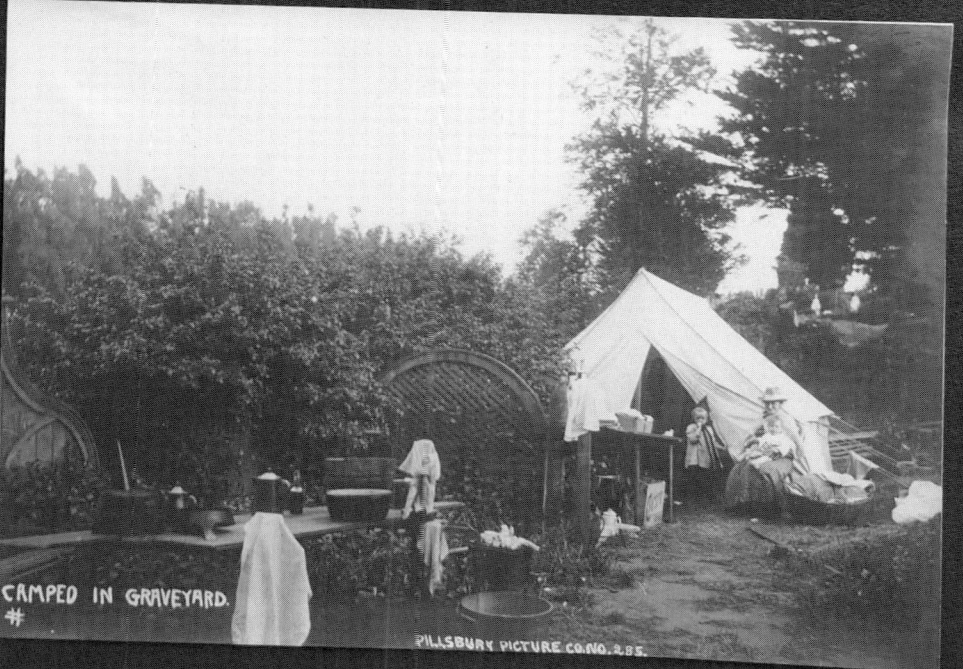

CAMPED IN GRAVEYARD.
#

PILLSBURY PICTURE CO. NO. 285.

The Album

"Golden Gate Ave opposite Jefferson Square"
Following the earthquake and fire, Jefferson Square became a large homeless encampment. Located fairly close to Van Ness, where explosives were used to make a large fire break, one can see smoke moving in closely. Note the white horse-drawn ambulance with the man standing on its back step.

"Buying relics of the fire"
A policeman stands watch at right as women purchase replacement crockery.

"Camped in Graveyard"
As public spaces filled up after the earthquake, survivors pitched tents wherever open space was available—even in cemeteries. (Pillsbury)

23

When San Francisco Burned

"Market St ablaze below 1st St."
Here the street is burning, apparently without an audience. It also seems that a safe has been moved onto the sidewalk. Was it too much to move, too hot, or did thieves abandon it? (Pillsbury)

"Golden Gate Ave. people fleeing from fire"
As smoke bellows just a short distance away, this image shows flight from the fire zone in full swing. (Pillsbury?)

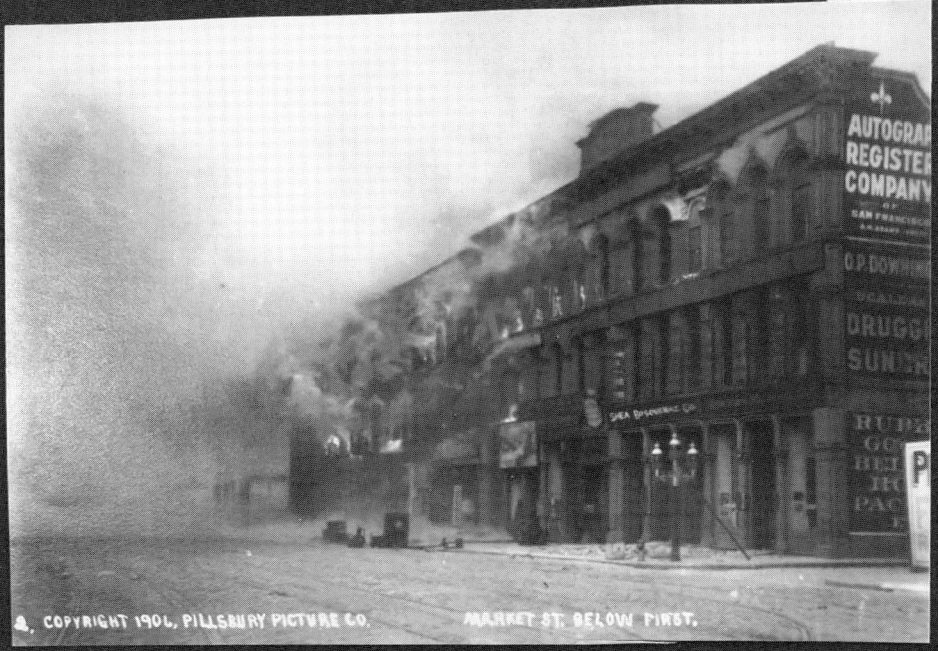

COPYRIGHT 1906, PILLSBURY PICTURE CO.   MARKET ST. BELOW FIRST.

Market St. ablaze below 1st St.

Golden Gate Ave. people fleeing from fire

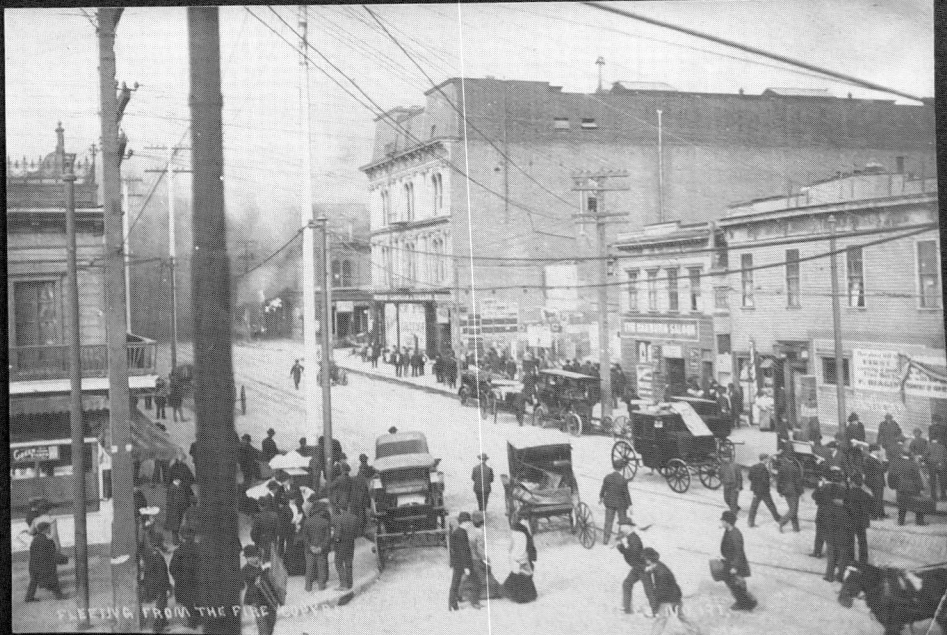

FLEEING FROM THE FIRE

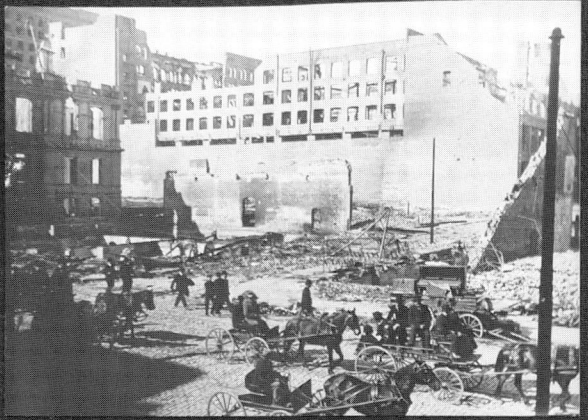

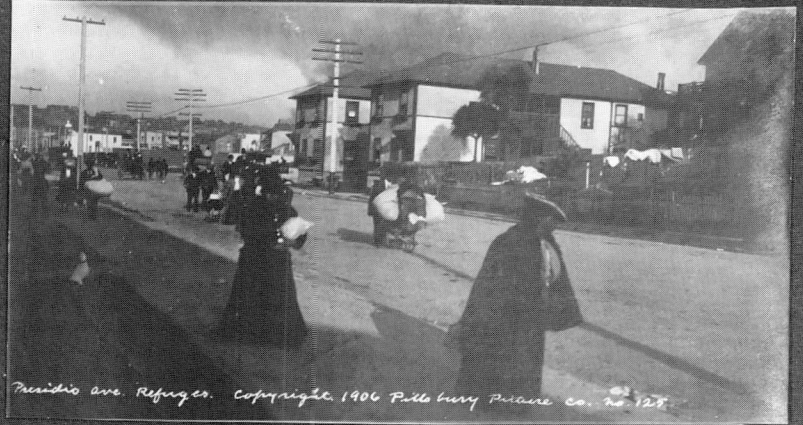

Presidio Ave. Refuges. Copyright 1906 Pillsbury Picture Co. No. 128.

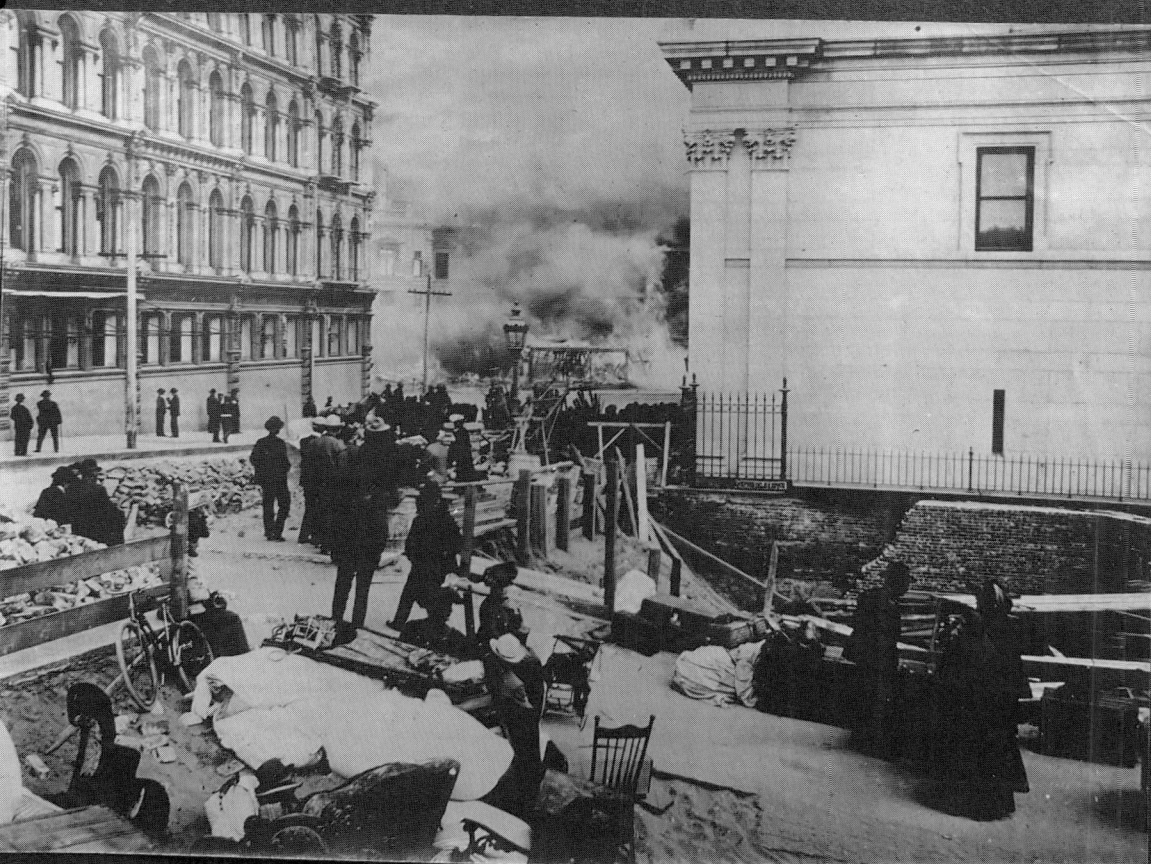

Watching fire opposite Hibernia Bank

[Untitled]
A post-fire scene, showing much rubble cleared from the ground.

"Presidio Ave. Refuges [sic]" Survivors, carrying their hastily-assembled belongings, try to stay a few steps ahead of the advancing fire. (Pillsbury)

"Watching fire opposite Hibernia Bank" In this view, the flames seem to be closing in fast. The Hibernia Bank, a longtime San Francisco landmark designed by Albert Pissis, is located where Market, McAllister, and Jones streets converge. It survived 1906 and operated for many years thereafter. It is currently undergoing renovation.

When San Francisco Burned

"Damage by Earthquake Delmonico's..." Close by this famous eatery, the Alcazar Theatre's vertical sign is visible, with the Call Building in the background.

"Hale Brothers' just before fire reached it" This wraparound department store was located on Market near Sixth. The building was restored and continues in use.

"Ruins of California Theatre & Hotel" A man points out this ruined complex, located on Bush between Kearny and Grant streets.

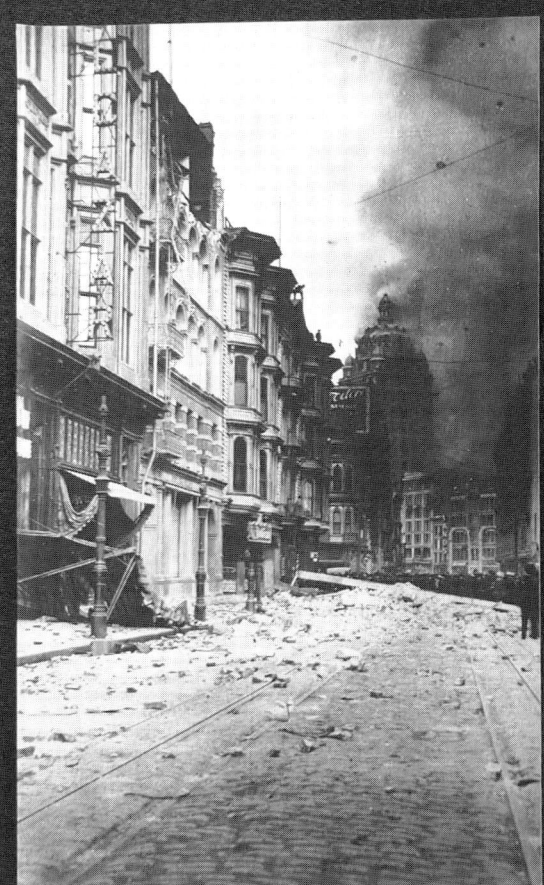

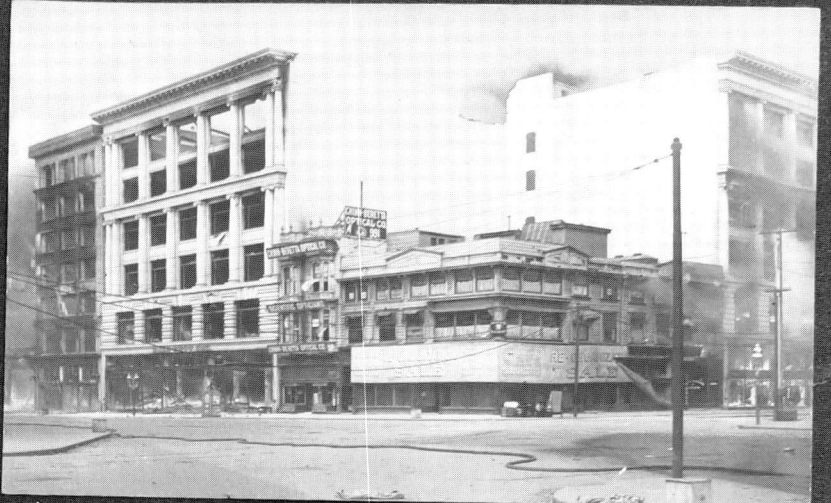

"Hale Bros" just before fire reached it

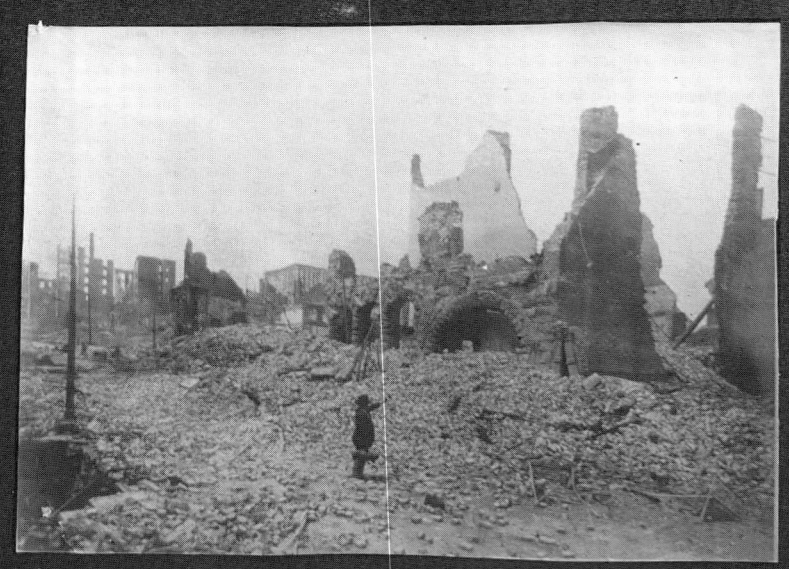

Damage by Earthquake Delmonico's Restaurant O'Farrell St.

Ruins of California Theatre & Hotel

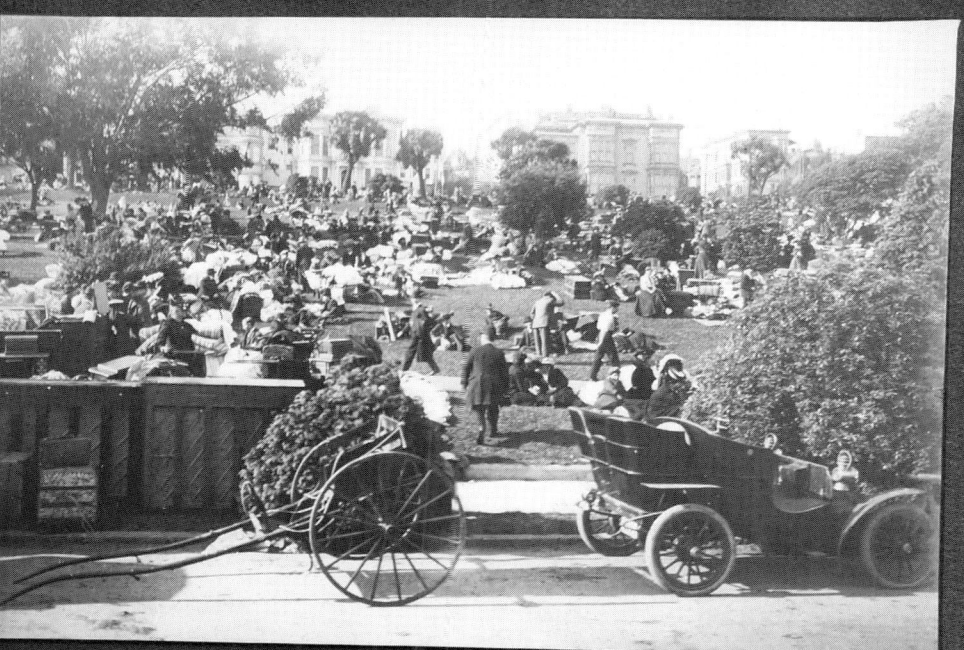

Resting while their homes burn
Jefferson Square

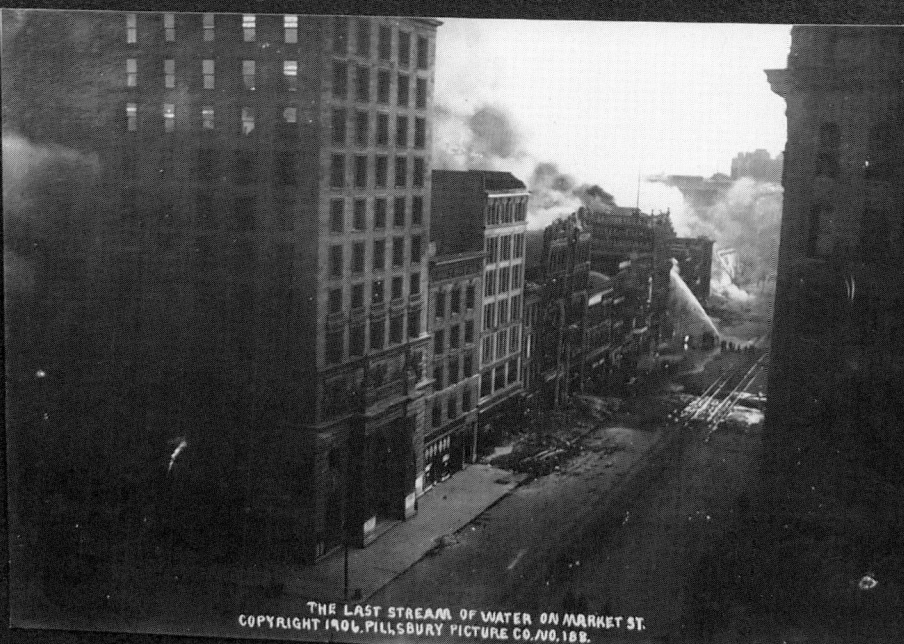

THE LAST STREAM OF WATER ON MARKET ST.
COPYRIGHT 1906, PILLSBURY PICTURE CO. NO. 188.

The last stream of water on Market St.

"Resting while their homes burn…" Another view of Jefferson Square, thick with refugees.

"The last stream of water on Market St." Taken at the moment the fire hoses went dry. The Call Building stands at left. The last stream of water is poured on buildings still burning along Market Street. This photo was probably taken from the Chronicle Building at Market and Kearny streets. (Pillsbury)

When San Francisco Burned

"Buildings burning in Wholesale district" This photograph shows men assembled to watch the fire advance on Sansome at Bush Street. The buildings around them have already burned. (Whigham)

"View down Geary St." This view down Geary toward the Call Building shows the street's total ruin. One lone man picks his way through the rubble.

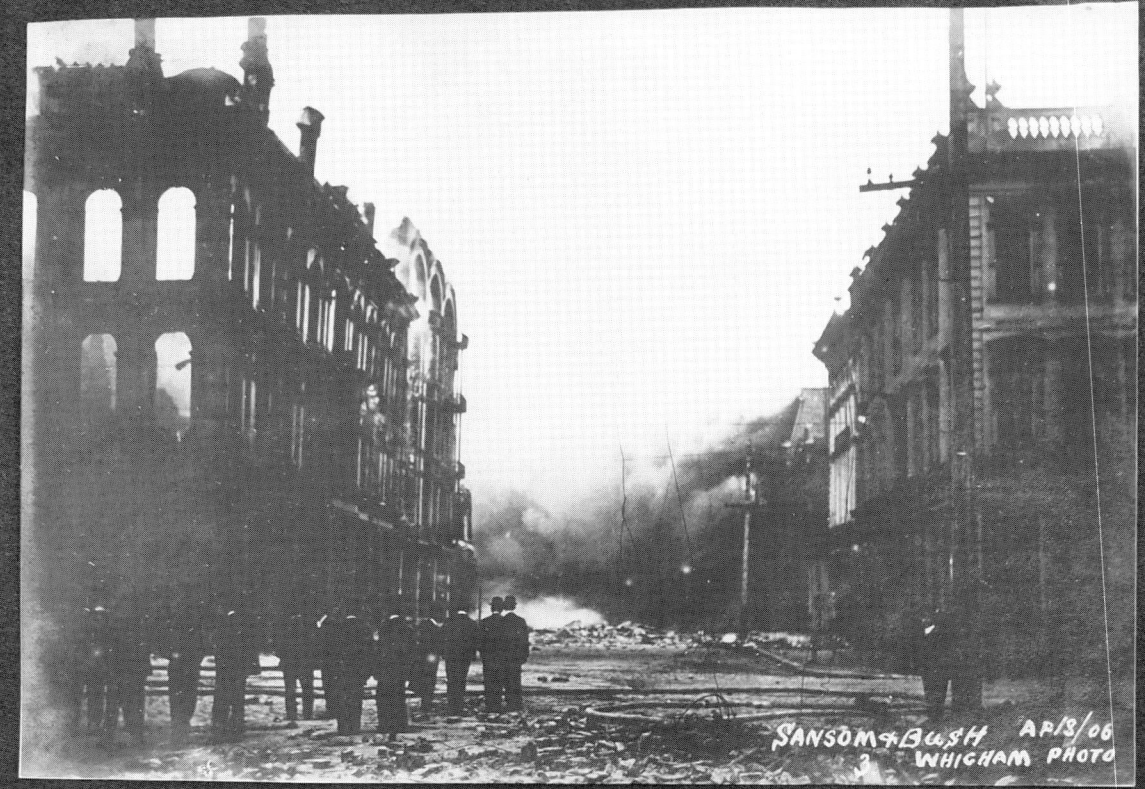

Buildings burning in Wholesale district

SANSOM & BUSH AP 13/06
WHIGHAM PHOTO

View down Geary St.

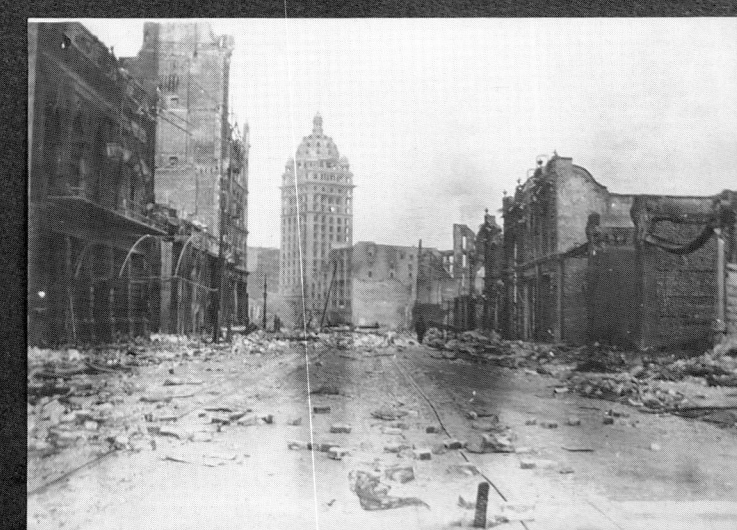

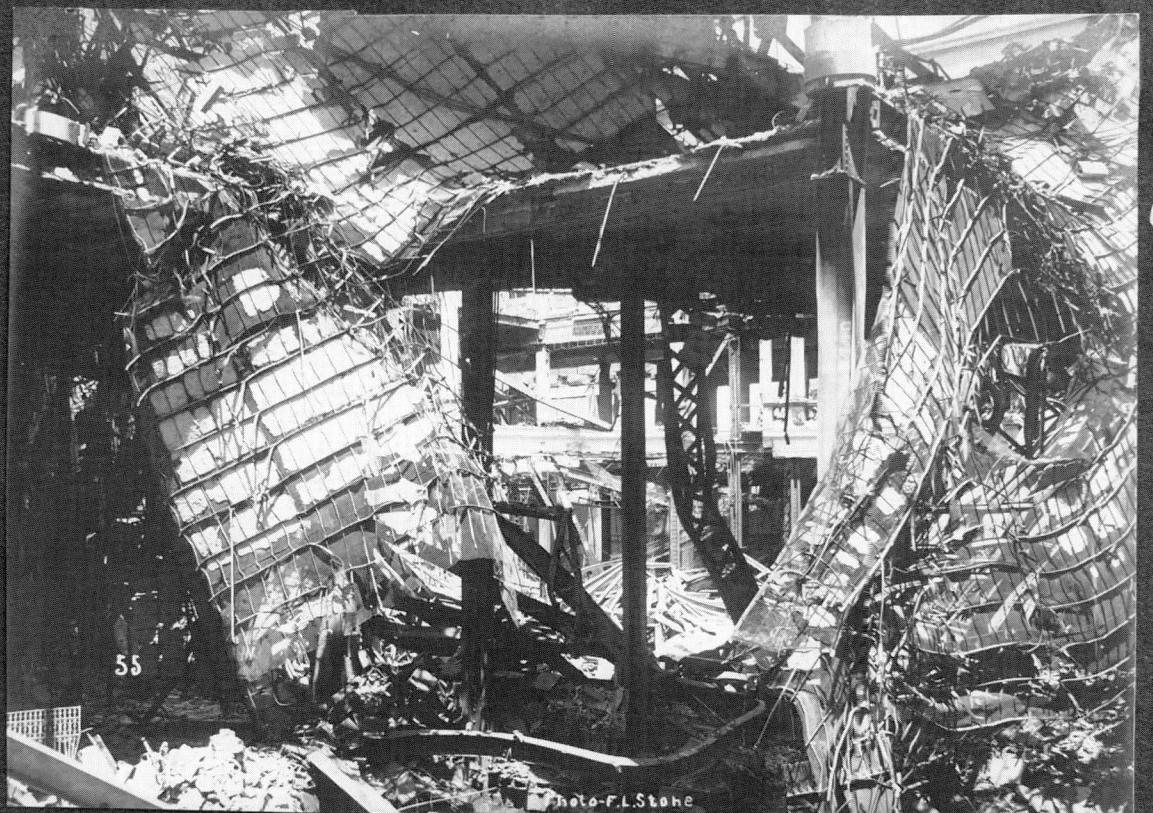

Interior of Emporium

55

Photo-F.L.Stone

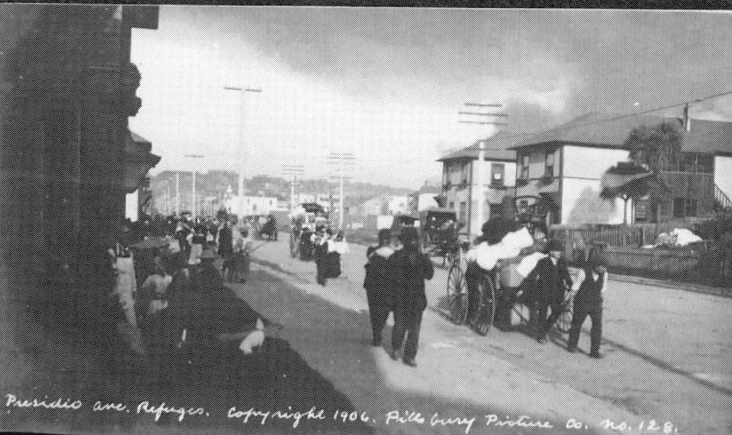

Presidio ave. Refuges. Copyright 1906. Pillsbury Picture Co. no. 128.

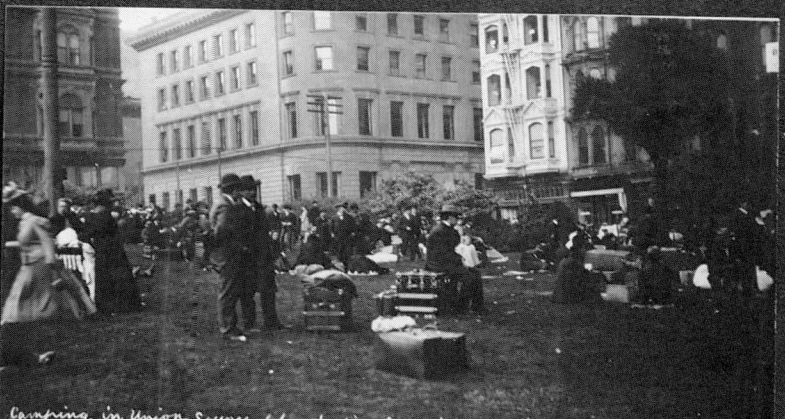

Camping. in Union Square, before the fire, Copyright 1906. Pillsbury Picture Co. no. 210

Presidio Ave Refugees　　　*Camping in Park, before the fire*

The Album

"Interior of Emporium"
Located on Market, this famed San Francisco department store took a terrible pounding during the earthquake. (Stone)

"Presidio Ave Refugees"
Similar to the photo on page 25, using the same vantage point and taken probably just a few minutes before or after the other image. (Pillsbury)

"Camping in Park, before the fire"
In this case the "park" is Union Square, still one of San Francisco's most notable and recognizable public spaces. (Pillsbury)

When San Francisco Burned

"Presidio Ave Refugees"
Also similar to the images on pages 25 and 29. (Pillsbury)

"The homeless reaching for Eggs." Sailors and volunteers appear to be handing out provisions in a neighborhood left intact. (Pillsbury)

"The Call Building afire…" In this view, taken high above Kearny Street, the Call Building is completely ablaze. At right, Raphael's (later known as the White House department store) and the M. A. Gunst cigar store are visible.

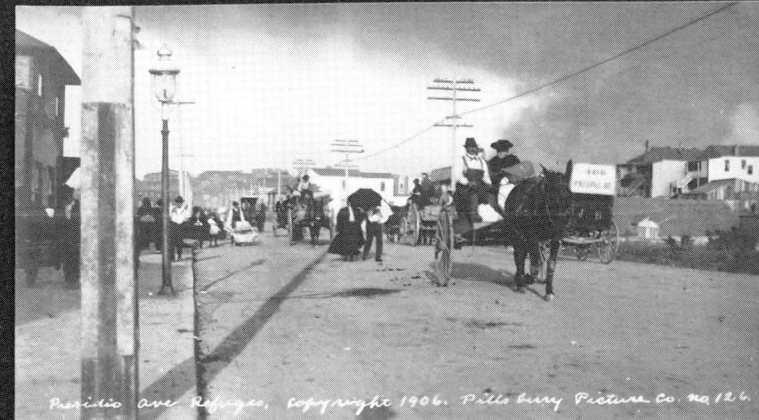

Presidio Ave. Refugees

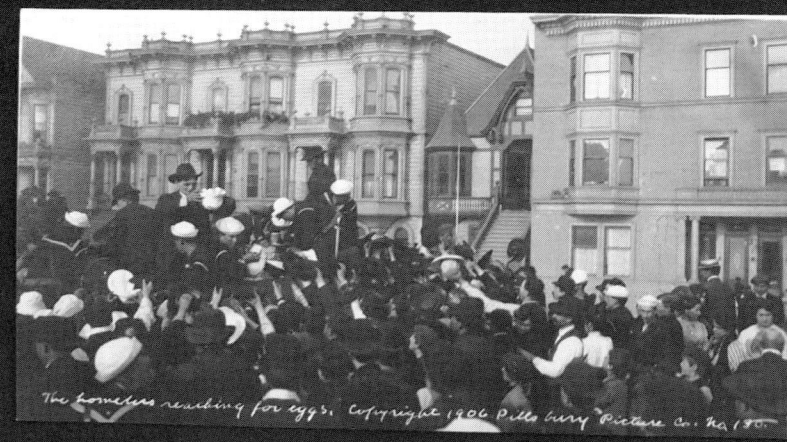

The homeless reaching for Eggs.

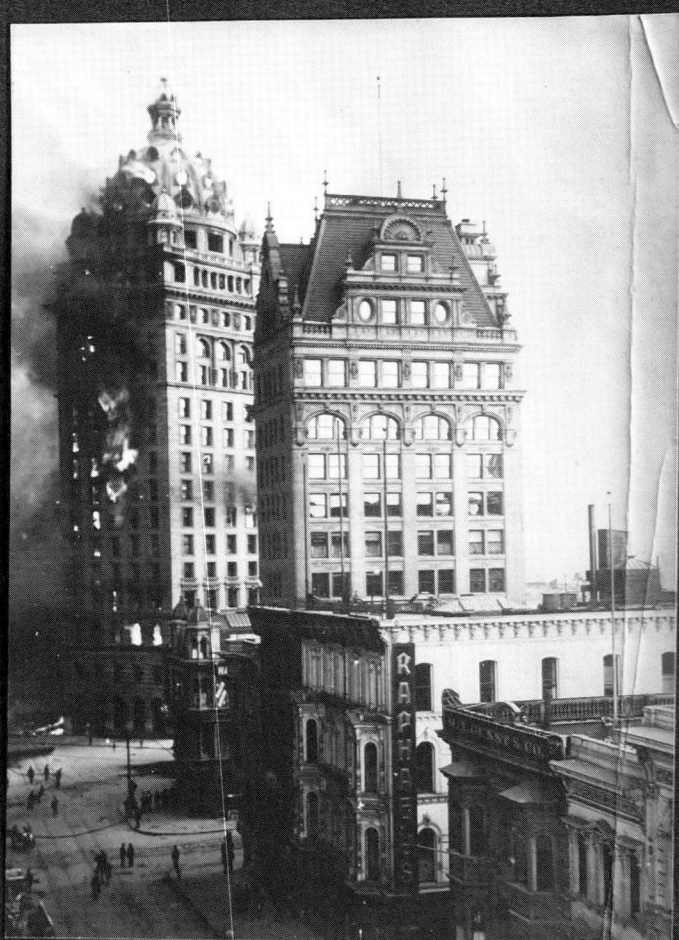

The Call Building afire.
View from Kearny St.

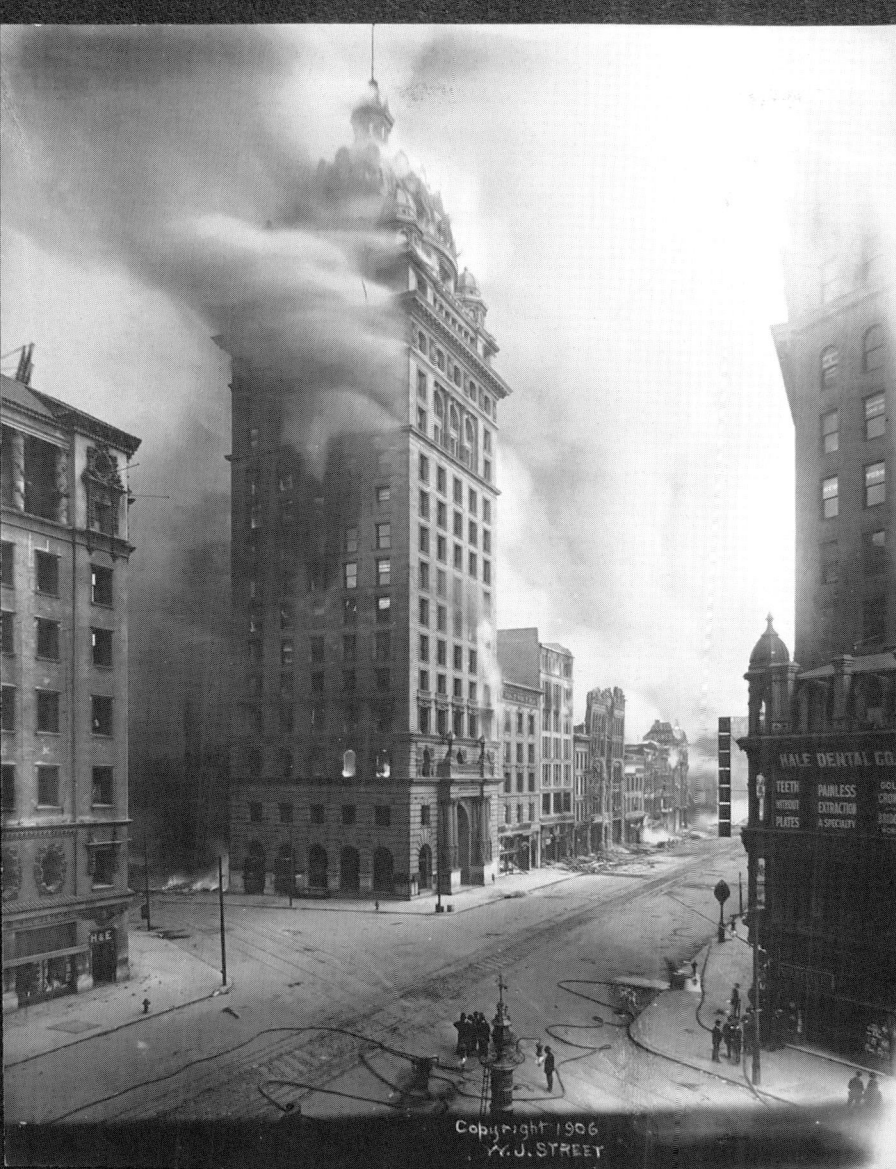

Copyright 1906
W. J. STREET

The Call Building afire

"The Call
Building af
A different,
detailed vie
burning bui
looking rou
southwest a
Market. Th
Dental Co.
be seen on
opposite co
(Street)

When San Francisco Burned

"Market St. James Flood Bldg…" An impromptu store is open for business. Scorched in the fire, the Flood Building continues in service as a mixed-use complex.

"Earthquake damage…" Buckled pavement and billowing smoke aplenty.

"Killed by falling bricks" Another sad image of animals felled by the earthquake.

"Grant Ave during fire" Looking toward Market from Post. Barely visible is the Hammam [Turkish] Baths. (Pillsbury)

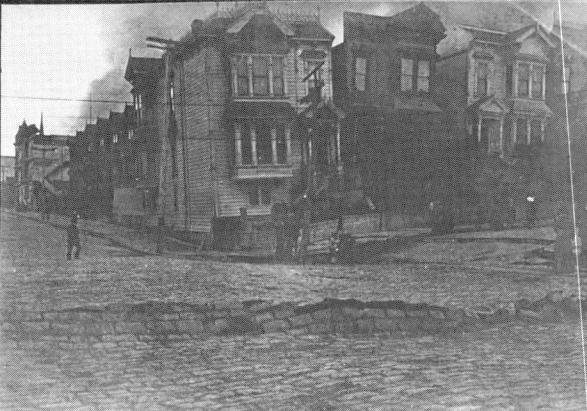

Earthquake damage Van Ness Ave & Vallejo Sts

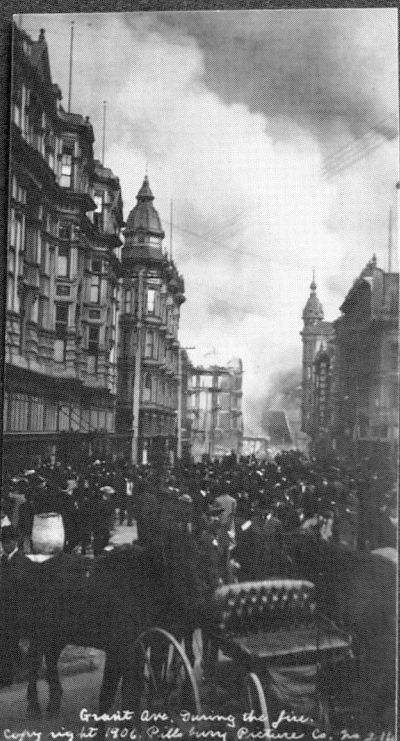

Grant Ave. during the fire. Copyright 1906. Pillsbury Picture Co. No 21

Grant Ave during fire

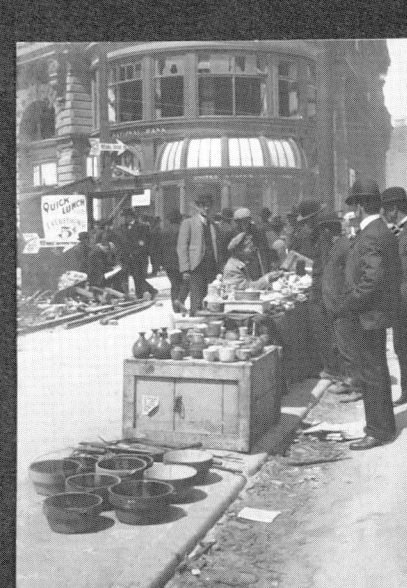

Market St James Flood Bldg after fire

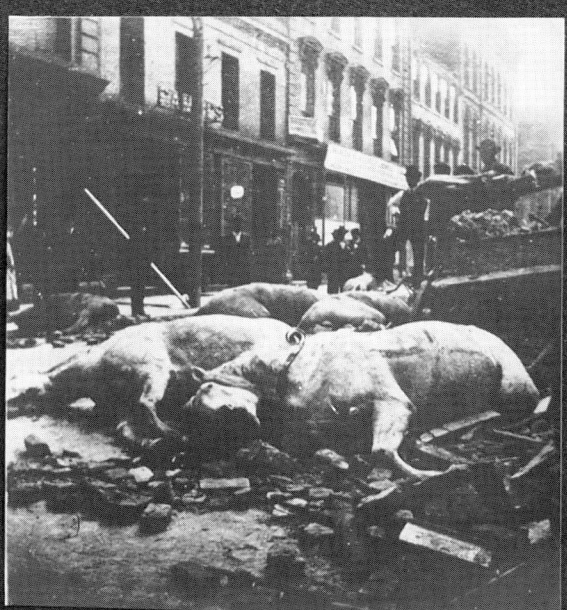

Killed by falling bricks

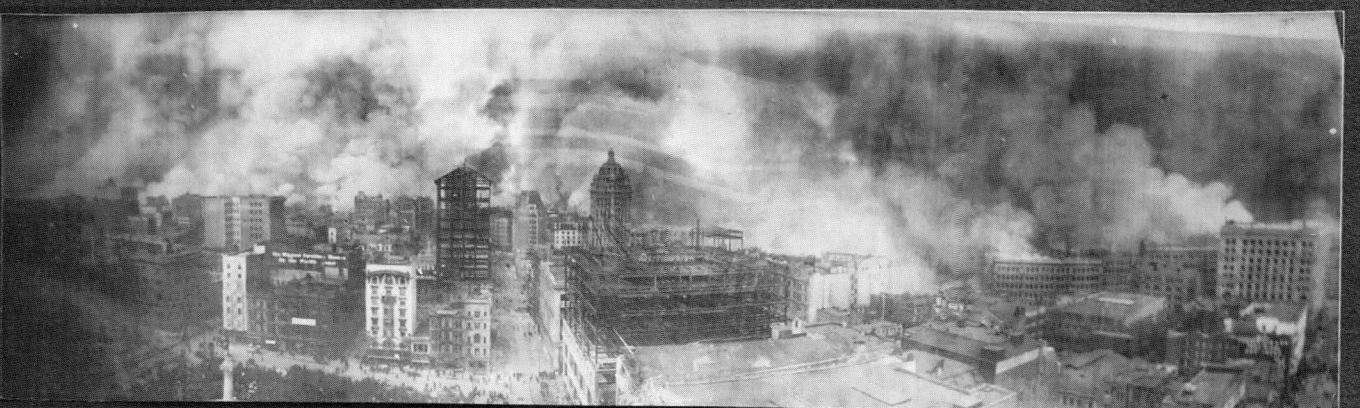

- View from St Francis Hotel - as city burned -

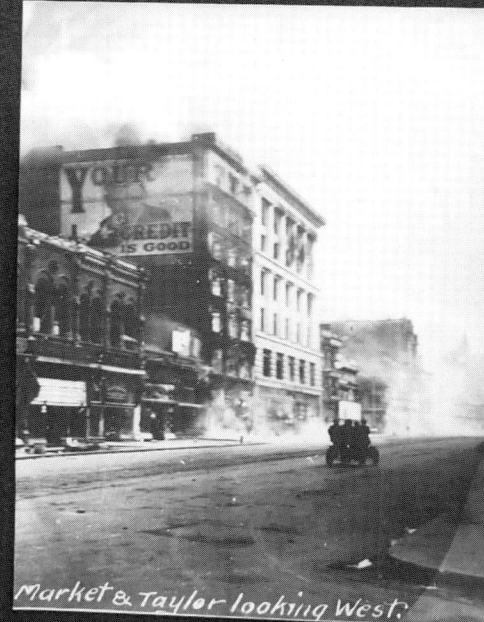

Market & Taylor - Looking West

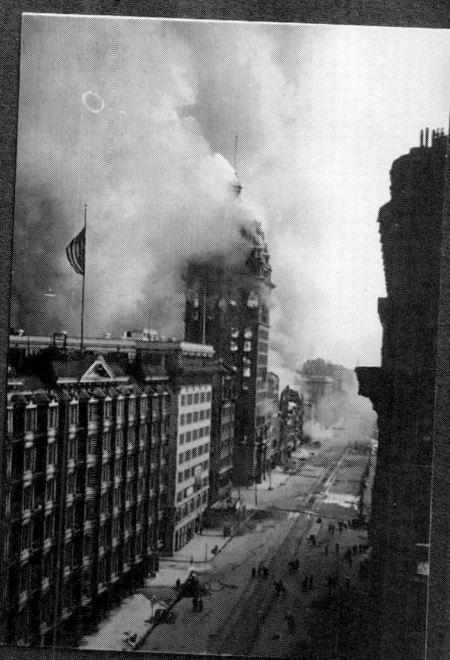

View of Market St. during fire

The Album

"View from St Francis Hotel as city burned" A panoramic, high-level vista of destruction, looking eastward from Powell Street and Union Square across the smoke-filled skies. The Call Building on Market Street is nearly at dead center.

"Market & Taylor— Looking west" As smoke surrounds the buildings, a company of motorists heads down the otherwise-empty street.

"View of Market St. during fire" In this image, the Palace Hotel is as yet unscathed, while the Call Building farther down Market is engulfed in flames.

33

When San Francisco Burned

"Call Building after fire" The gutted structure is seen amid nearby ruins and reconstruction activities.

"South side of Market St. ablaze" As fire rages within the Call Building, the Palace Hotel continues to fly its flag proudly, before it also burns. Fire hoses are snaked uselessly across Market Street. (Street)

Call Building after fire

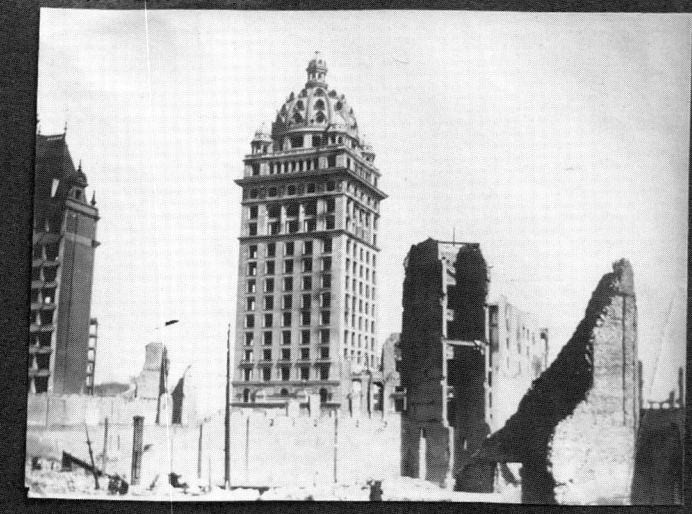

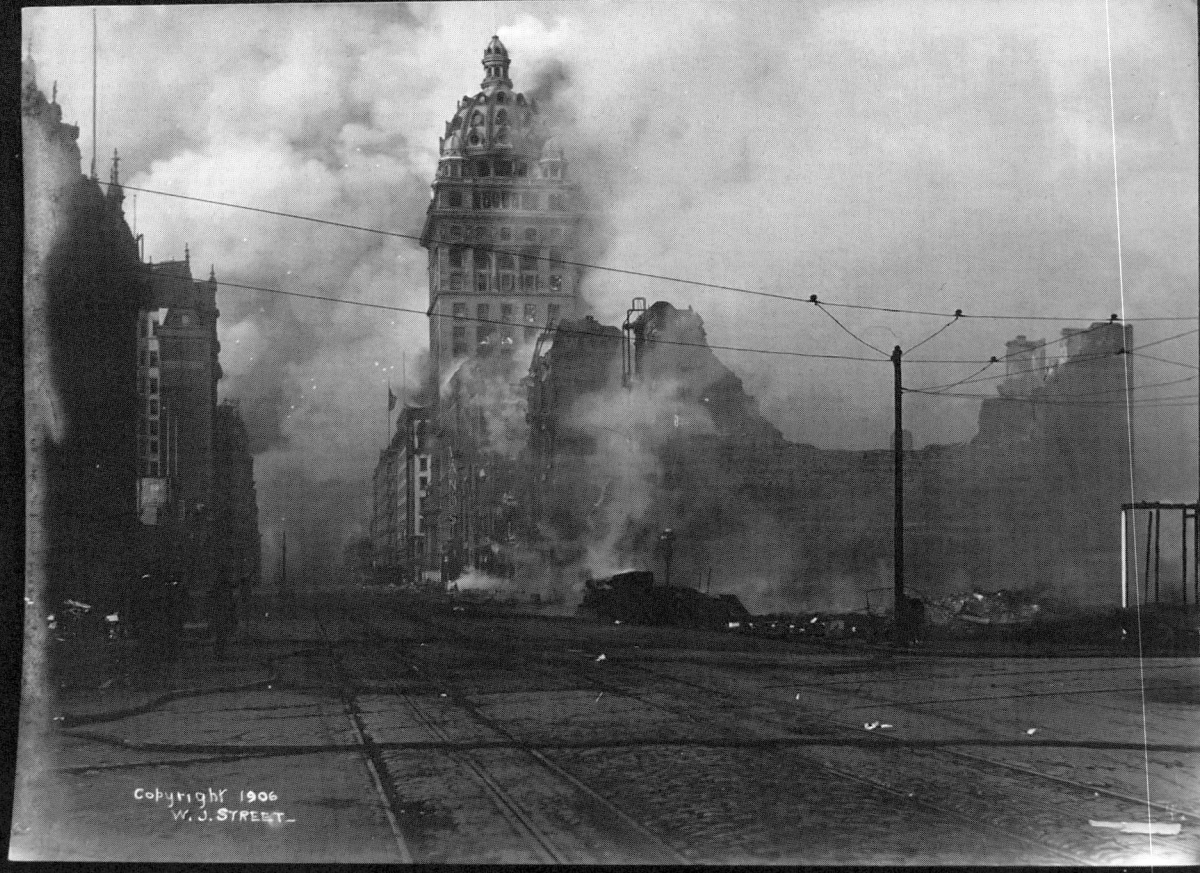

South Side of Market St. ablaze

Copyright 1906
W. J. STREET

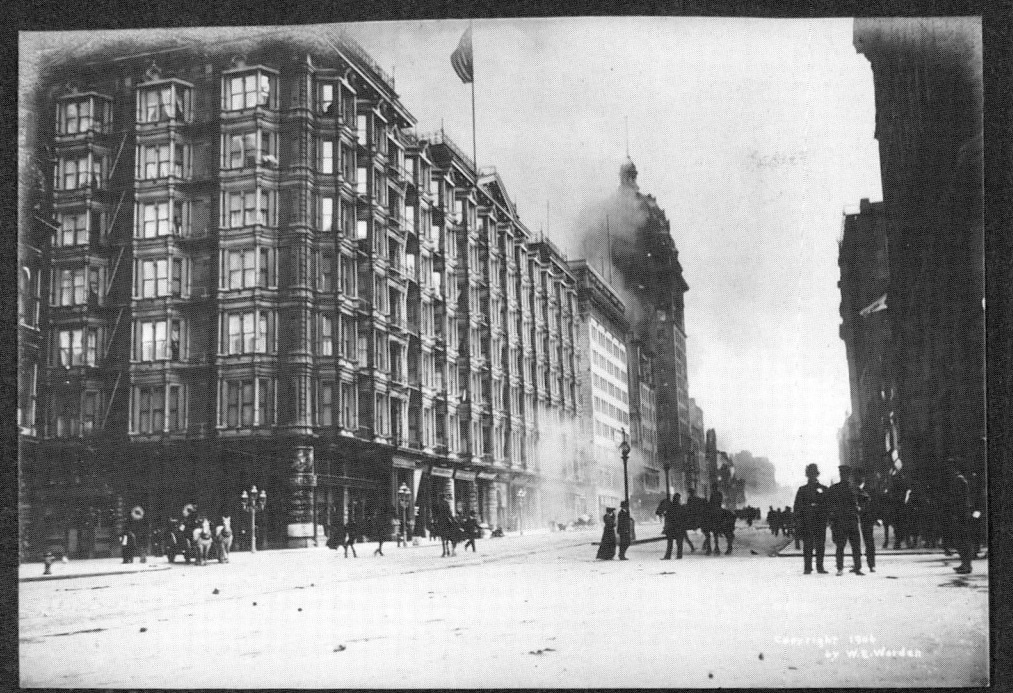

Palace Hotel before fire reached it

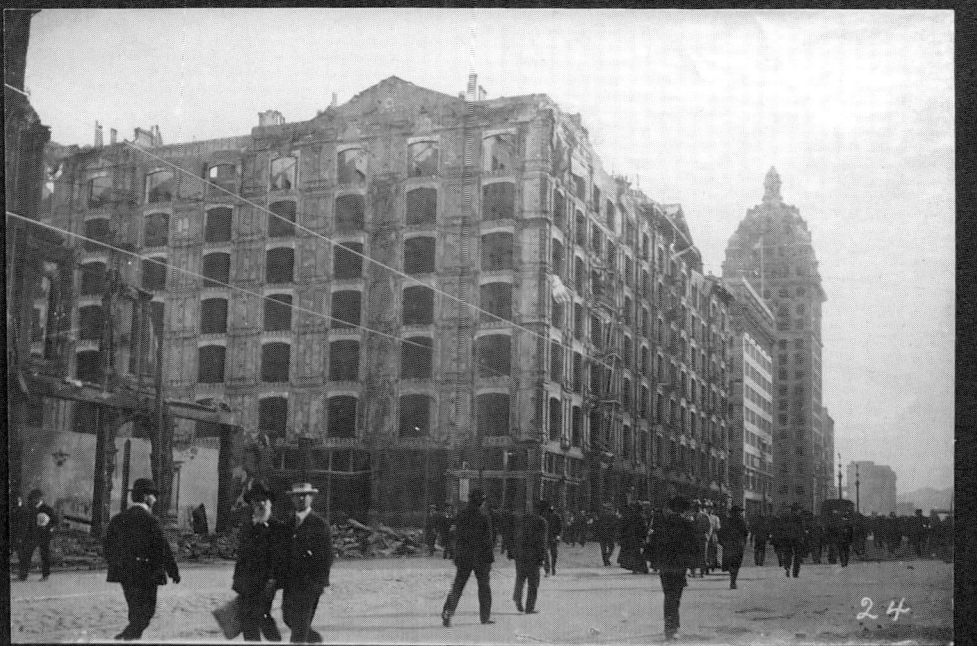

Palace Hotel after fire

"Palace Hotel before fire reached it" (Worden)

"Palace Hotel after fire"

These views document how the hotel went from internationally-famous showplace to burned-out hulk in a matter of hours.

When San Francisco Burned

"Fire approaching Larkin St." A dark view showing a debris-laden street and the fire's rapid advance.

"After the fire" A striking view of the destruction, with the ruins still smoldering.

"Powell St. before fire" The relative calm suggested by this photo might indicate it was taken before the earthquake and fire.

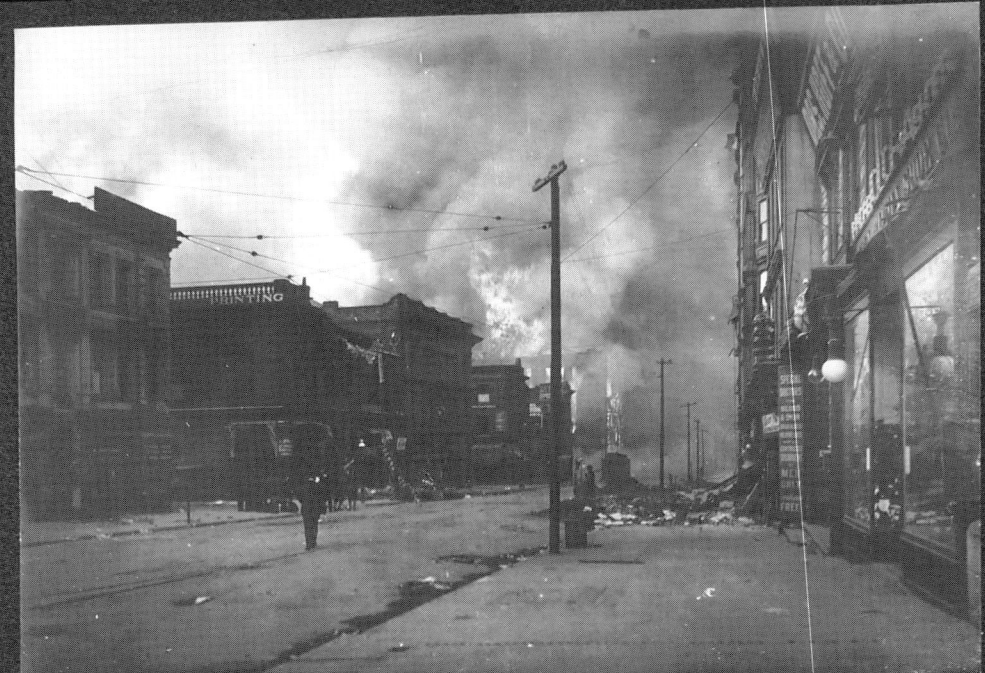

Fire approaching Larkin St.

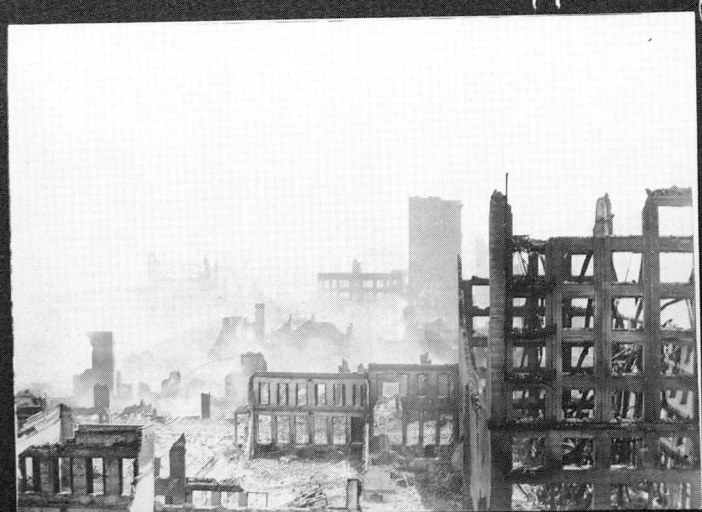

After the fire

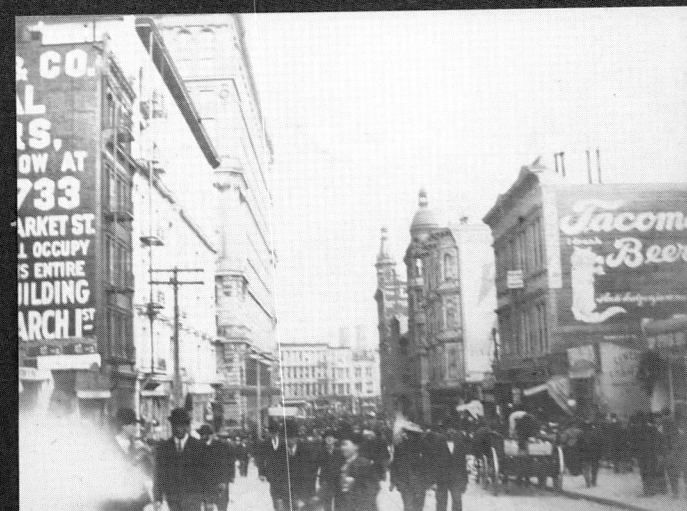

Powell St. before fire

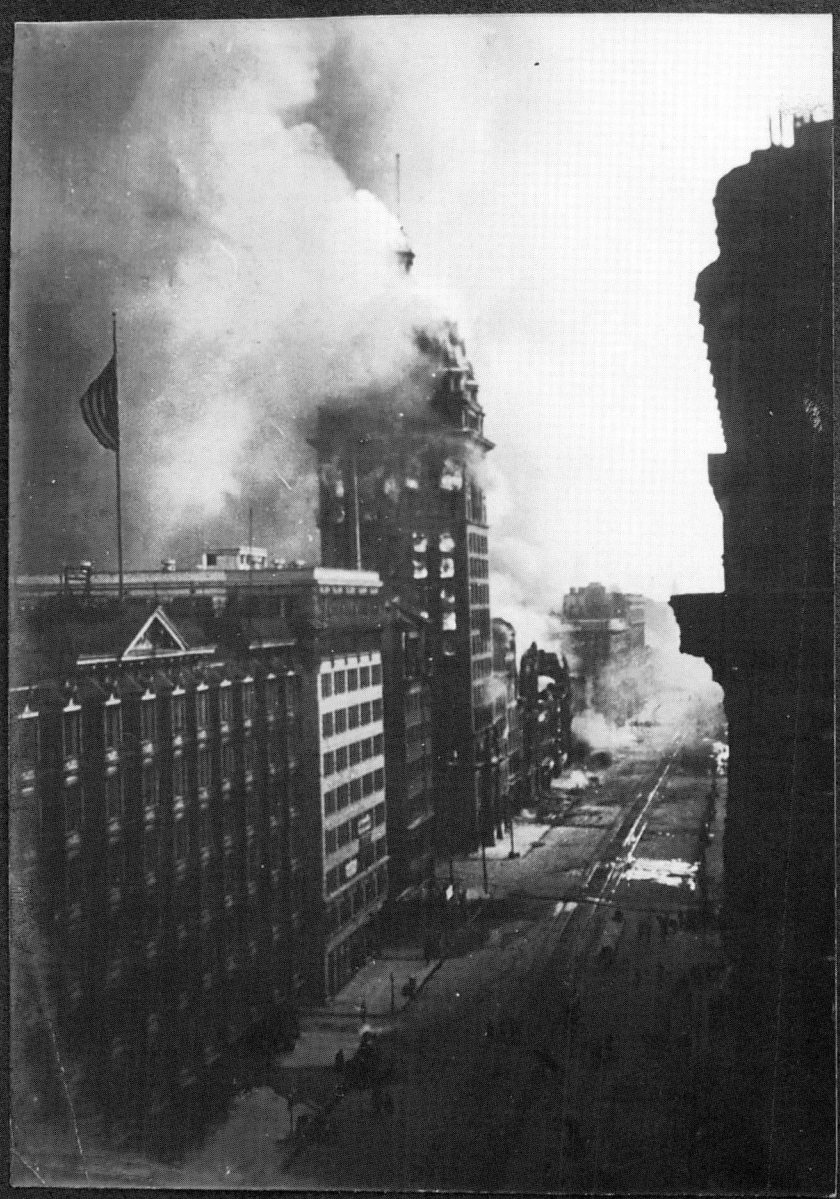

Just before the fire reached the Palace Hotel

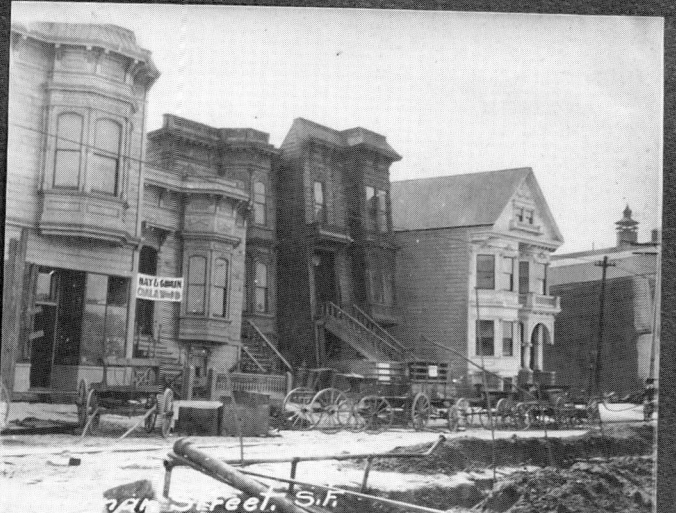

Earthquake damage on Brannan St.

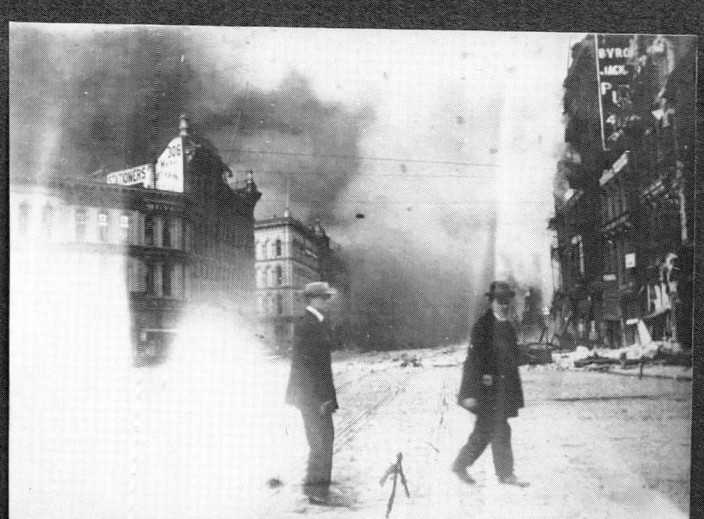

Market St. from Sansome

"Just before the fire reached the Palace Hotel" Similar, if not identical to, the view on page 33.

"Earthquake damage on Brannan St." Another shot of buildings turned awry. While street excavations suggest this photo was taken post-disaster, it might have a date closer to April 18 as most of Brannan was wiped out by the fire.

"Market St. from Sansome" Here, two Selby brothers inspect the Market Street ruins as fire rages behind them. No others seem to be present on the street.

37

When San Francisco Burned

"St Ignatius Ruins"
Another side view of the devastated coplex.

"Market St from 4th"
This shows smoke and flames beginning to lap at the southern side of Market, looking east toward the Call Building.

"Fire coming up Larkin St."
Fire moves up the street toward City Hall, on the left, while a wagon loads and waits to make a fast getaway. The City of Paris French Laundry is on the right.

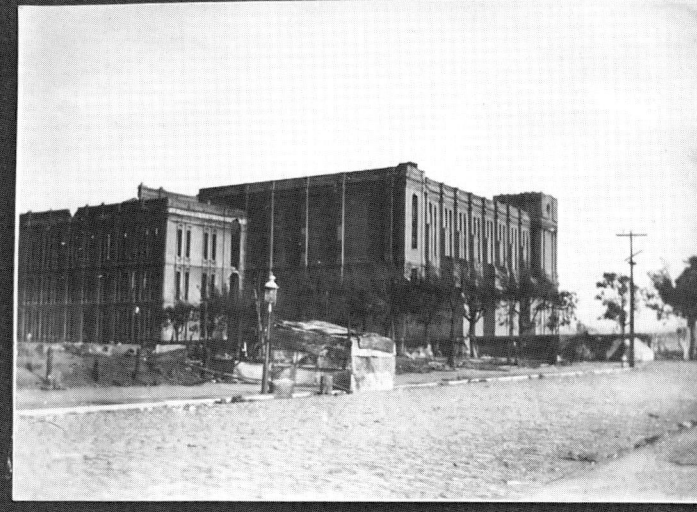

St Ignatius ruins

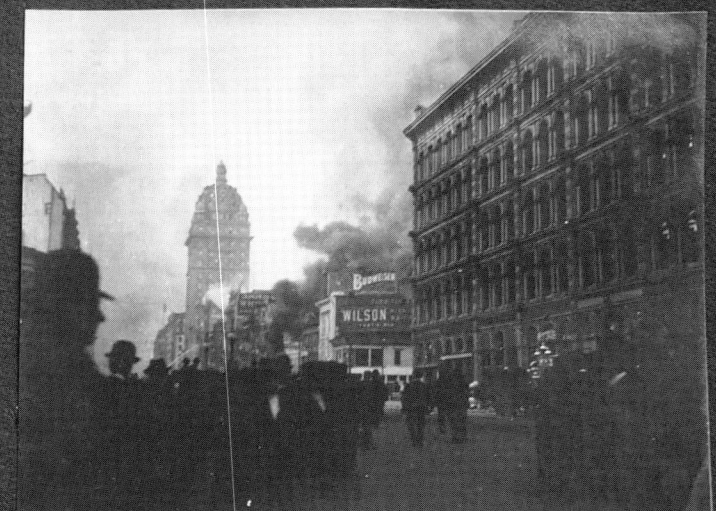

Market St from 4th

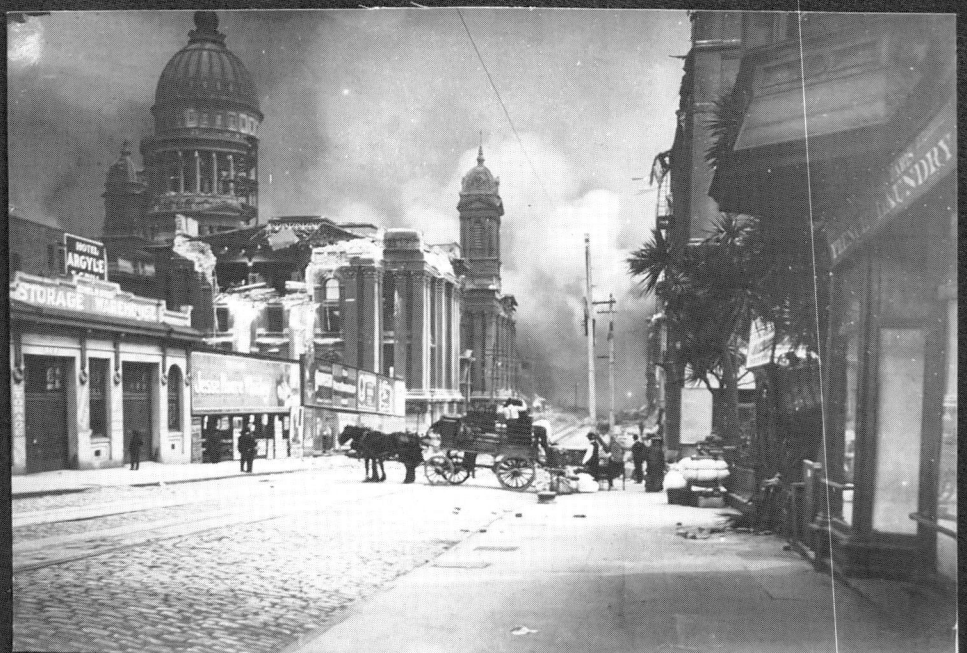

Fire coming up Larkin St.

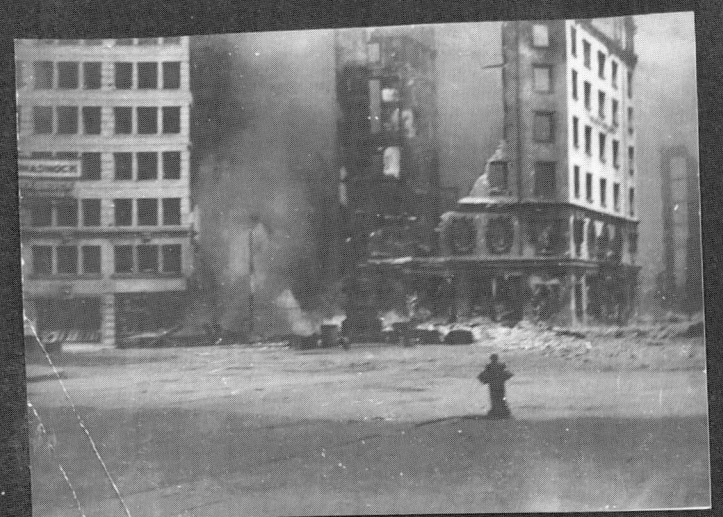

Examiner Building before dynamited

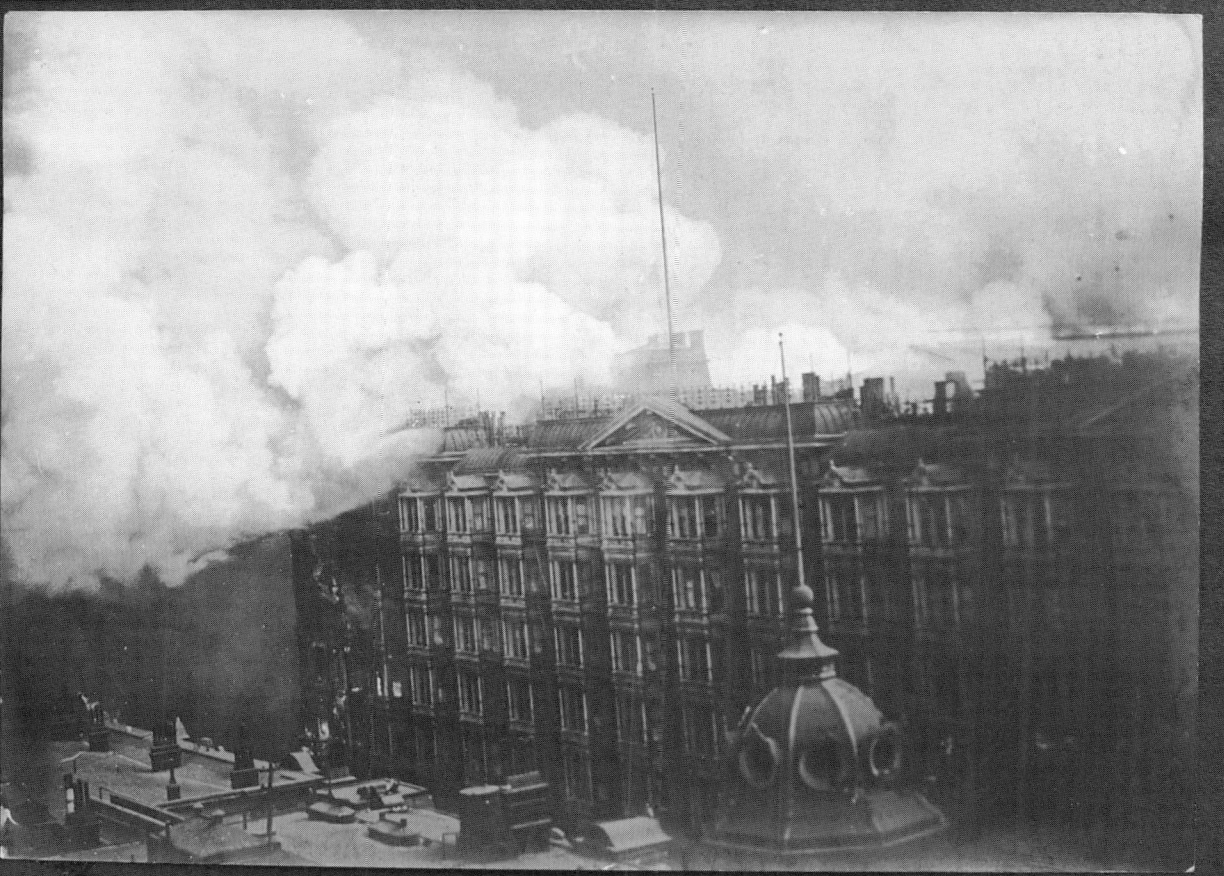

Palace Hotel burning rear view

"Examiner Building before dynamited" Located at the corner of Market and Third, the Examiner (Hearst) Building was an imposing building designed by A.C. Schweinfurth of New York. Rendered a complete loss, it was soon rebuilt and still stands today. The Monadnock Building stands at left.

"Palace Hotel burning rear view" Flames advance on the building from behind Market Street.

When San Francisco Burned

"Earthquake damage Girls' High School" Located on Scott Street, between Geary and O'Farrell, this building was only fourteen years old when the quake took its toll. It was later rebuilt and eventually merged with the coeducational city school system. (Noel)

"Rescuing the dead & injured…" A dramatic photo of rescue work in progress at the badly damaged Brunswick Hotel, located at Howard and Sixth.

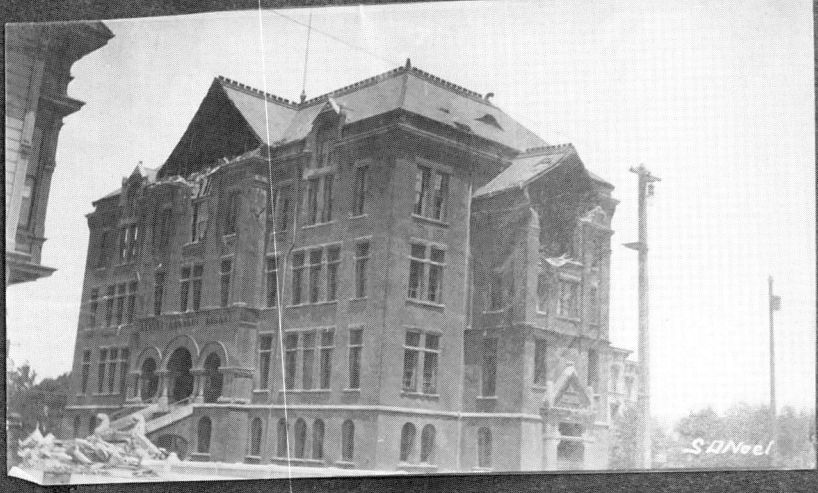

Earthquake damage Girls' High School

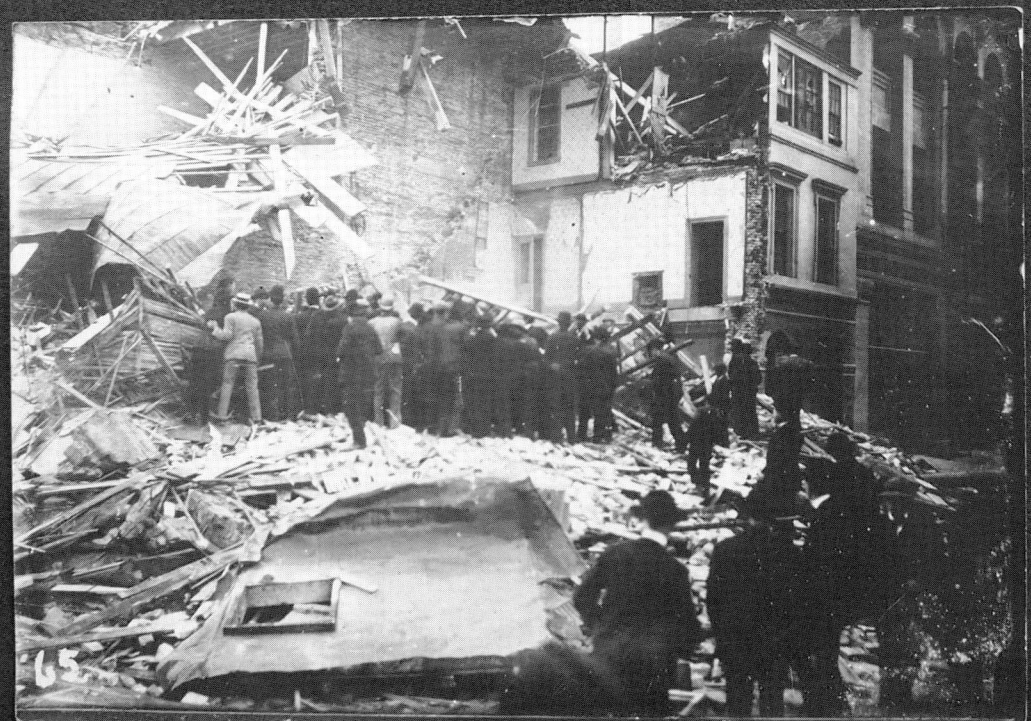

Rescuing the dead & injured (shortly after the earthquake *Brunswick Hotel*

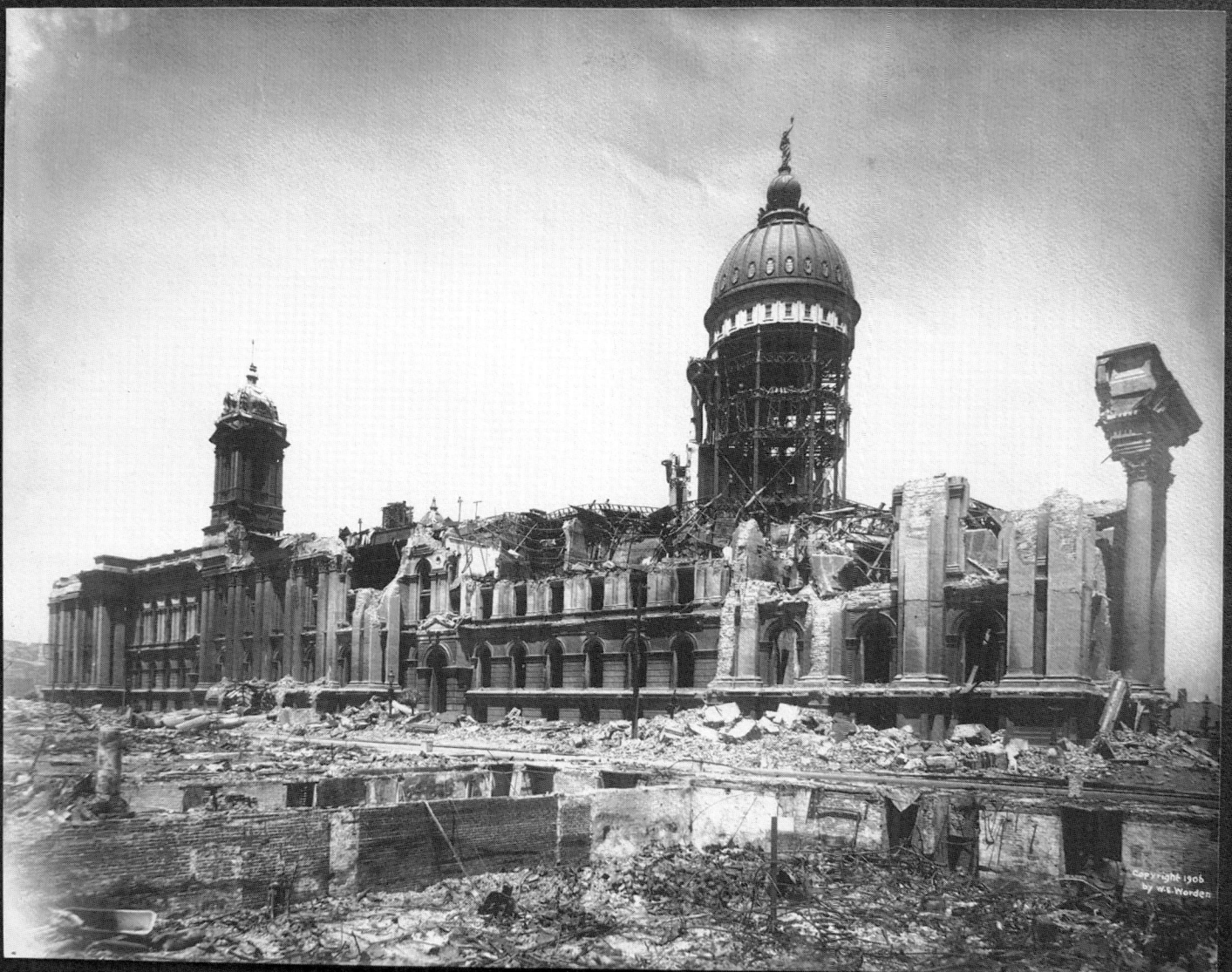

View of City Hall Ruins from Larkin & McAllister Sts.

"View of City Hall ruins…" San Francisco's "old" City Hall rose between 1872 and 1899 on a triangle bounded by City Hall, McAllister and Larkin streets. Constructed on the cheap, the earthquake managed to knock most of it down in seconds. It was located approximately a block east of today's City Hall, and near the old Hall of Records and the Mechanics' Pavilion. (Worden)

When San Francisco Burned

"As the streets appeared after fire" This view looks north toward Vallejo Street, where the St. Francis Pro-Cathedral is barely visible on the right.

"Looking down Market St" The distinctive, burned-out profile of Old St. Mary's Church is visible on the far left.

"Hotel ablaze" The fire is at dead center, visible between the Examiner (Hearst) and Call buildings.

"Watching Palace Hotel burn from Montgomery St." The arrow seems to indicate a Selby brother.

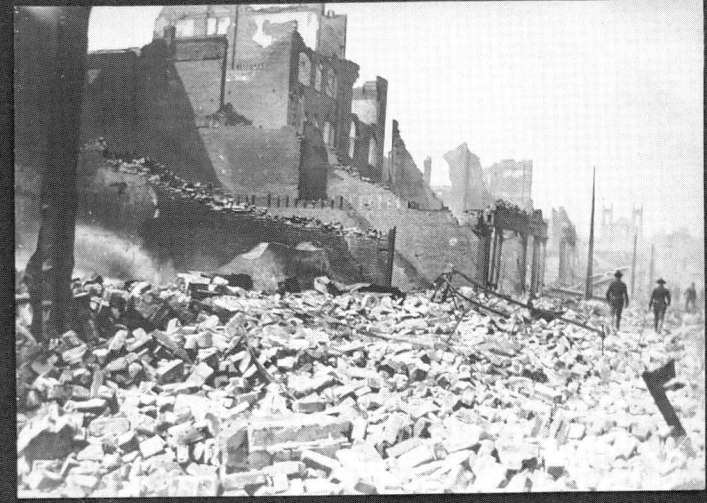

As the streets appeared after fire

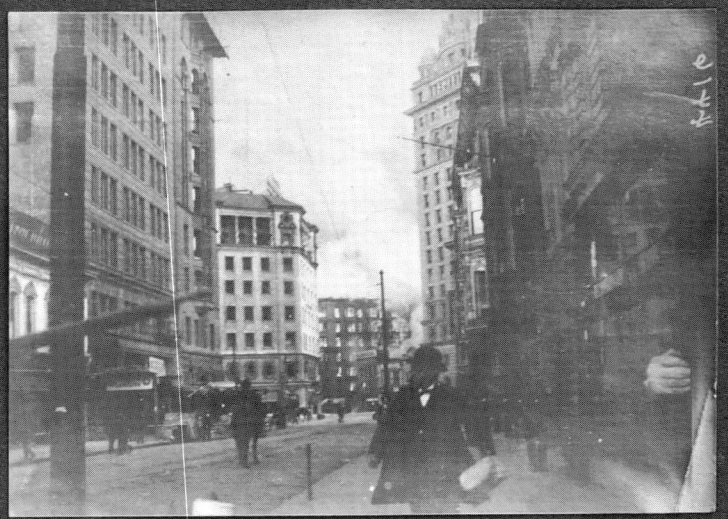

Hotel Ablaze

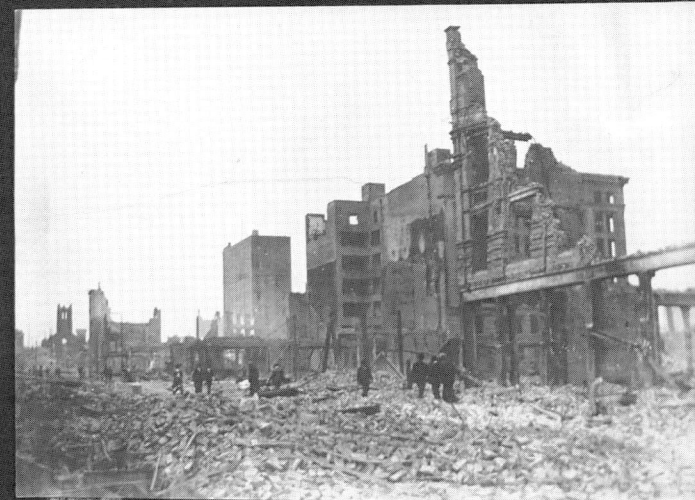

Looking down Market St

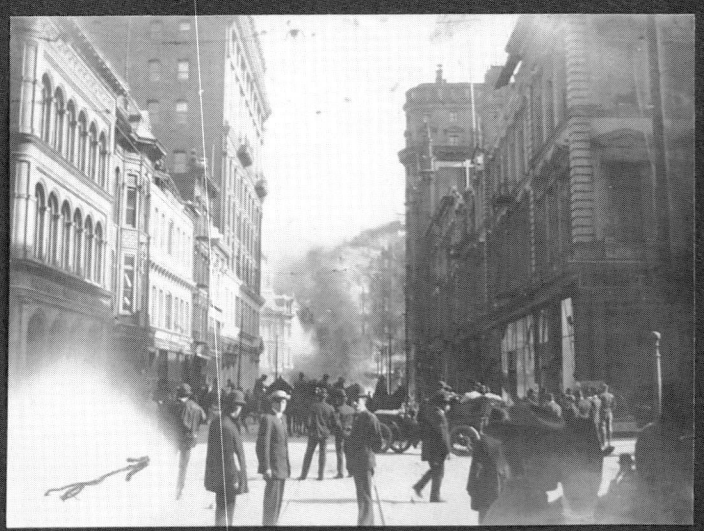

Watching Palace Hotel burn from Montgomery St.

42

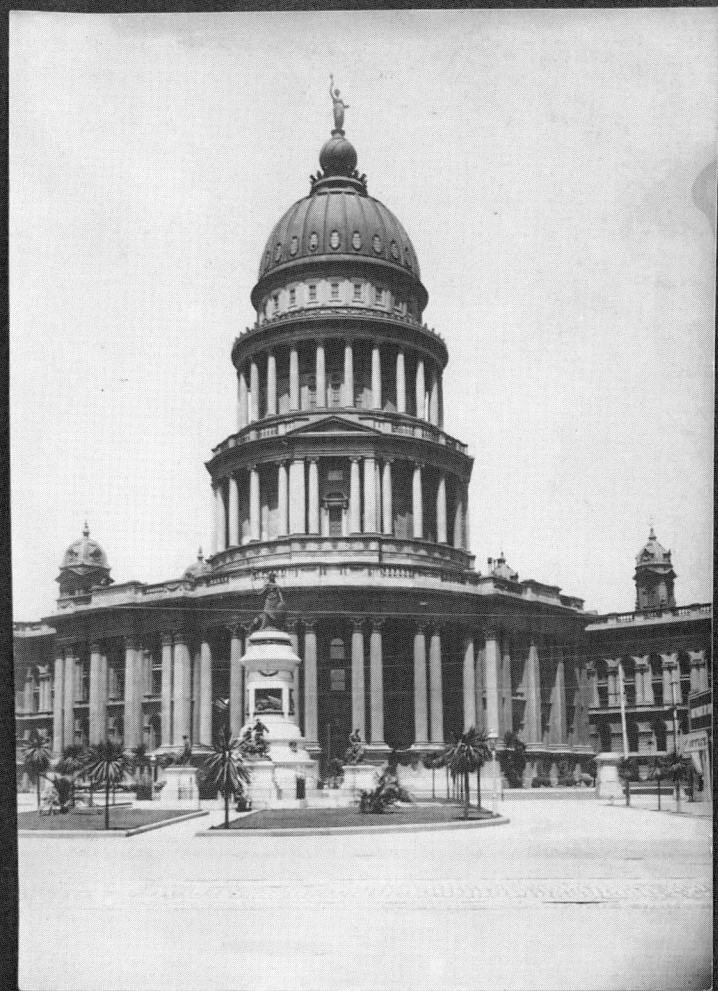

*City Hall
before Earthquake*

*City Hall
after Earthquake*

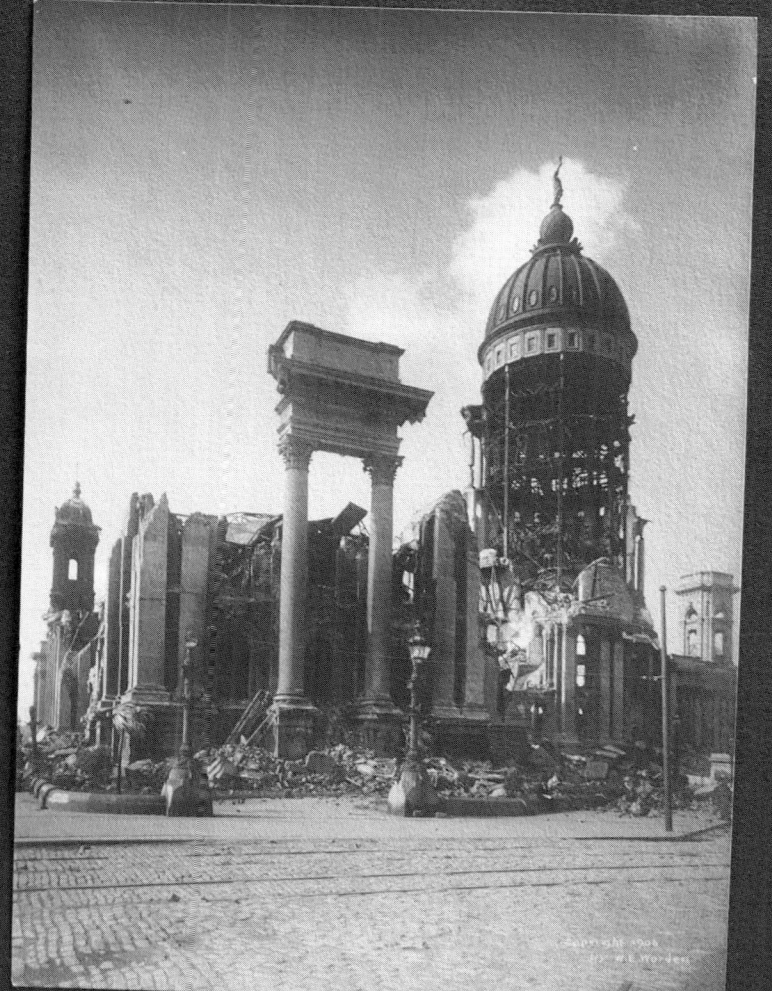

"The City
Ablaze…"
This photo looks
ast toward City
ll, whose dome
s barely visible
ugh the smoke.
The people in
the street are
staging a fast
vacuation and
ing to beat the
s. See page 16
a smaller-scale
version of this
same view.
(Blumberg)

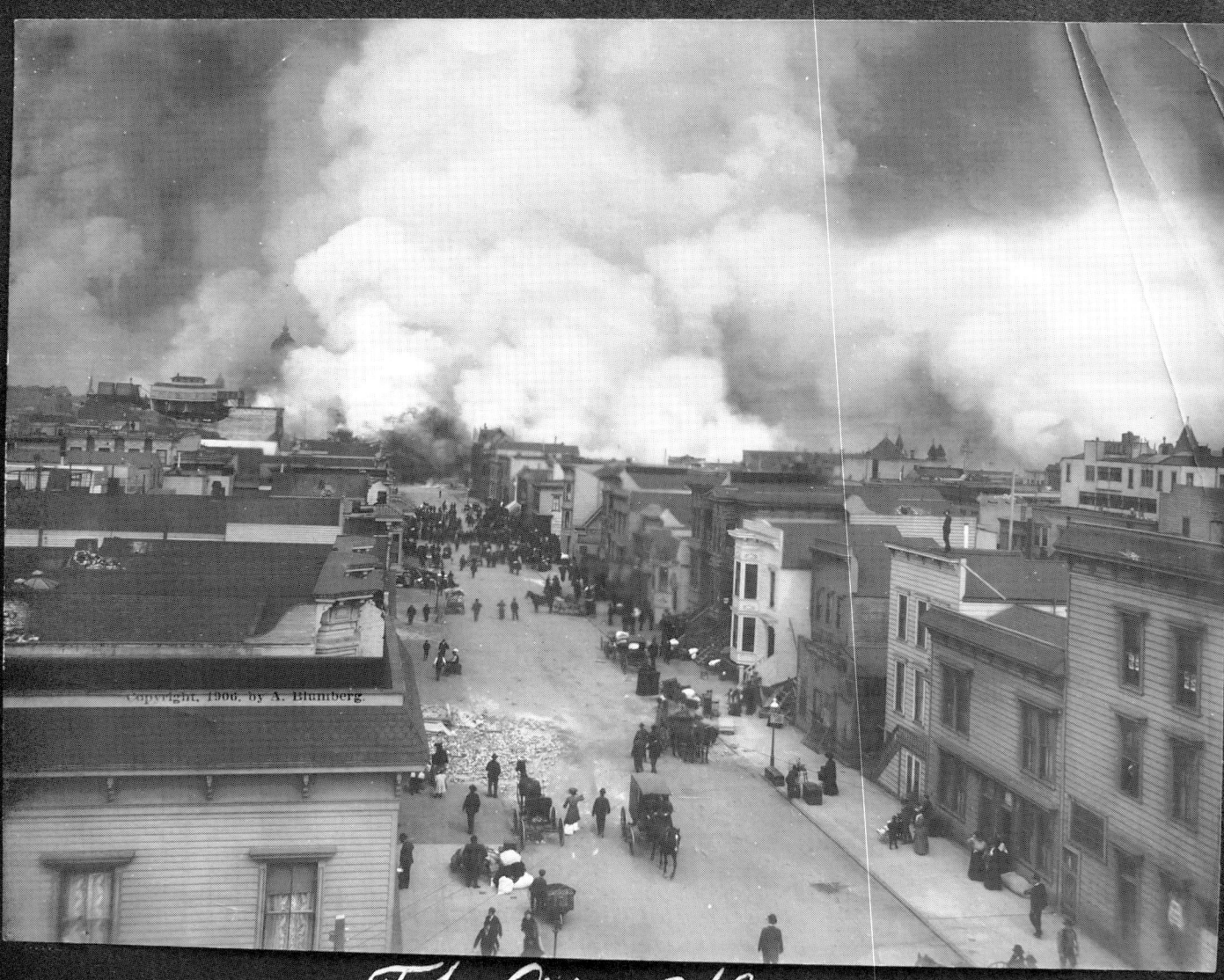

Copyright, 1906, by A. Blumberg.

The City Ablaze
Looking up Grove St.

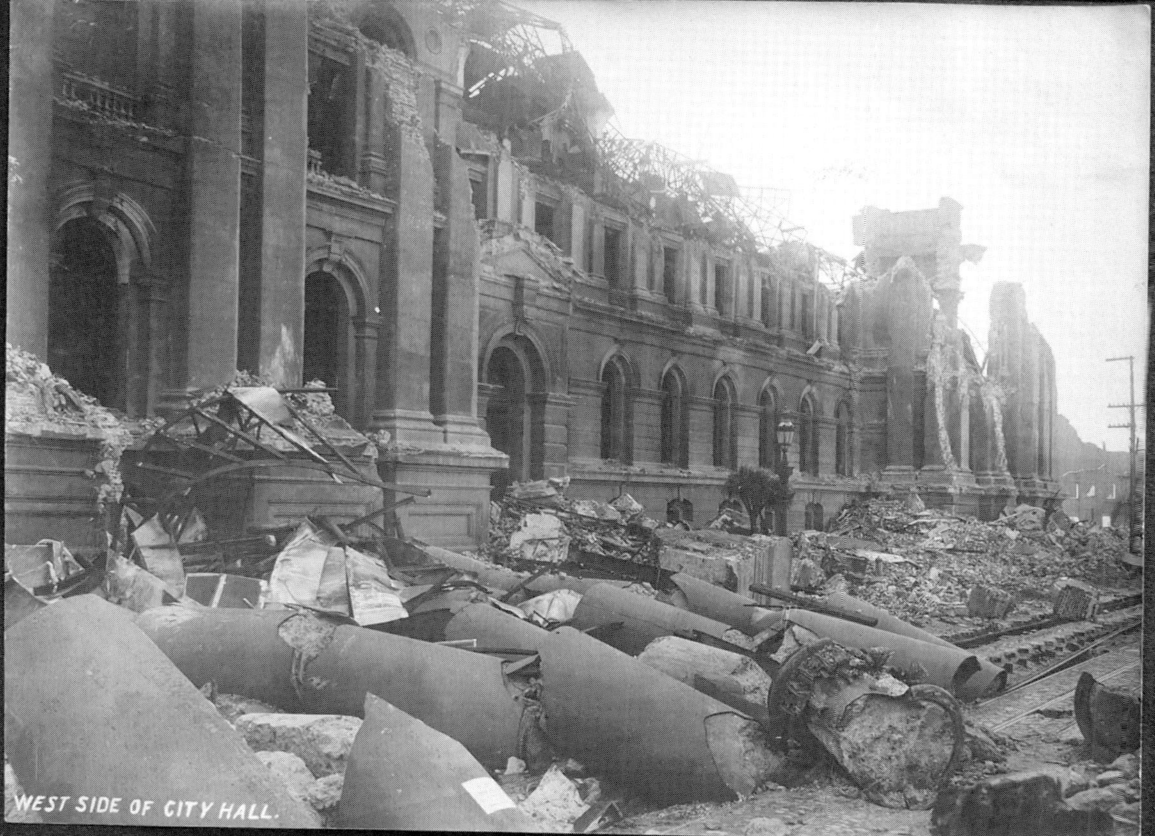

City Hall.
destruction

Larkin St.
view

WEST SIDE OF CITY HALL.

"City Hall
destruction
Larkin St. view"
The building's
heavy devastation
is once again
evident in this
photo. (Stoddard)

"Fire on Howard
St. near 8th St."
In this photo,
no one is in sight,
as the street has
become a tinder-
box. Ironically,
one of the city's
principal water
mains was located
here and had been
rendered unusable

Fire on Howard St.
near 8th St.

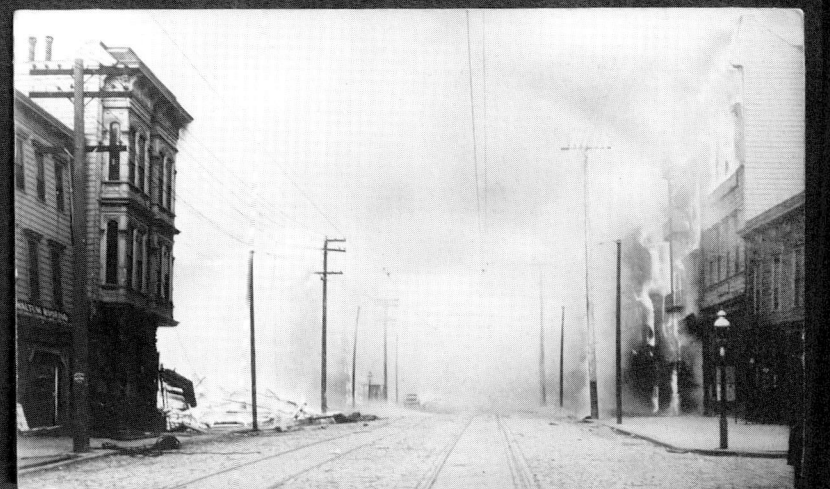

When San Francisco Burned

"Gymnasium Stanford University" This large structure on Stanford's campus, hit hard by the shocks, was one of the Peninsula's more spectacular ruins. (Bailey)

"Fillmore St. after the Earthquake" Located west of Lafayette Park, Fillmore Street was outside of the fire zone. This view reveals a neighbor-hood left relatively untouched by the twin disasters. (Pillsbury)

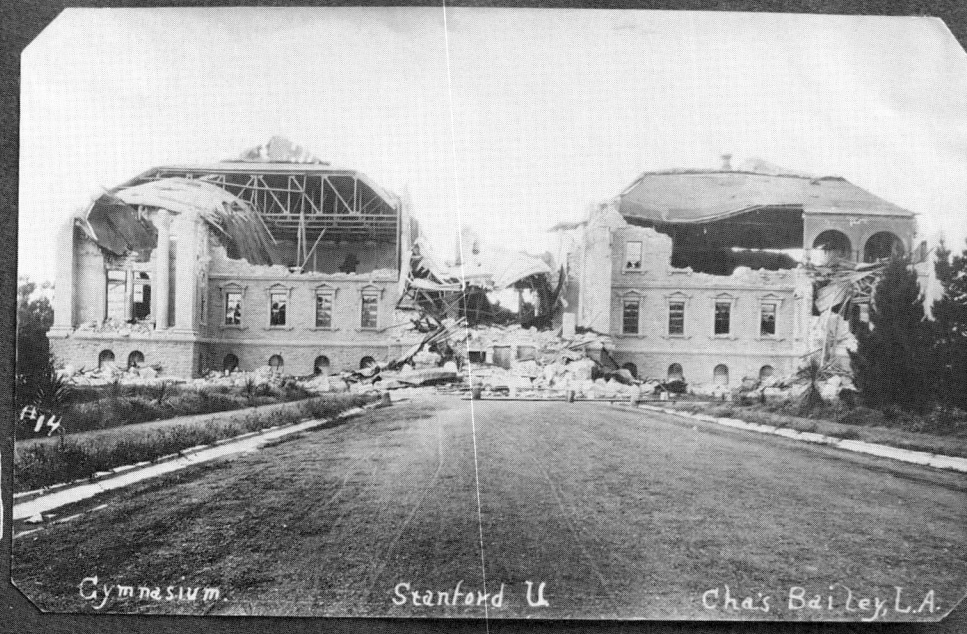

Gymnasium Stanford University

Gymnasium.   Stanford U   Cha's Bailey, L.A.

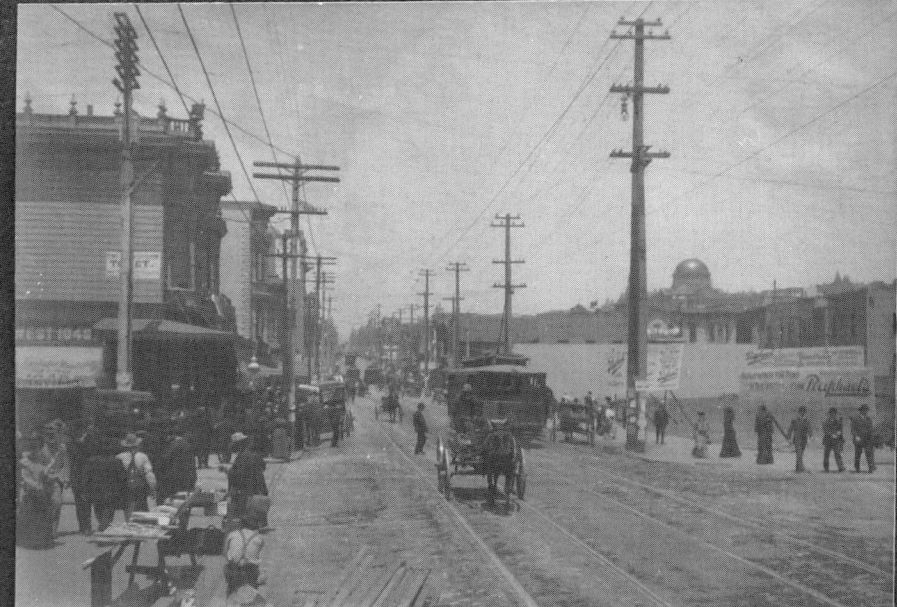

Fillmore St. after the Earthquake

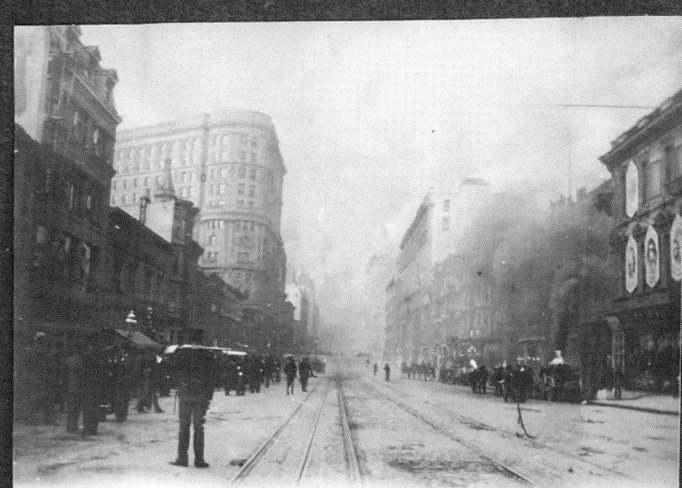

Market St. Emporium on fire

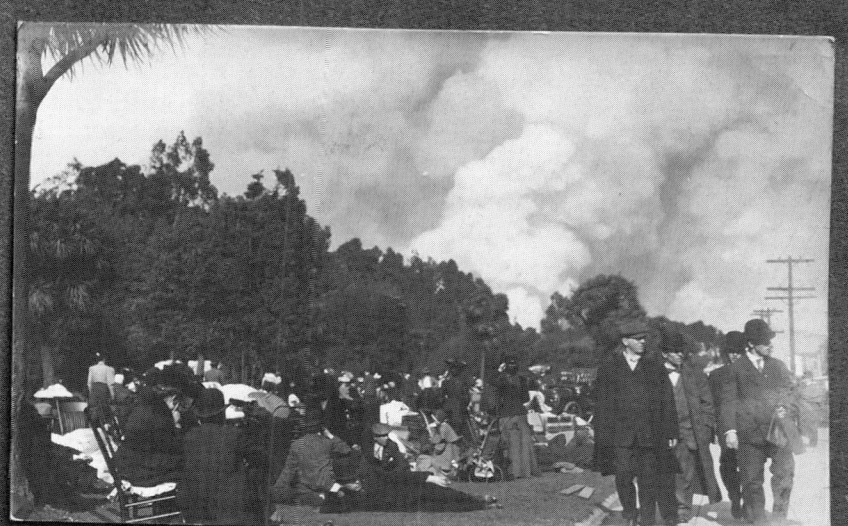

Refugees — Jefferson Square

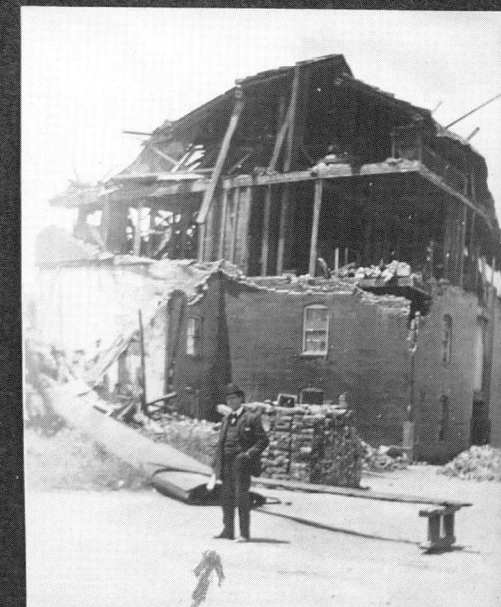

Earthquake damage — Santa Rosa

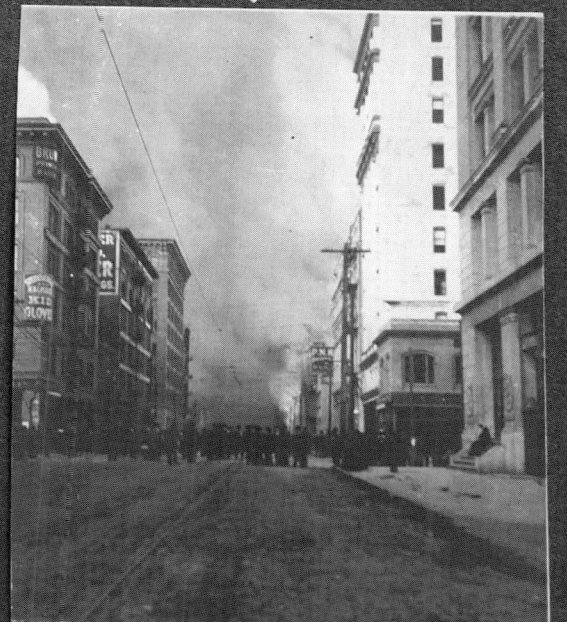

View down Market St.

Tl

"M
Fir
as
eve
Ma
ap
Em
Jar
Bu
aci
wh
Bu
the
the

"E
ag
Pr
tou
hit
ear
A
sta
un
ag

"R
Jef
Sm
hir
clu
op

"V
Ma
A
to
sm
co
blo

When San Francisco Burned

*"Observatory,
[Stra]wberry Hill…"
A spectacular
[sce]ne of ruination
[i]n Golden Gate
Park. Note the
decorative post
[at] right, uprooted
[but] standing at an
[a]ngle. (Worden)*

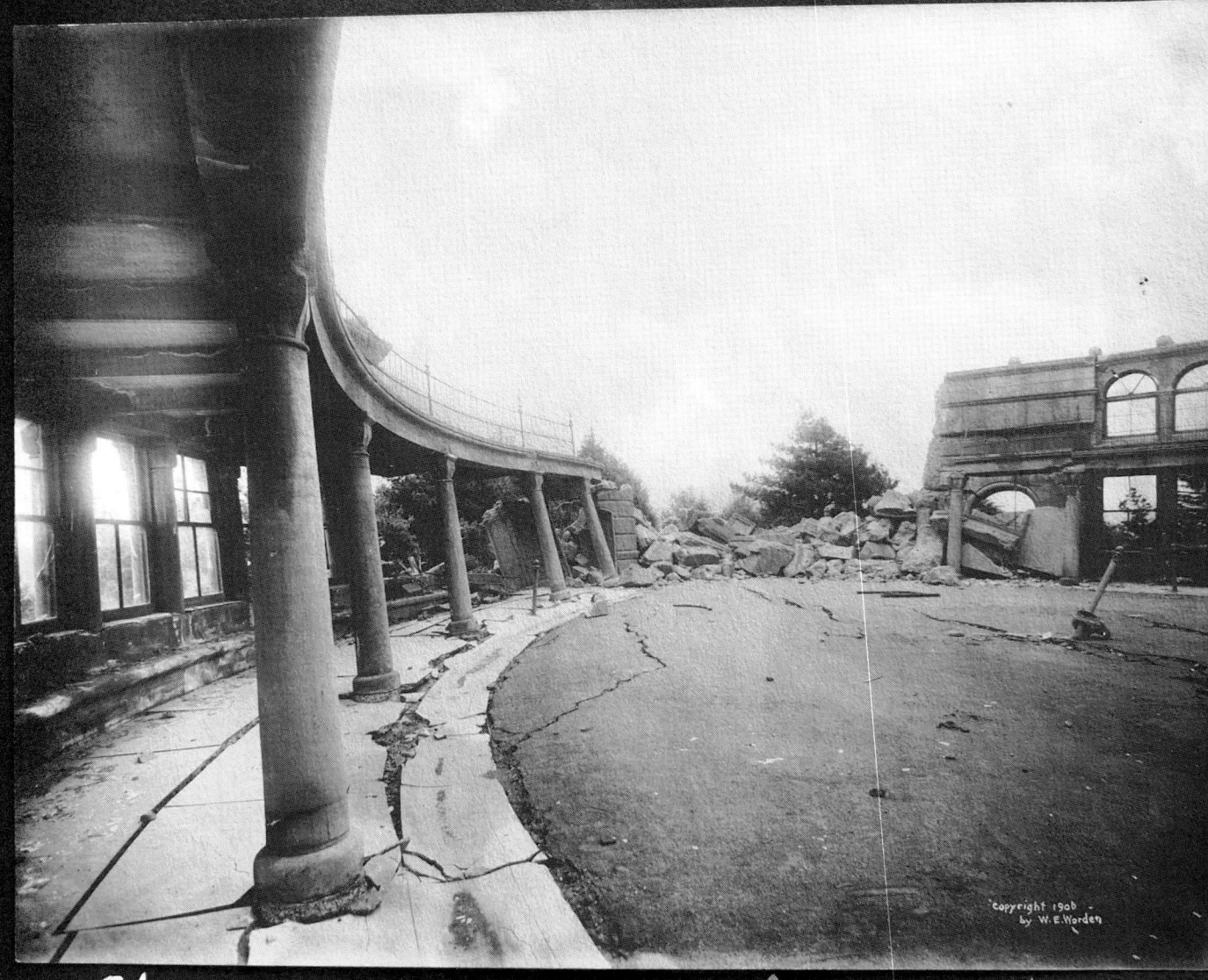

*copyright 1906
by W.E.Worden*

Observatory

Golden Gate Park

Strawberry Hill

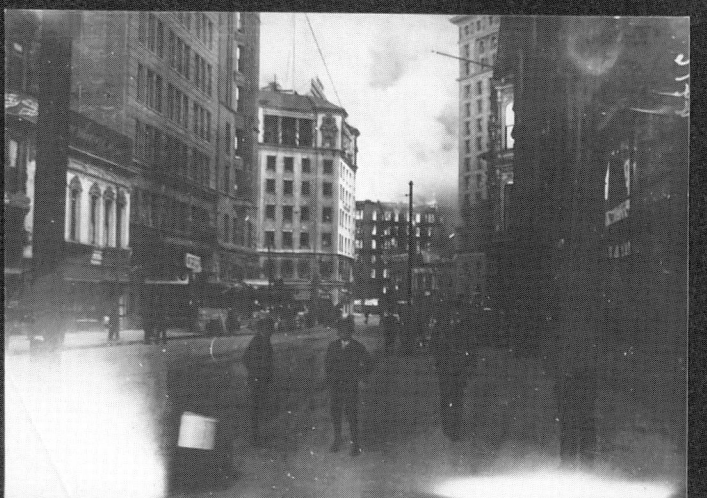

S.F. fire view from Kearny St.

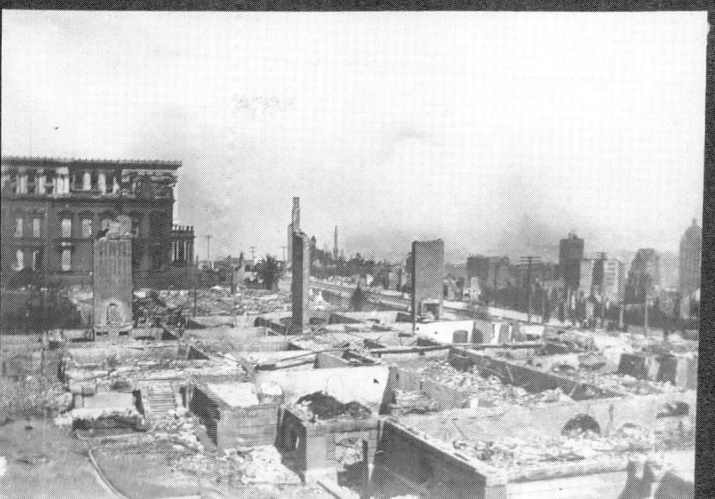

Apartment Houses—Ruins

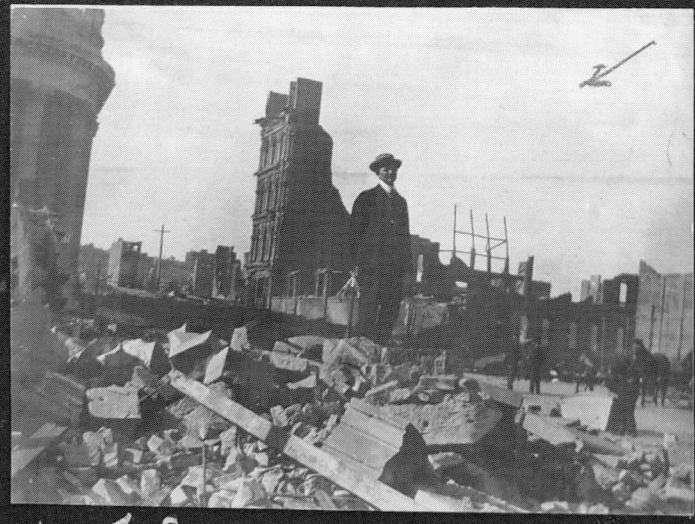

D.F.S. amidst S.F. Ruins

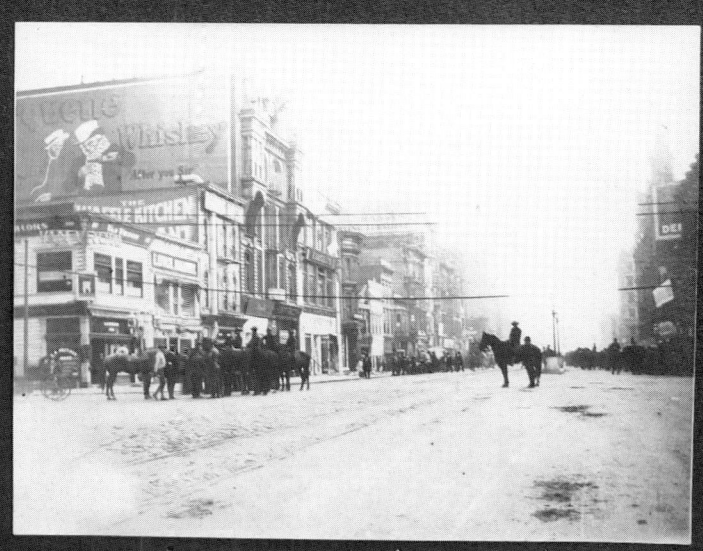

Market St. from 6th before fire reached it

The Album

"S.F. fire view from Kearny St." Looking south toward Market. Similar to the photo on page 42.

"D.F.S. amid S.F. Ruins" David Selby poses atop some ruins near the Hibernia Bank building at Market and Jones. He is most likely perched on the remains of the Selby Candy Store, which were strewn only feet away from those of the bank.

"Apartment Houses—Ruins" Photo taken somewhere north of Market, with the Call Building at extreme right.

"Market St. from 6th…" Mounted soldiers patrol the western reaches of Market ahead of the fire.

"Jewish
Synagogue After
Earthquake"
A more detailed
view of the damage
inflicted on Temple
Beth Israel,
situated on Geary
between Steiner
and Fillmore
streets. See pages
19 and 103 for
a different
perspective.
(Pillsbury?)

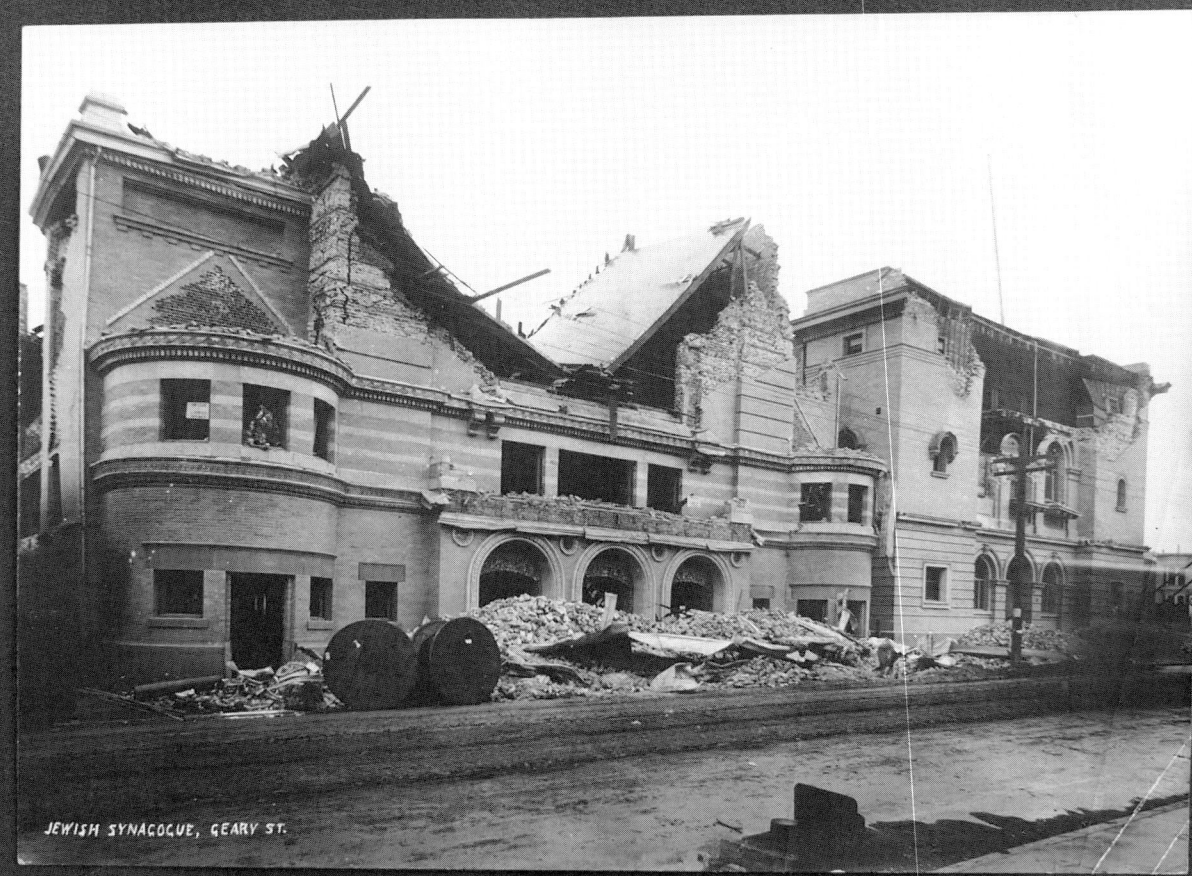

JEWISH SYNAGOGUE, GEARY ST.

Jewish Synagogue After Earthquake

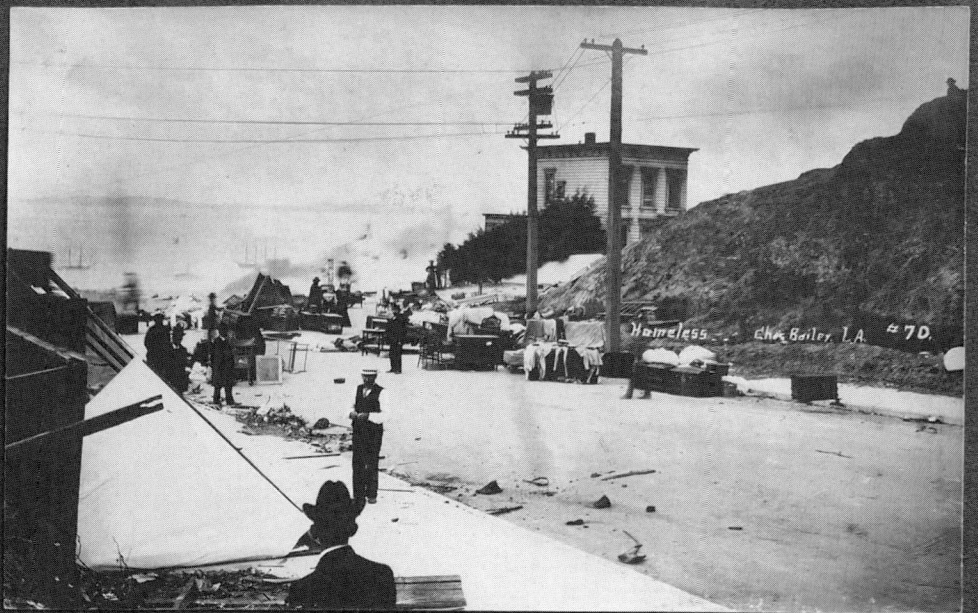

Homeless at North Beach

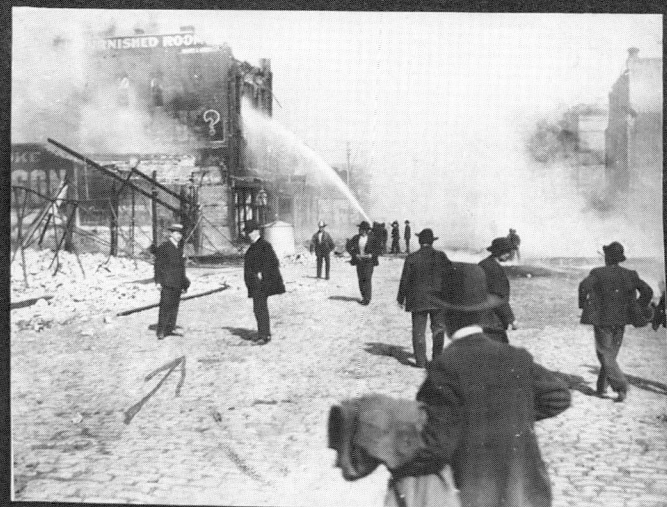

The fire South of Market St.

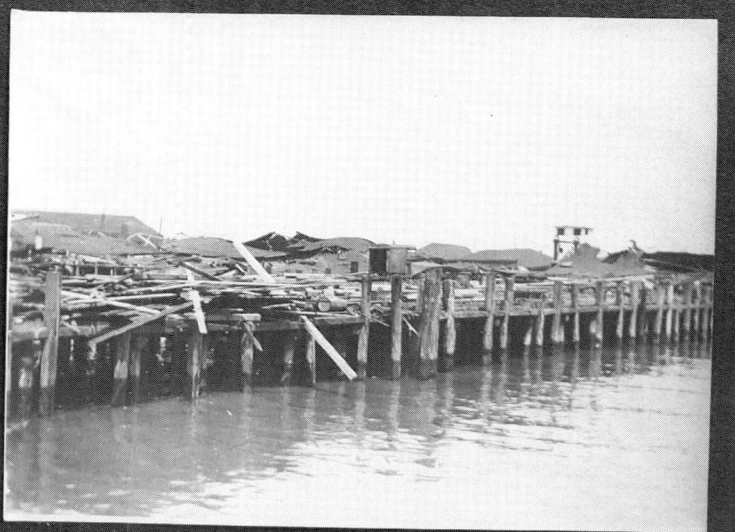

Earthquake destruction Mission St Wharf

"Homeless at North Beach" This photo was taken on Clay Street Hill and overlooks the devastated Marina District. Angel Island is visible in the distance at far left.

"The fire south of Market St." One of the Selby brothers, indicated by arrow, watches with others as operational fire hoses try to extinguish flames.

"Earthquake destruction Mission St Wharf" After the earthquake hit, little remained of the flimsy wooden buildings situated here, just south of the Ferry Building. Today, the rebuilt neighborhood is home to businesses and shopping, and bears no resemblance to its pre-1906 appearance.

When San Francisco Burned

"Earthquake damage 18th near Capp St" Another view of buckled pavement and twisted ironwork.

"Dynamiting the 'Monadnock'" Despite the caption, this image shows the Monadnock Building standing, with the Examiner (Hearst) Building at center succumbing to a dynamite charge. The Monadnock survived the disasters and still stands on Market Street. (Pillsbury)

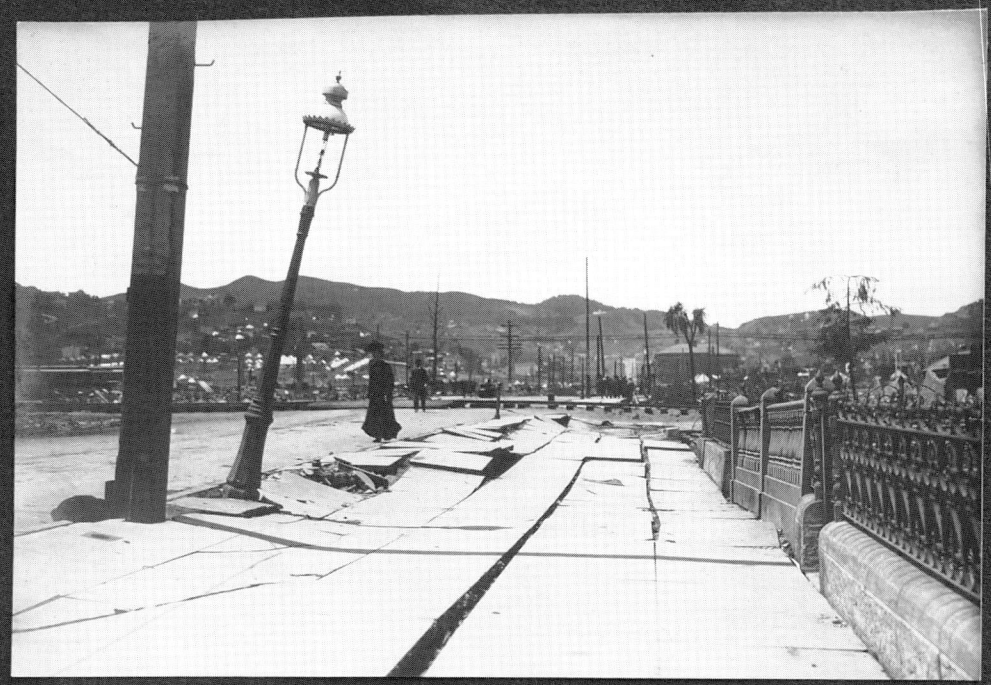

Earthquake damage 18th near Capp St

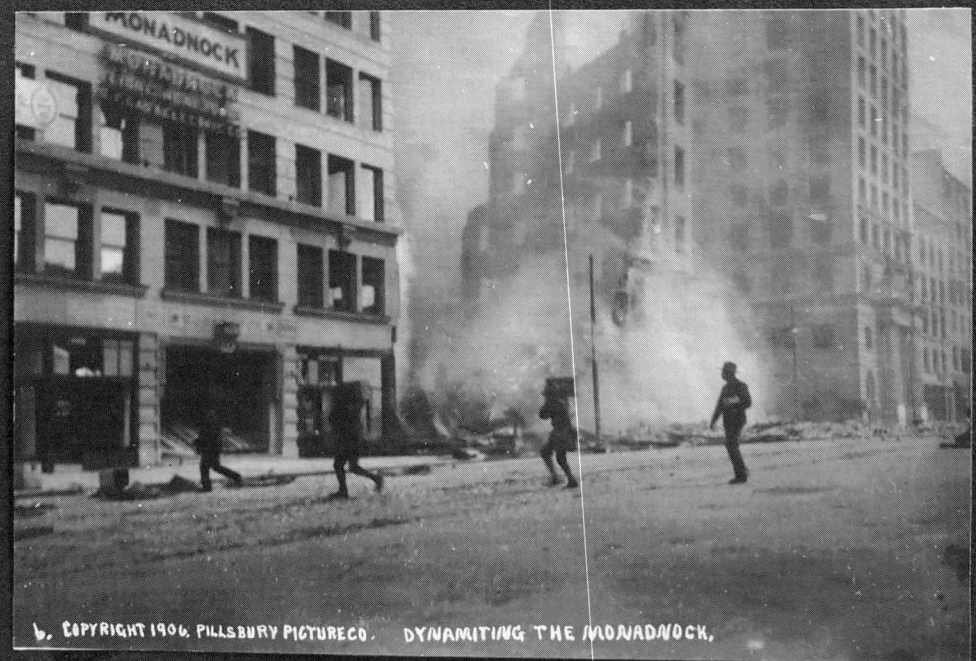

Dynamiting the "Monadnock"

b. COPYRIGHT 1906. PILLSBURY PICTURE CO.   DYNAMITING THE MONADNOCK.

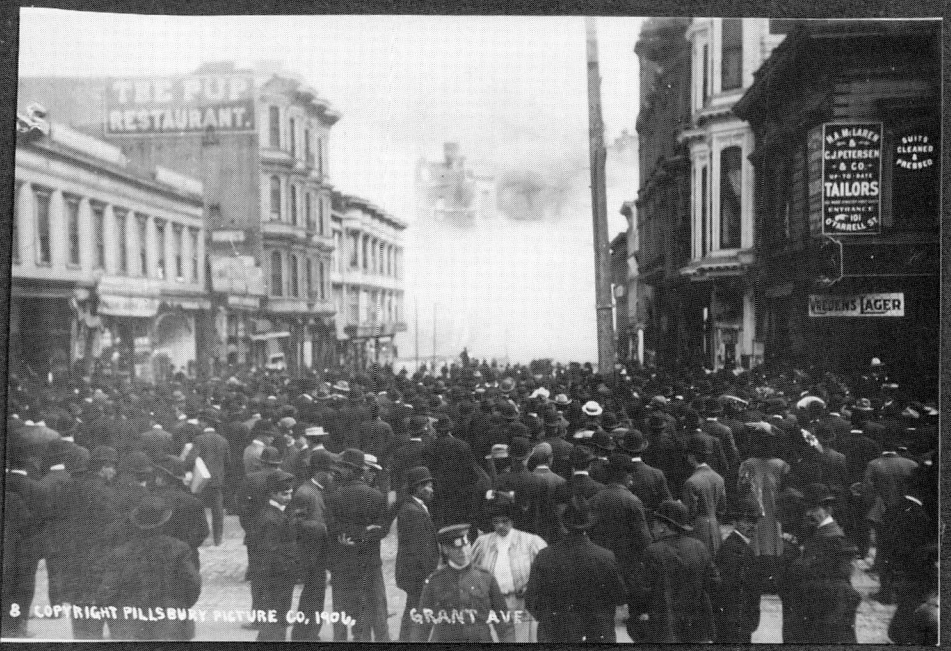

*Stockton St.
near
Market St.*

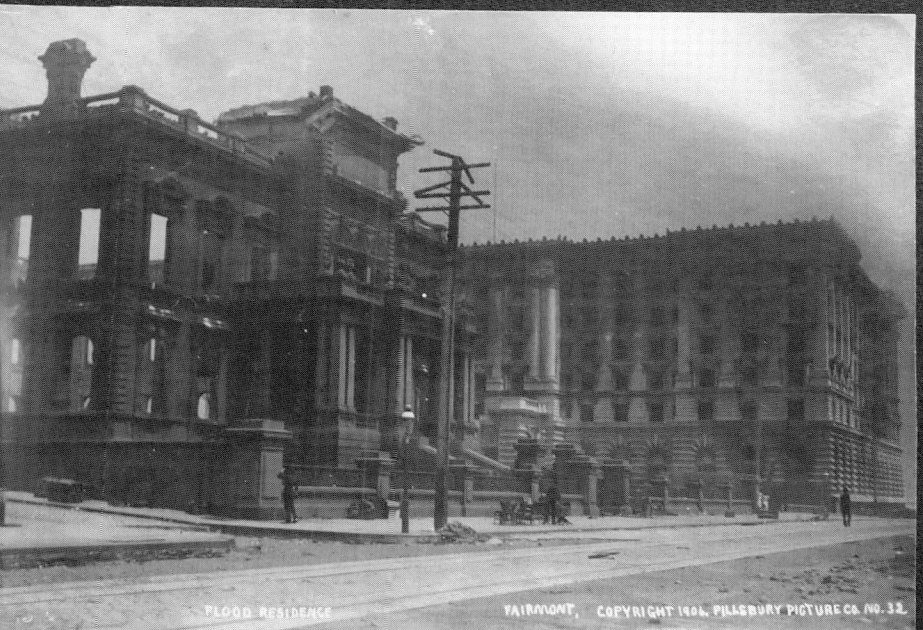

*Ruins of Flood Mansion
Fairmont Hotel*

The Album

"Stockton St. near Market St." Despite this photo's surface labeling as "Grant Ave.," this appears to agree with Louis Selby's captioning, as The Pup restaurant (visible at left) was situated near this corner, and the McLaren and Petersen tailor shop was on O'Farrell Street, in the foreground. (Pillsbury)

"Ruins of Flood Mansion & Fairmont Hotel" At left stands James Flood's elegant Nob Hill mansion and at right the Fairmont, both burned-out but with walls intact. The rebuilt mansion now houses San Francisco's Pacific Union Club, and the rehabilitated Fairmont remains one of the city's grand hostelries. (Pillsbury)

53

When San Francisco Burned

"Mission St. near 30th…" In this photo, most of the people are headed north as they attempt to flee the city. Dense smoke fills the background.

"Opening of the Hibernia Bank" Anxious San Franciscans mob the bank when it opens its doors for the first time after the earthquake and fire. Market Street remains choked by rubble and debris. (Pillsbury)

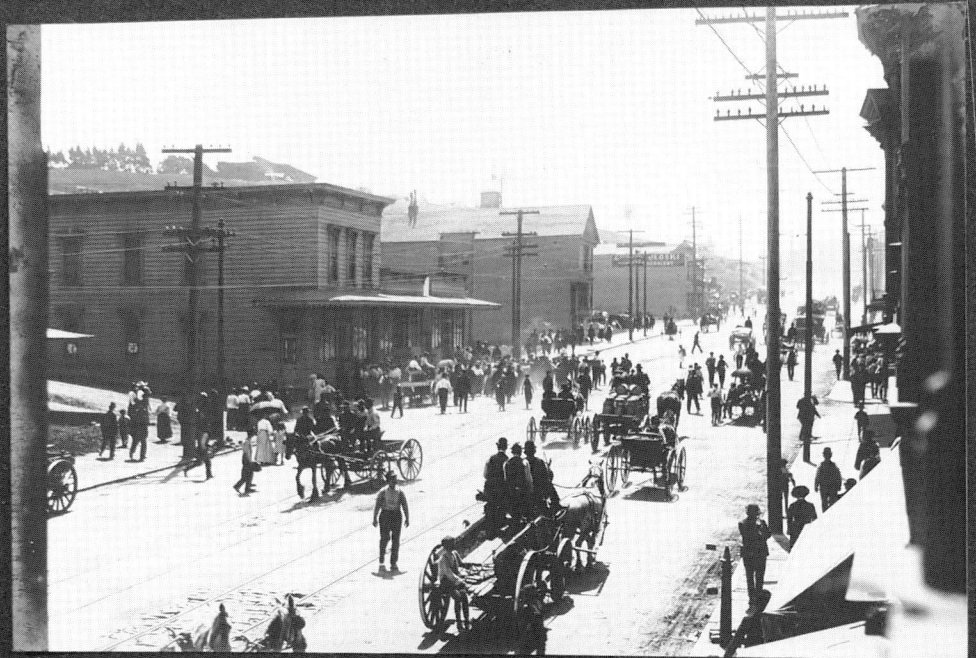

Mission St. near 30th - people fleeing from City

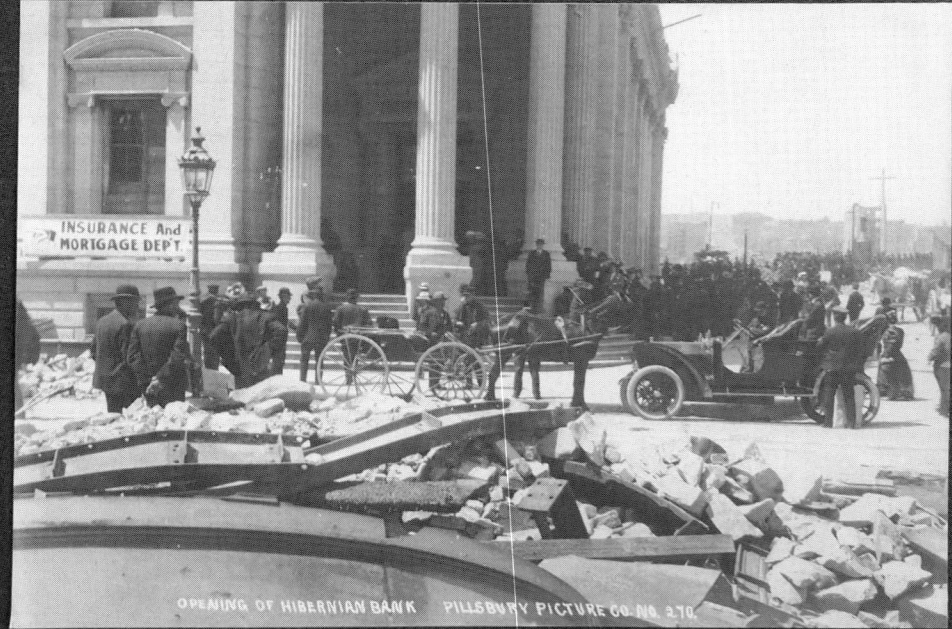

Opening of the Hibernia Bank

OPENING OF HIBERNIAN BANK   PILLSBURY PICTURE CO. NO. 270.

INSURANCE And MORTGAGE DEPT.

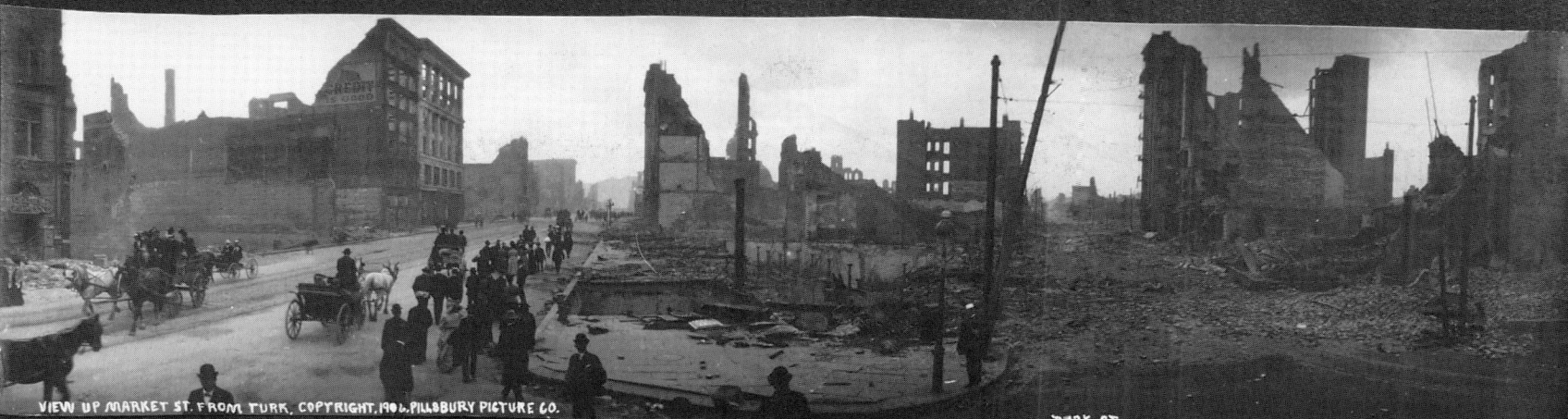

VIEW UP MARKET ST. FROM TURK, COPYRIGHT, 1906, PILLSBURY PICTURE CO.

TURK ST.

NO. 57.

View up Market St from Turk St

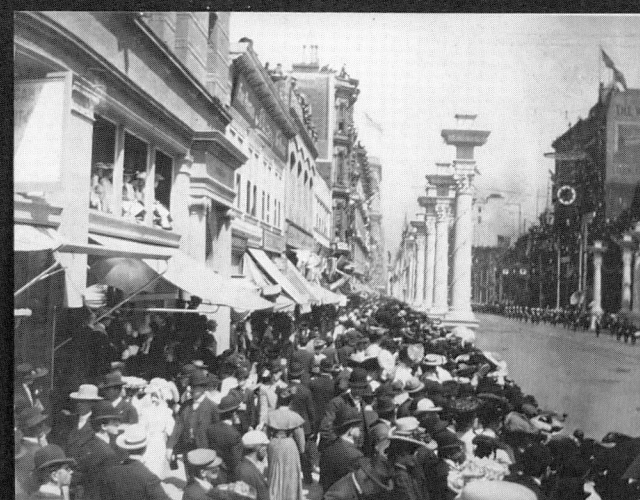

San Francisco in her glory
View on Market St.

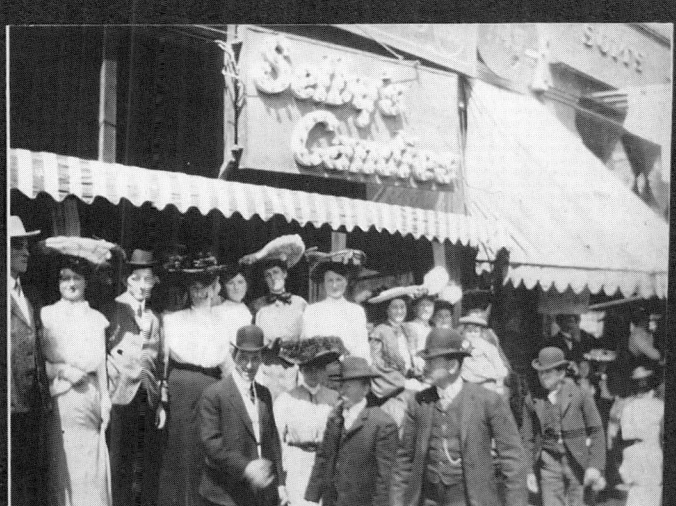

"Selby's Candy Store" on Parade Day

"View up Market St from Turk St" A haunting scene of complete desolation and destruction. (Pillsbury)

"San Francisco in her glory…"

"'Selby's Candy Store' on Parade Day"

These views appear to predate the earthquake and fire. Selby brothers are present in the Parade Day image, which is also seen on page xviii.

California St. 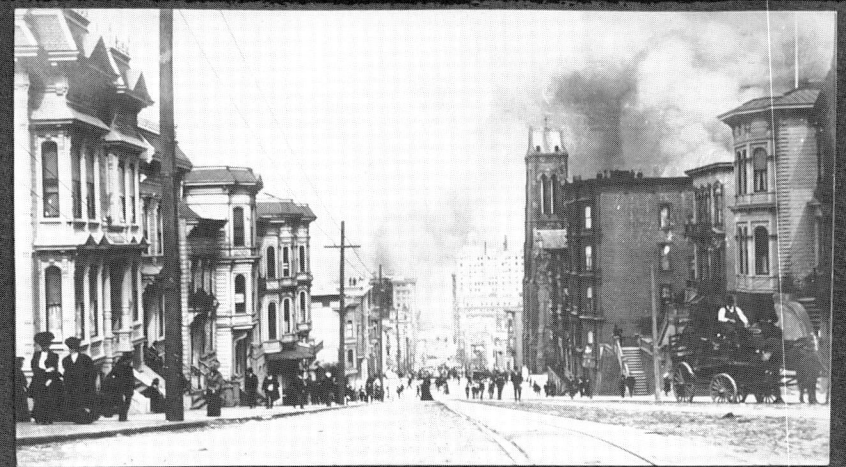 from Powell St.

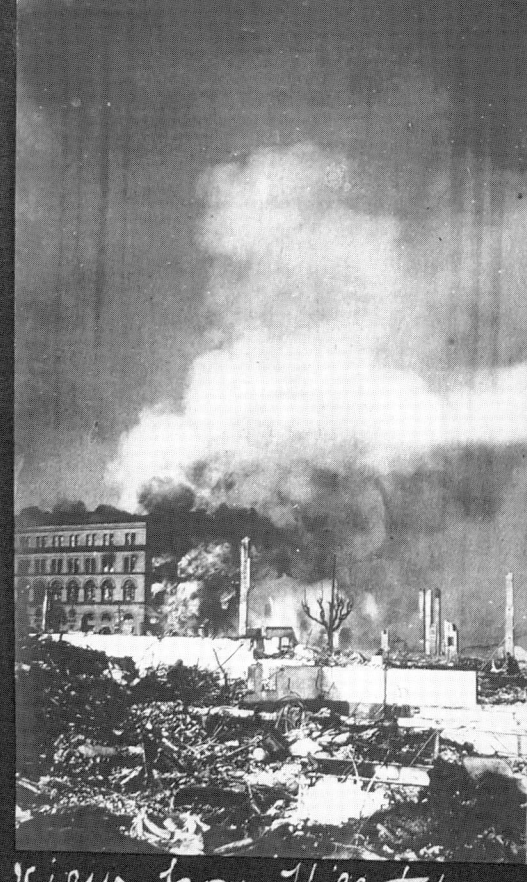

view from Hill top

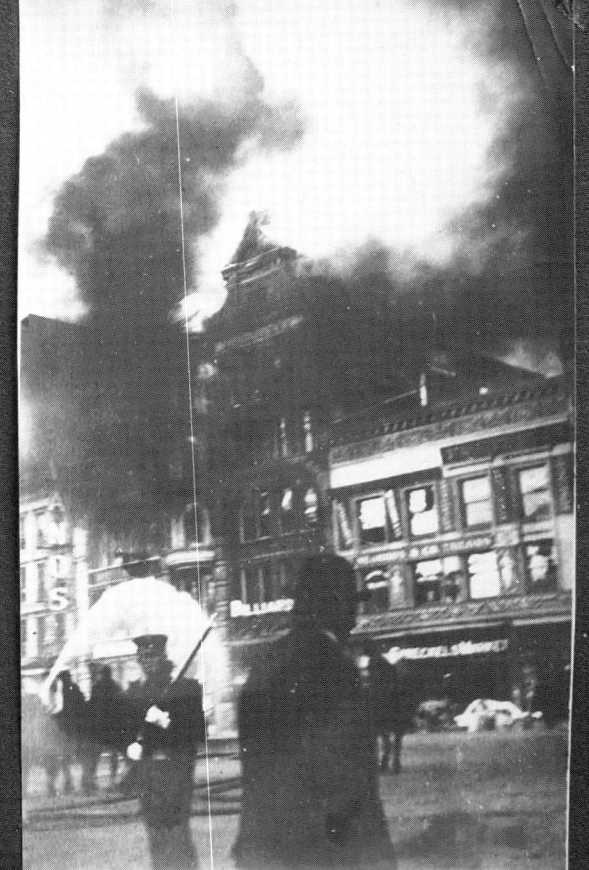

Academy of Science Market St. Ablaze

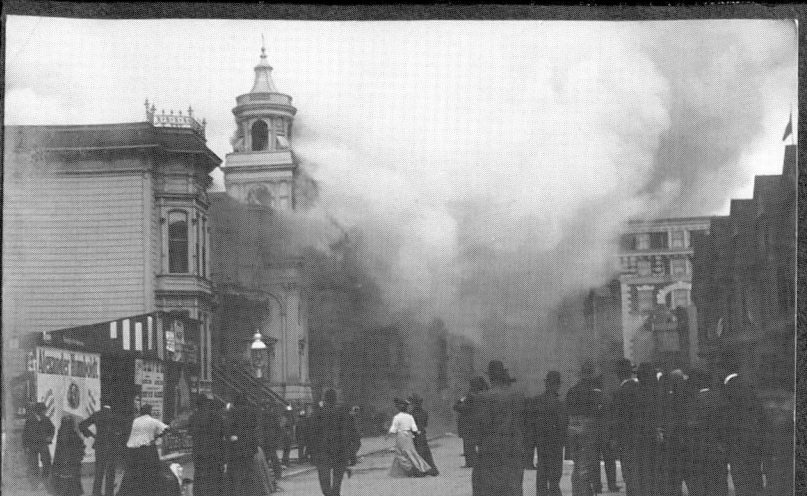

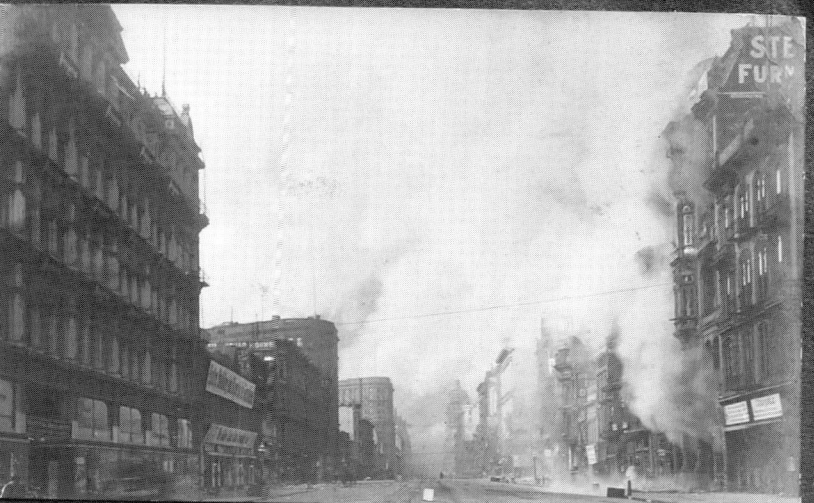

Fell St. near Gough

Market St on fire—from 7th St

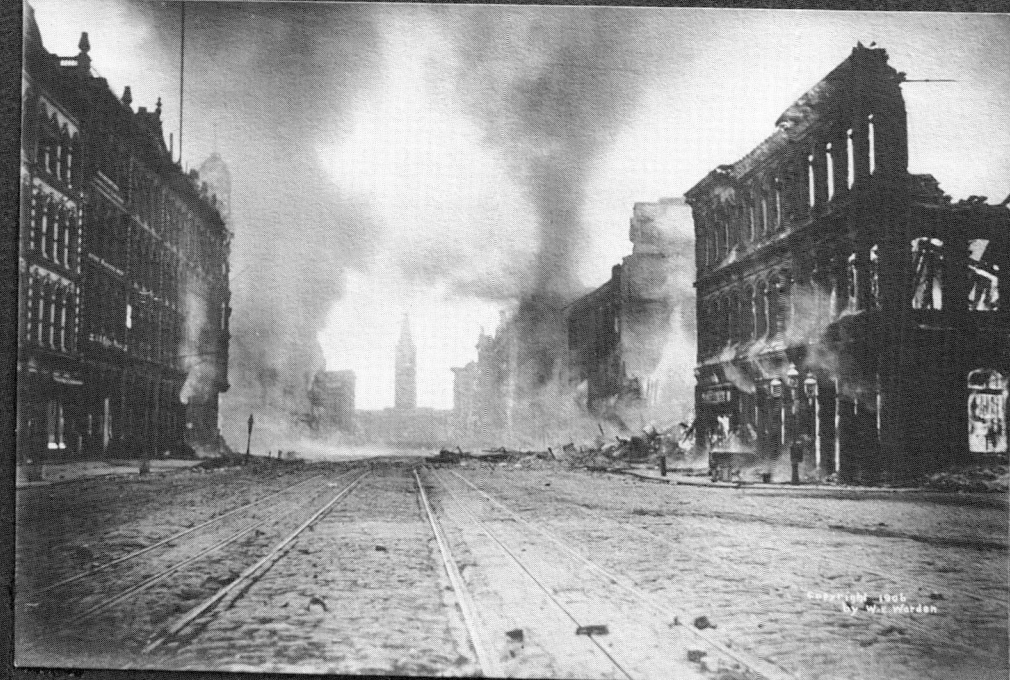

Market St afire showing Ferry Building through the smoke

The Album

"Fell St. near Gough"
The crowd here seems calm and unrushed. Perhaps the water mains were sprung, and little could be done to fight the fire. Tellingly, there is not a piece of fire apparatus or hose in sight.

"Market St. on Fire—from 7th St"
Here, the blaze seems more confined to the south side of the street. The Flood and Call buildings can be seen on opposite sides near the photo's center.

"Market St afire…"
An elegant portrait of tragedy: Market burning down, with smoke framing the Ferry Building to near-perfection. One of the more famous earthquake and fire images, taken by Worden.

When San Francisco Burned

"Reconstruction of tracks..." San Francisco was anxious to get up and moving after the last fires went out. Here, new streetcar tracks are being laid down near the burned-out Flood and Emporium buildings. *(Worden)*

"Fire coming up 3rd St." Wooden buildings are going up fast in this photo, taken south of Market. The Brode and Clark Iron Works can be seen on the left, which indicate the view is actually looking down Howard Street. The abandoned carriage adds a somber note. *(Pillsbury?)*

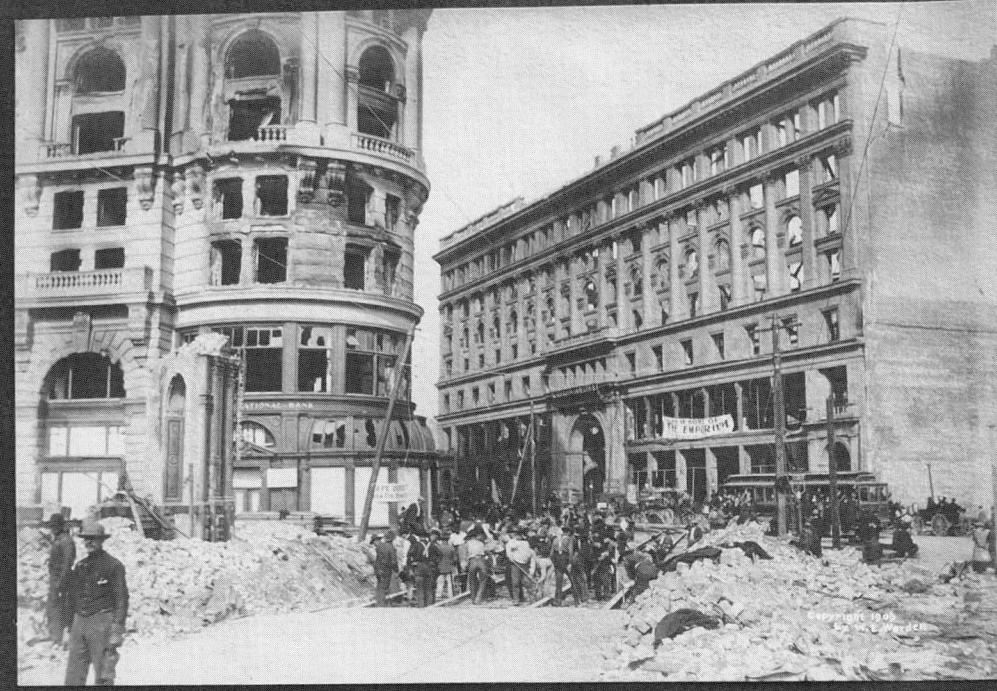

Reconstruction of tracks showing The Jas. Flood & Emporium Buildings

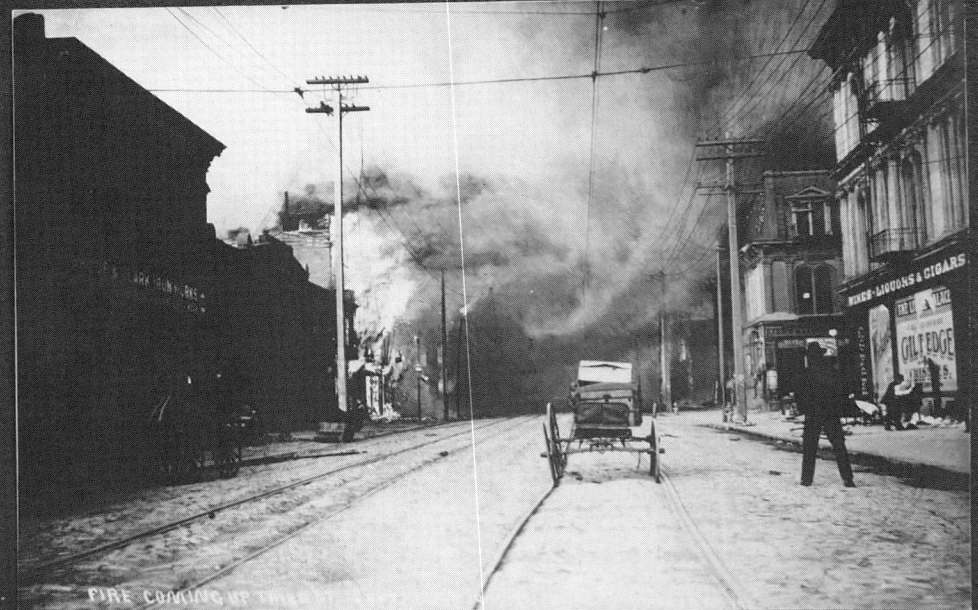

Fire coming up 3rd St.

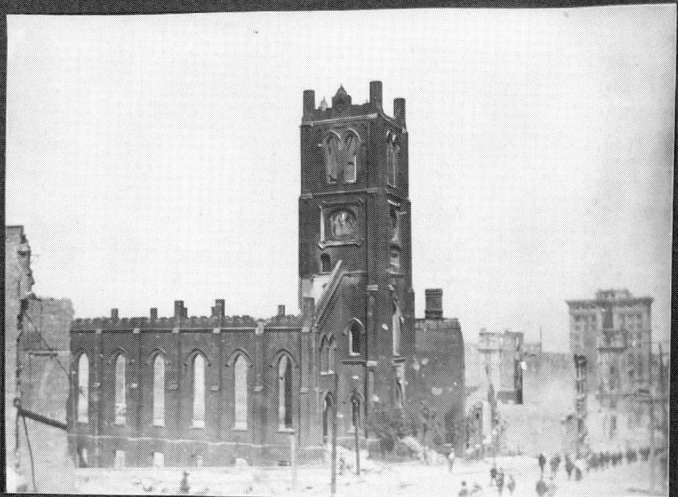

Ruins of old St Mary's Church
California St.

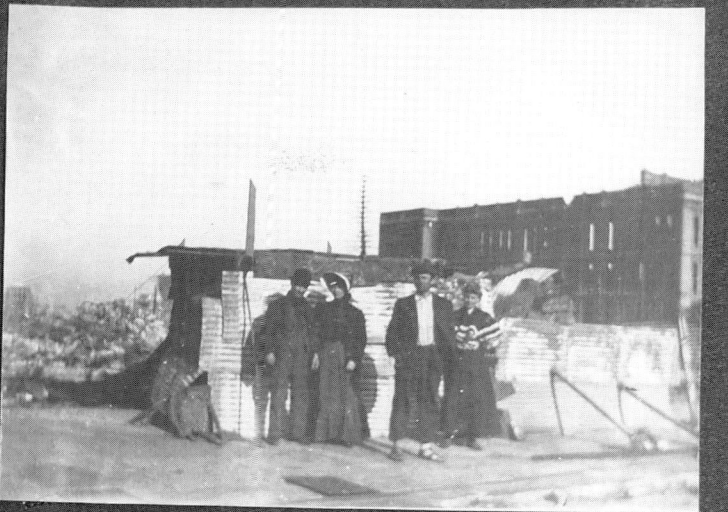

Refugees in their New Home

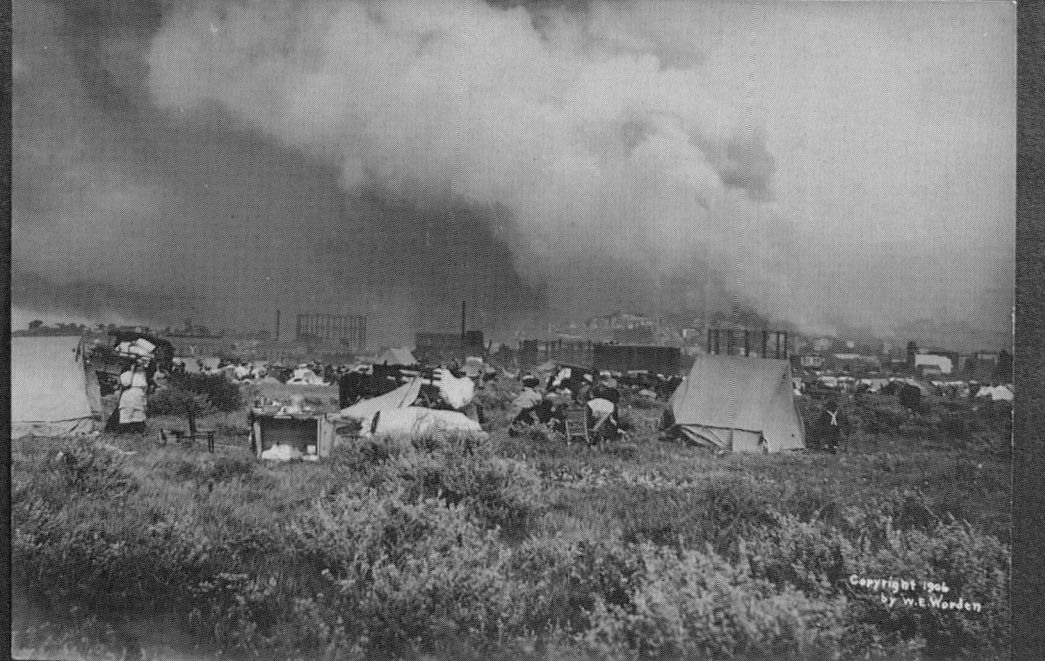

Copyright 1906
by W.E. Worden

Refugees camped near Presidio Fire in the background

"View of Old St. Mary's Church California St." A better view of the San Francisco landmark seen earlier on page 42. Actually a cathedral, the building was completed in 1854 and restored post-fire by 1909. Now located in San Francisco's Chinatown, it remains an active place of worship.

"Refugees in their new Home" Survivors pose proudly next to their new abode of corrugated iron and scavenged scraps.

"Refugees camped near Presidio…" All eyes remain fixed on the fires in this dramatic photo. (Worden)

When San Francisco Burned

"Valencia Street opposite Hotel Valencia" Another scene testifying to the earthquake's tremendous force, with buildings and telegraph poles pitched at odd angles and the roadway filled with crevices and potholes.

"Fire on Front St…" In this photo, fire consumes what was left of smashed buildings along Front Street, just off Market. This neighborhood, near the Ferry Building, was another built on fill and it fared poorly during the disasters.

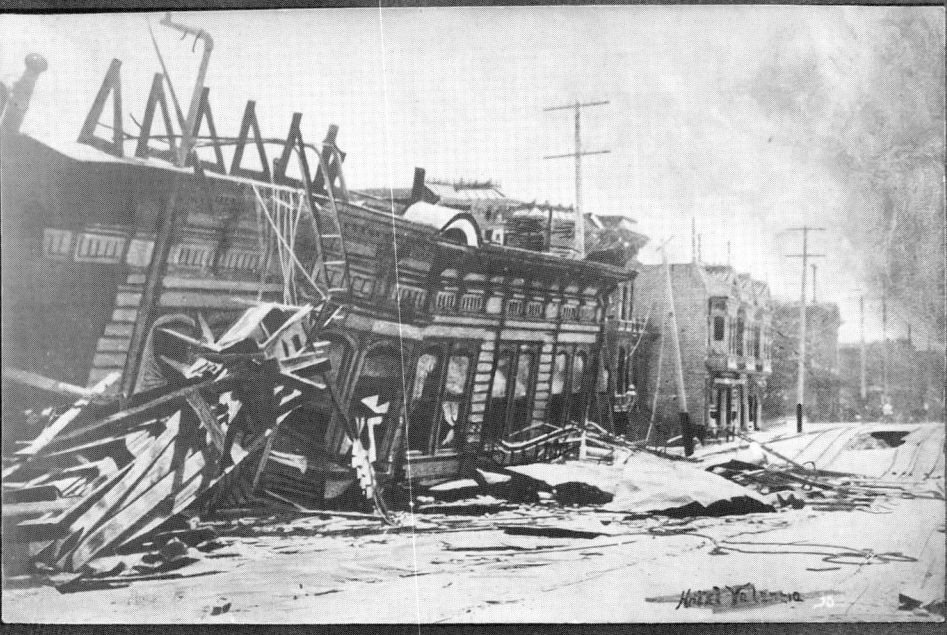

Valencia Street opposite Hotel Valencia

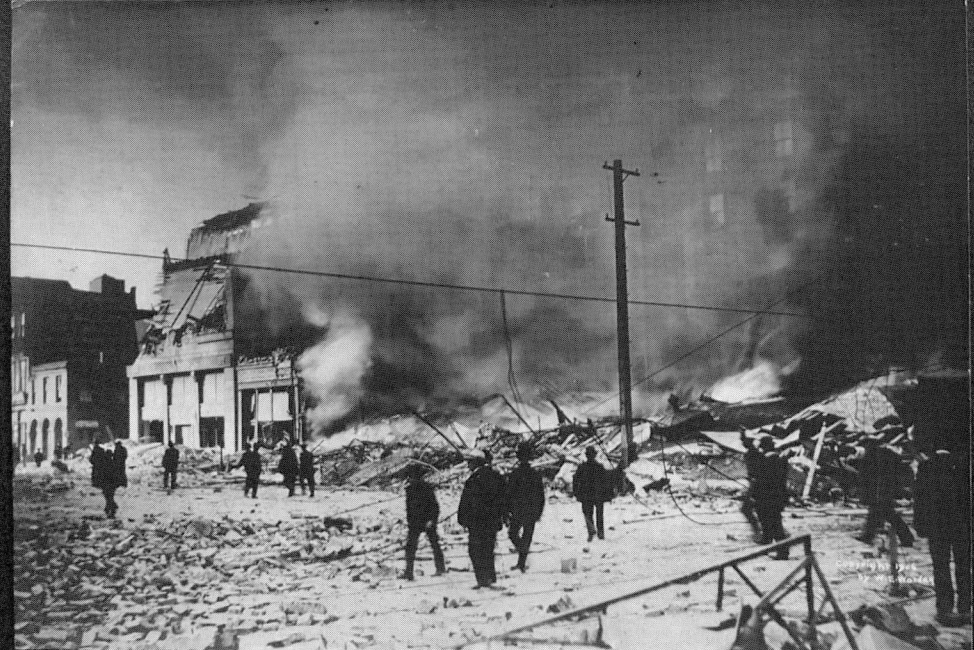

Fire on Front St. Showing buildings Shaken down by Earthquake

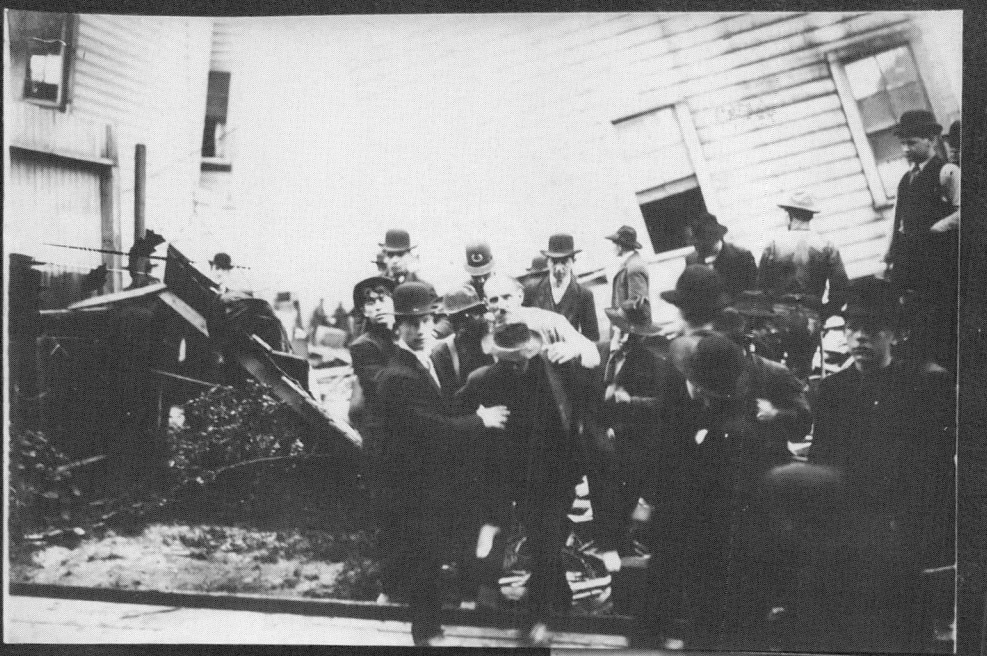

Rescuing the injured from Valencia Hotel before the fire reached it.

"Rescuing the injured from Valencia Hotel…" Another operation, similar to that undertaken at the Brunswick Hotel (page 40). Note policeman standing near center.

"The fire as seen from Mansions on Nob Hill…" This Worden photo looks down California Street, toward the main fire area. (Worden)

The fire as seen from Mansions on Nob Hill which were afterwards burned

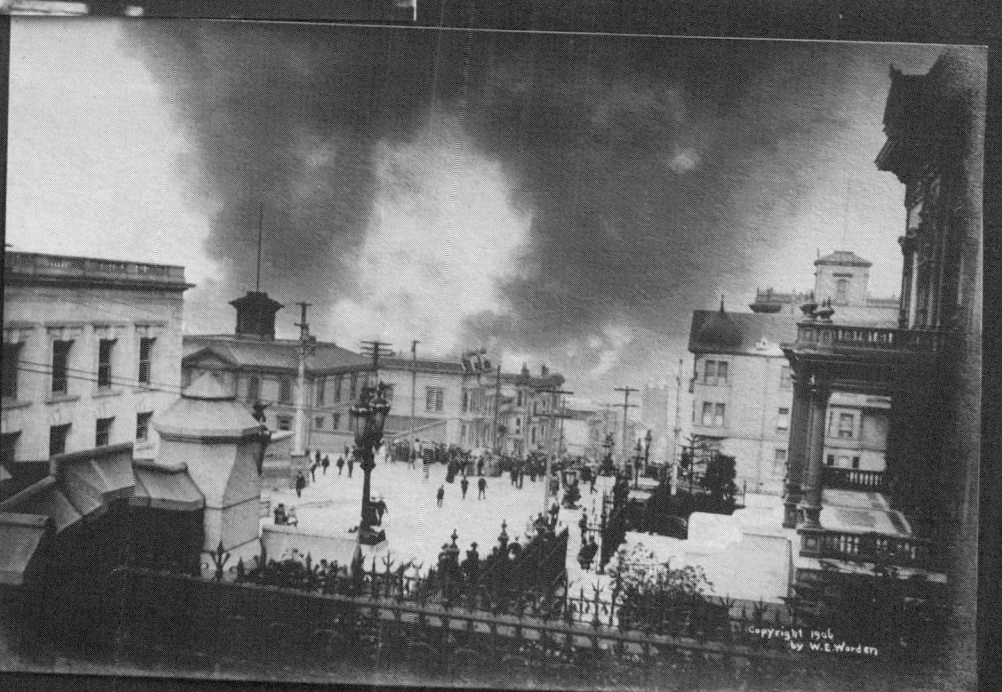

Copyright 1906 by W.E. Worden

When San Francisco Burned

"Dore Street after Earthquake" Another block of crooked, sagging homes unsettled by the earthquake. Note what appears to be a manhole cover in the fore-ground, with sur-rounding pavement torn up—perhaps indicating a frantic search for water. (Pillsbury)

"View of city burning from a skyscraper" The presence of the Pine Street Goldberg, Bowen & Co. gourmet grocery in the middle ground suggests a vantage point well north of Market Street. The Examiner (Hearst) and Call buildings are visible in the center.

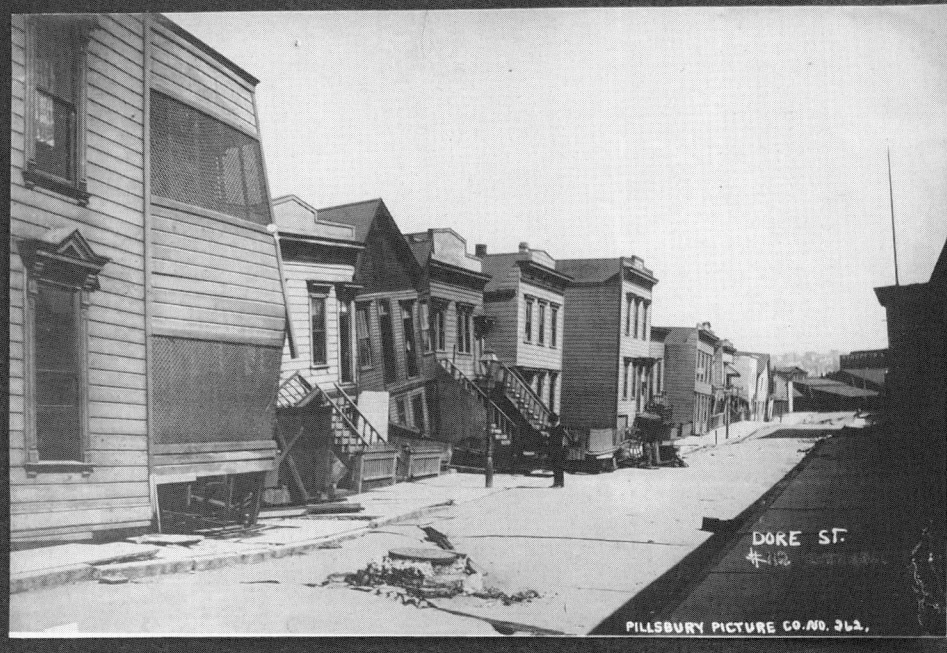

DORE ST.
PILLSBURY PICTURE CO. NO. 362.

Dore Street after Earthquake

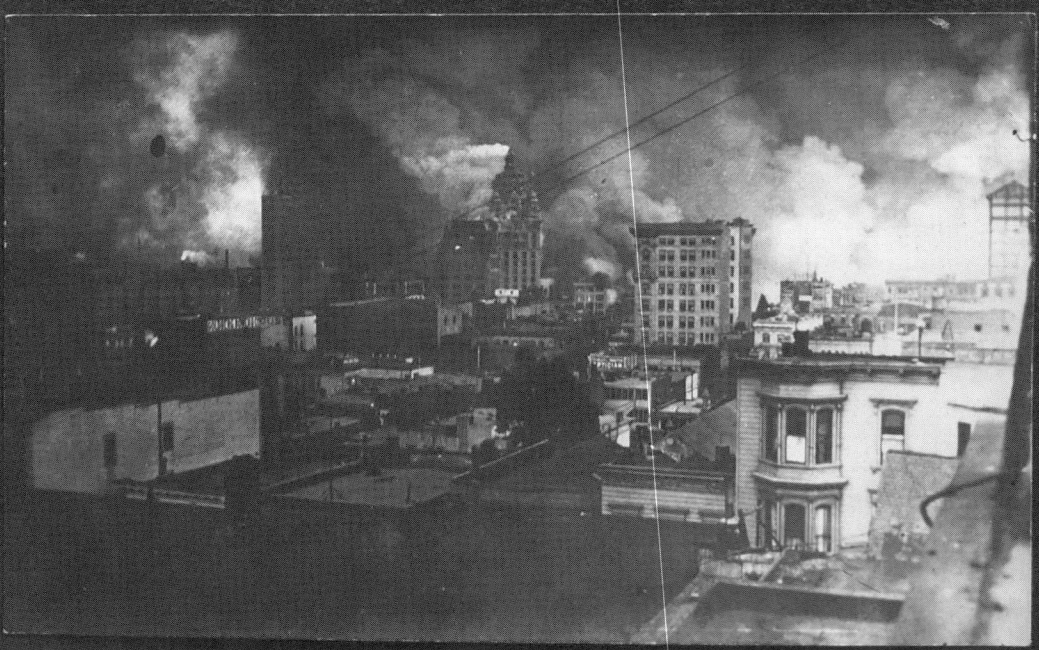

View of city burning from a skyscraper

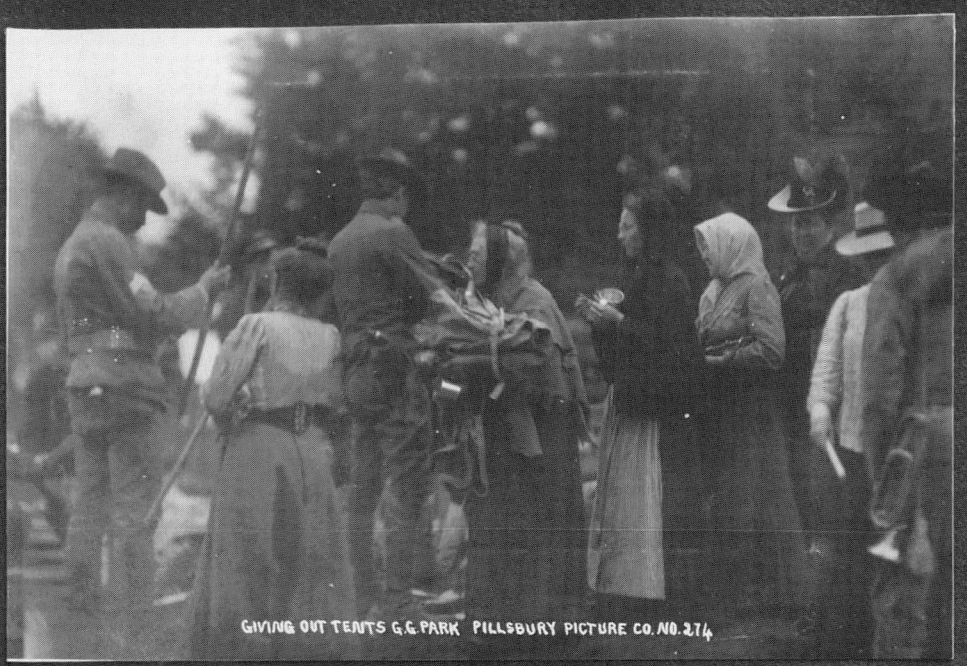

GIVING OUT TENTS G.G. PARK   PILLSBURY PICTURE CO. NO. 274

Giving out tents
Golden Gate Park

Moving the injured
in autos–

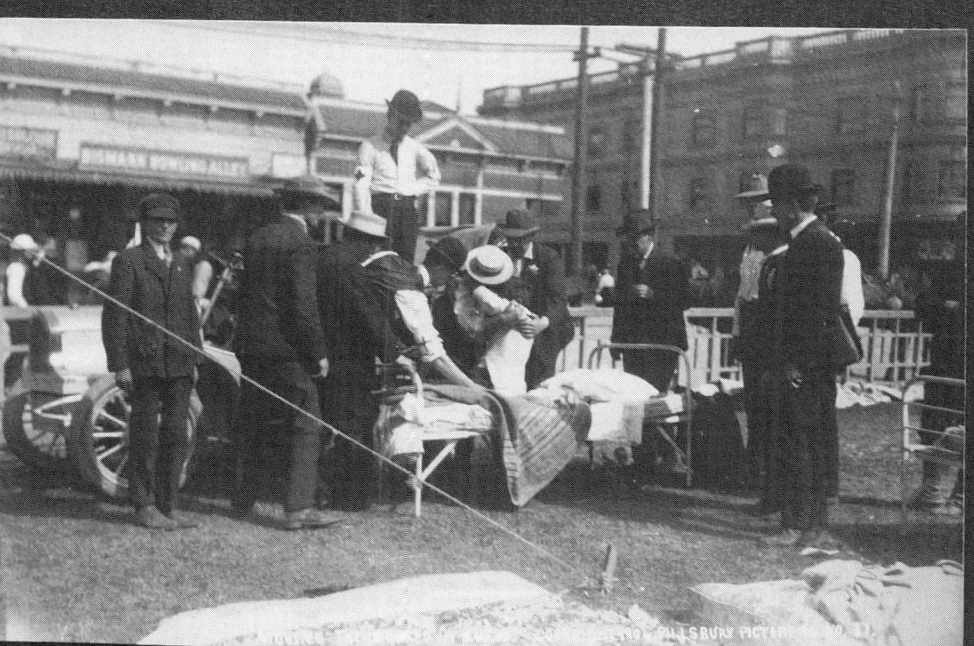

"Giving out tents Golden Gate Park" Soldiers assist in helping the newly homeless. (Pillsbury)

"Moving the injured in autos—" In this shot, a person is being moved from an automobile onto a hospital bed, within what appears to be an open-air, makeshift hospital. It seems remarkable that an automobile could navigate the debris-clogged San Francisco streets. (Pillsbury)

When San Francisco Burned

"Rescuing the injured…" A fireman and two others dig for survivors, and possibly corpses, in the Valencia Hotel's remains. See also page 61. (Whigham)

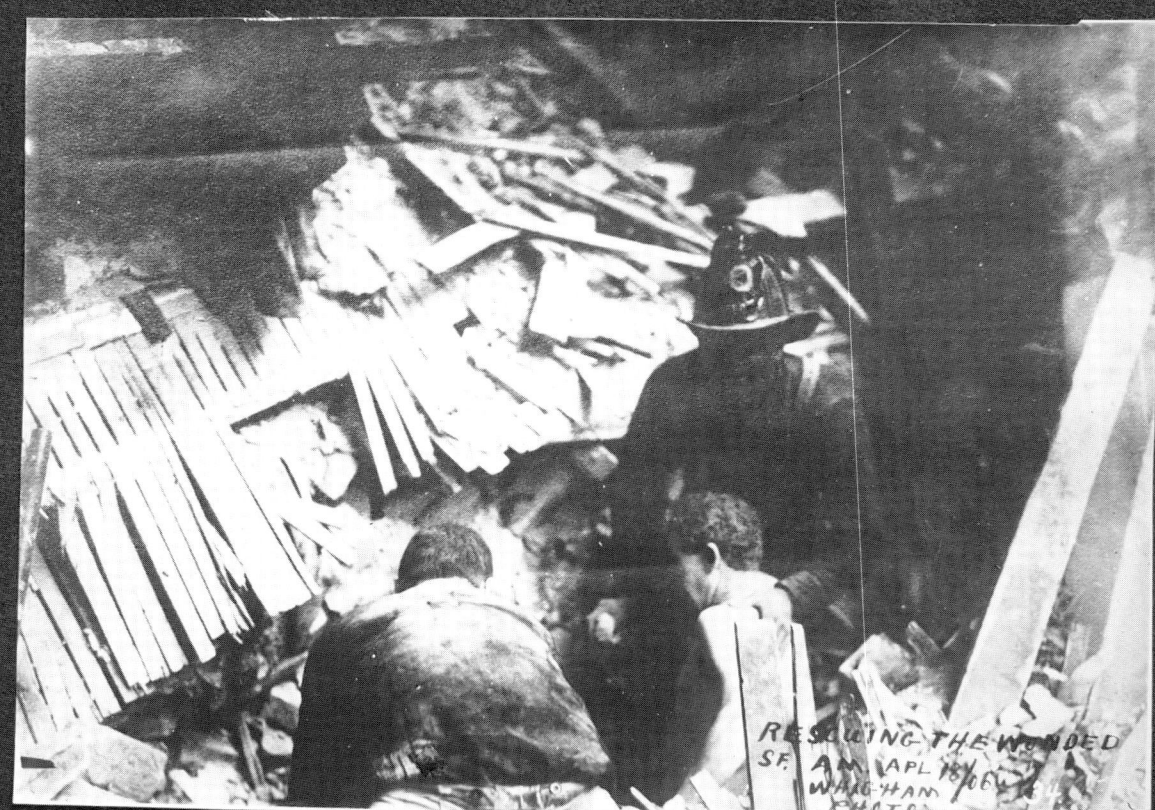

RESCUING THE WOUNDED
SF. AM APL 18/06
WHIGHAM
PHOTO

Rescuing the injured — before the fire reached them.
Valencia Hotel
"

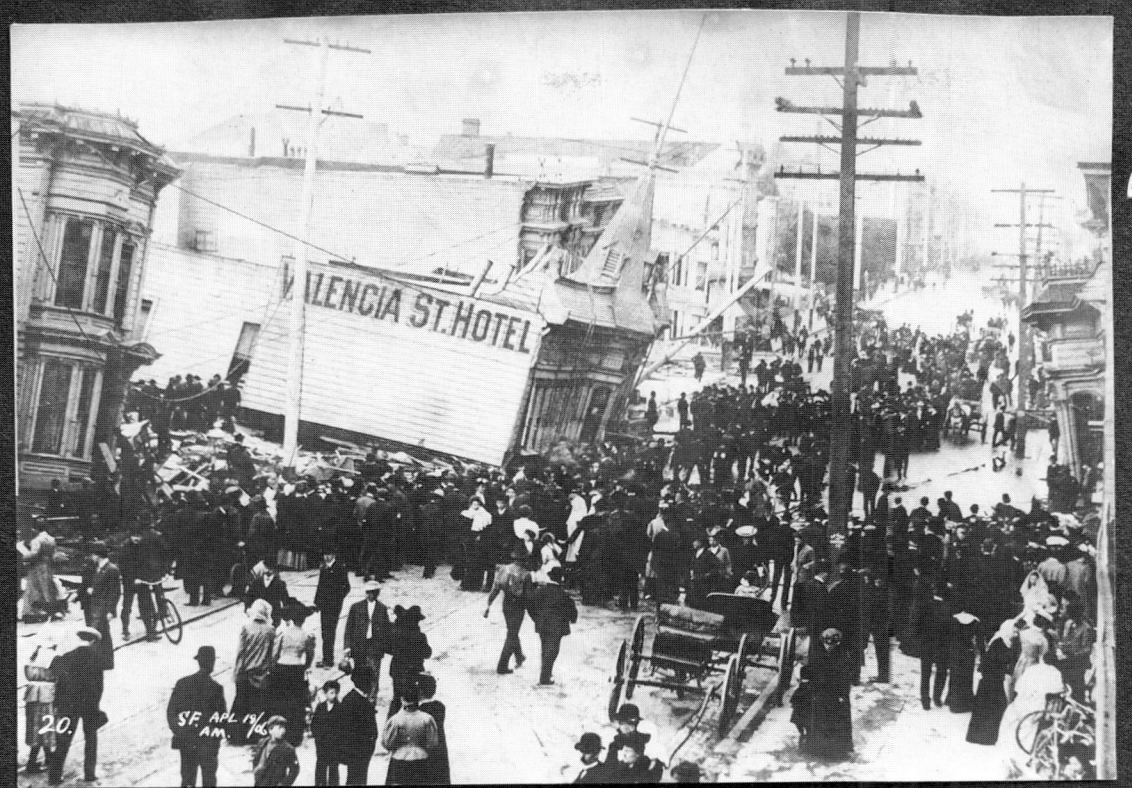

Valencia Hotel before fire reached it

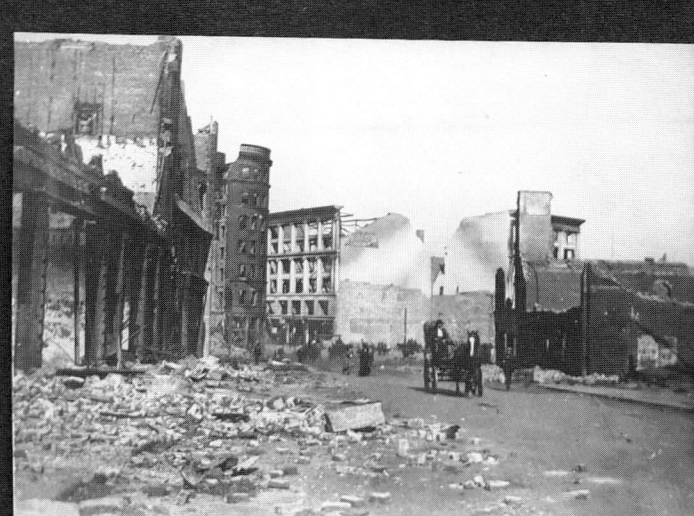

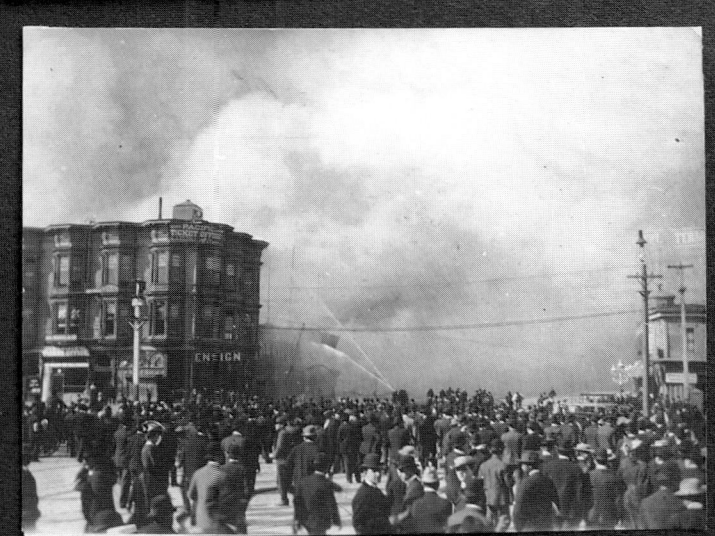

View of ruins from Golden Gate Ave

The start of the fire

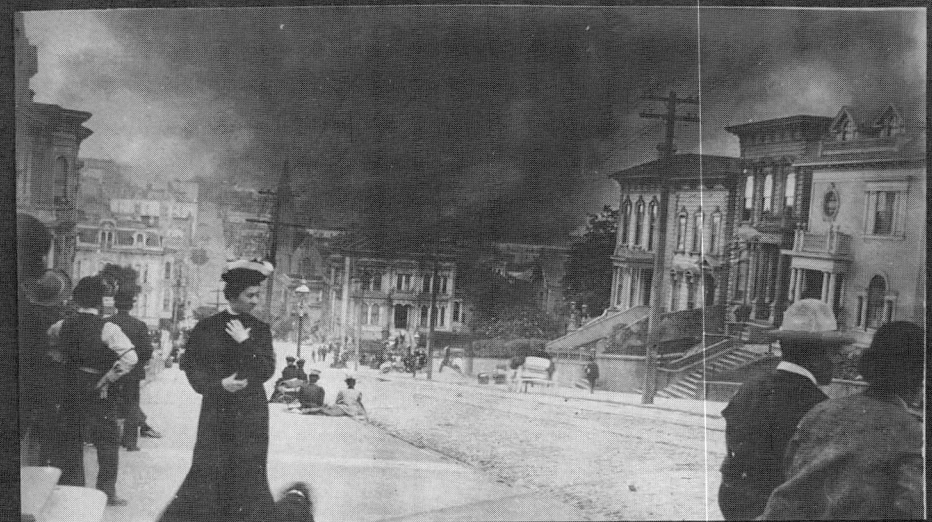

Watching the fire in the distance

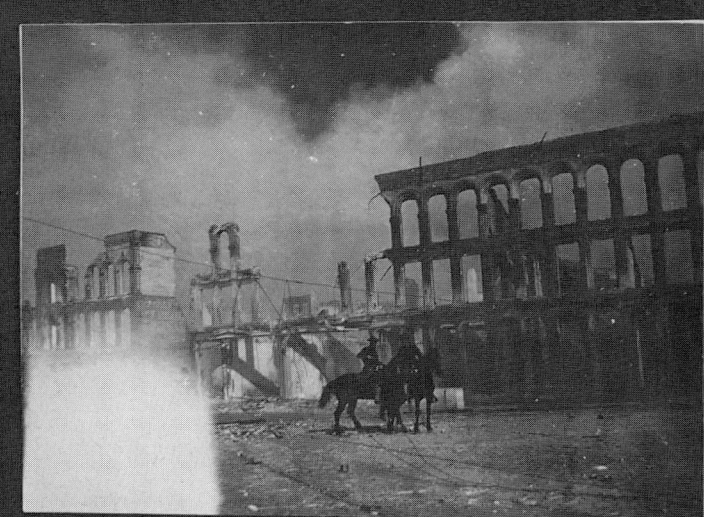

after the fire

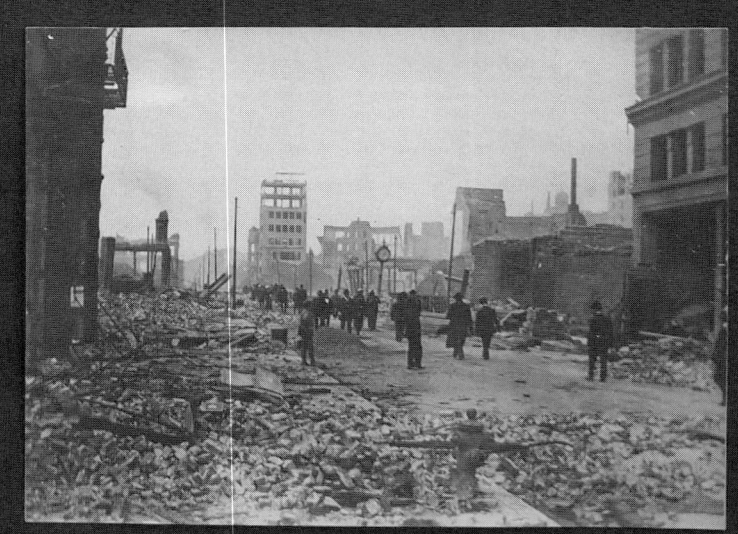

Visitors coming to see ruins

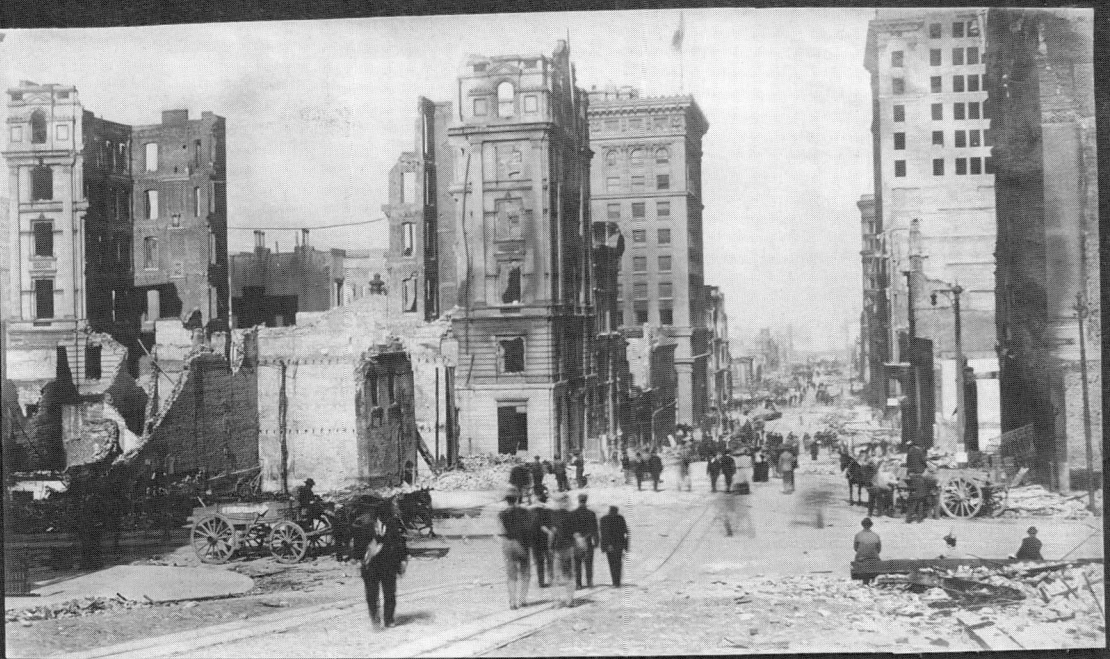

*View of
California St
Ruins from Kearney*

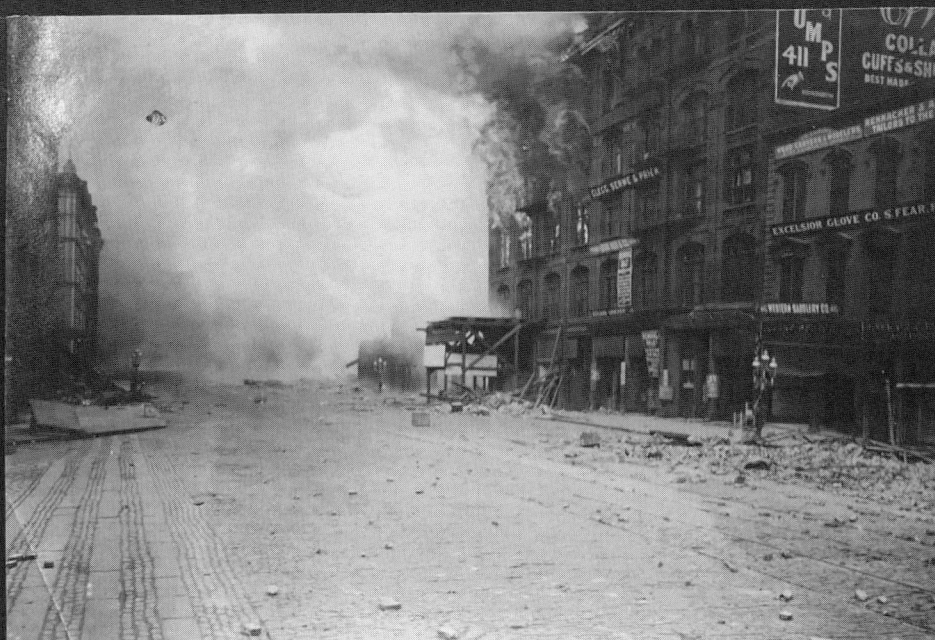

*Fire on Third St
near Howard St*

*"View of
California St
Ruins from
Kearny"*
Little other than
pure destruction
is visible in this
shot. The streets
appear passable,
with wagons and
crowds much in
evidence, suggest-
ing that this view
dates to several
weeks after
the disaster.

*"Fire on Third St
near Howard St"*
Flames consume
another city block,
without a single
person in sight.

When San Francisco Burned

"View of fire South of Market St…" This shot looks southeast on Mint Street, toward Mission. Created in 1854 to produce coinage from the California Gold Rush, the mint expanded and occupied this new Greek Revival building in 1874. While it survived the earthquake and fire, it was decommissioned in 1937 and has lately functioned as a historical museum.

"Taylor and Turk Sts…" A crowd surges to see the fire. Note mounted soldier at left center.

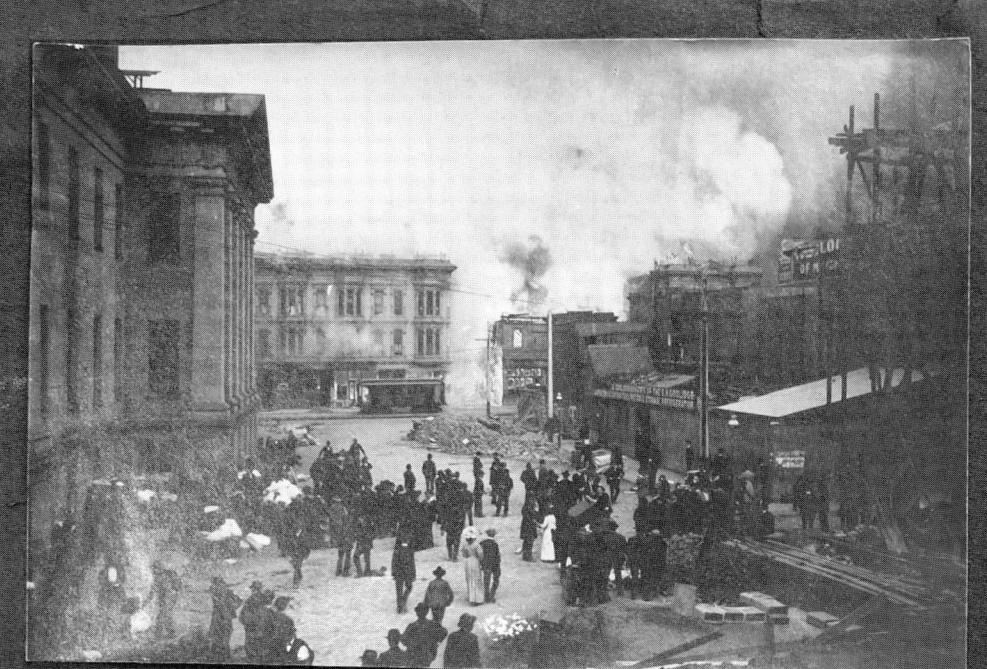

View of fire South of Market St. Taken from rear of U.S. Mint.

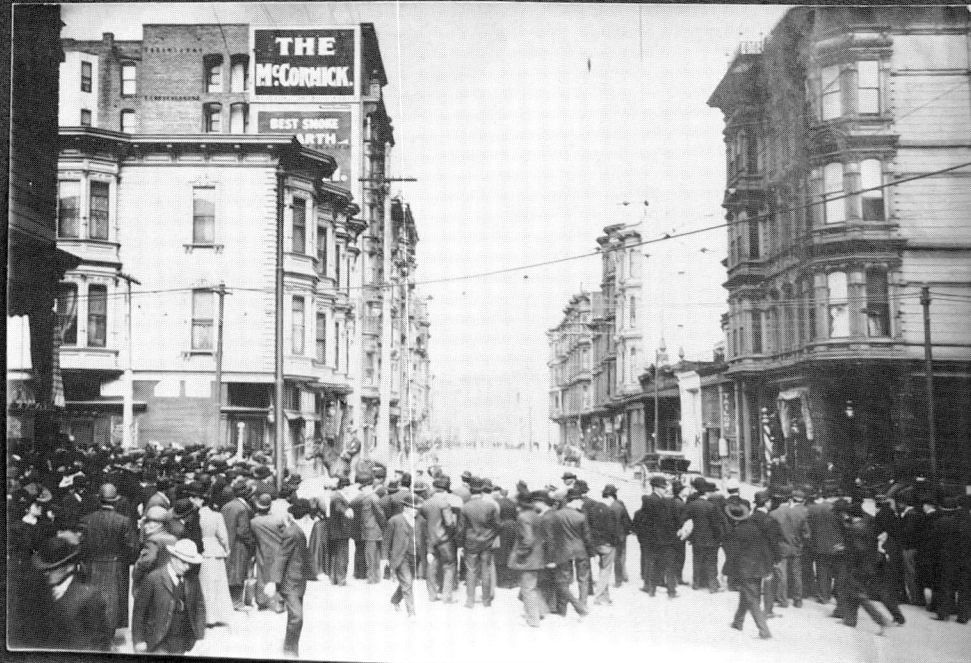

Taylor & Turk Sts all buildings burned twelve hours later

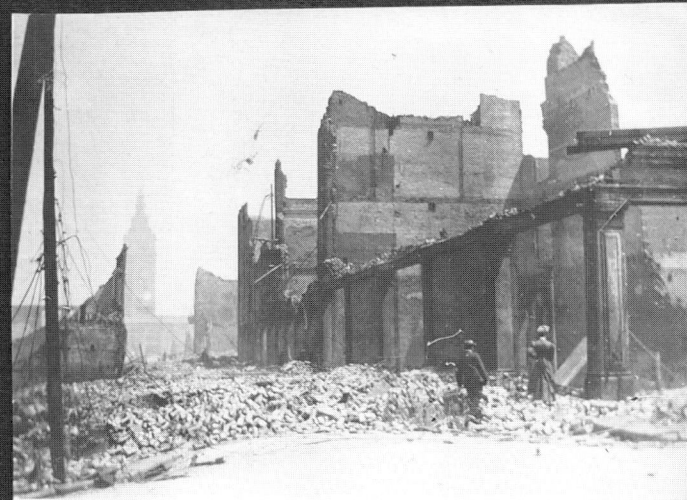

As S.F. streets appeared after the fire

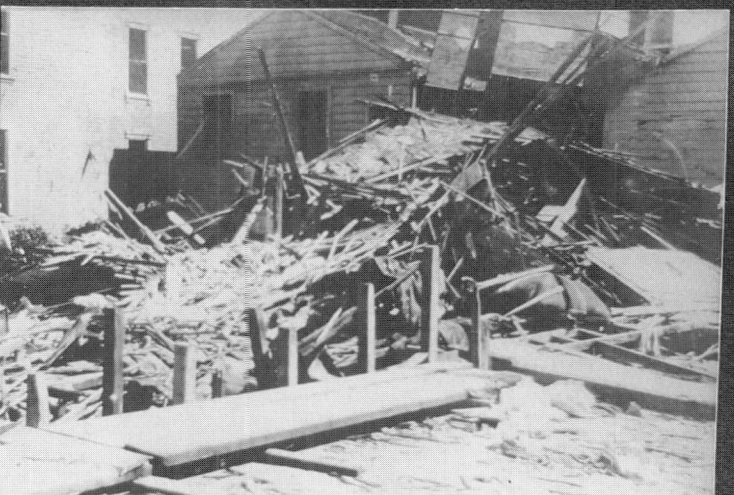

Earthquake damage

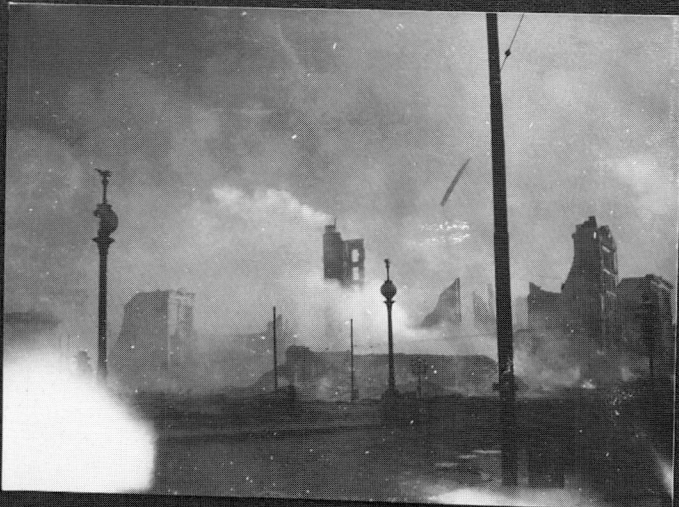

The last of the fire

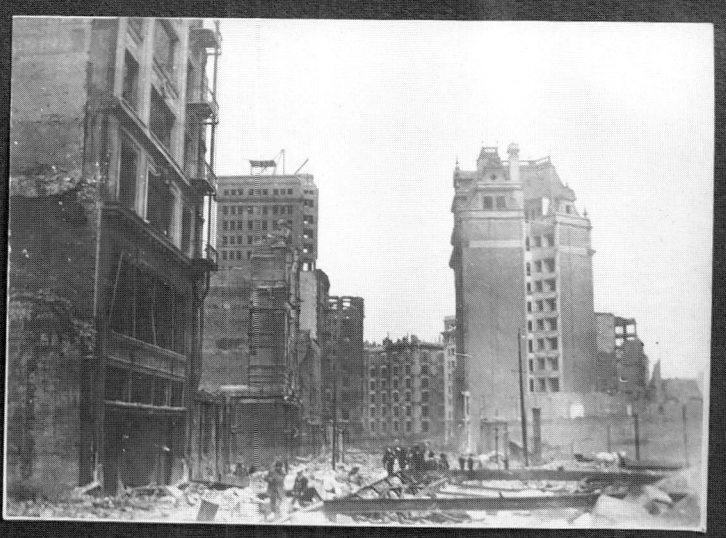

Geary St. after fire

"As S.F. streets appeared after the fire"
Looking east slightly north of Market, with the Ferry Building visible dimly in the left background.

"The last of the fire"
These dying smoke plumes were an indubitable relief to all San Franciscans.

"Earthquake damage"
A familiar scene of smashed wood and tilting structures.

"Geary St. after fire"
The Chronicle Building looms on the left, with the rear of the Mutual Bank Building at right. The burned-out Palace Hotel is at the center.

When San Francisco Burned

"Early morning scene on Market St…" Likely a bit after the caption time, as the earthquake commenced after 6 a.m.

"The Homeless Union Square…" The Call Building's undamaged dome, in the background, indicates this shot was taken on the morning of April 18, before fire hit Market Street in the afternoon.

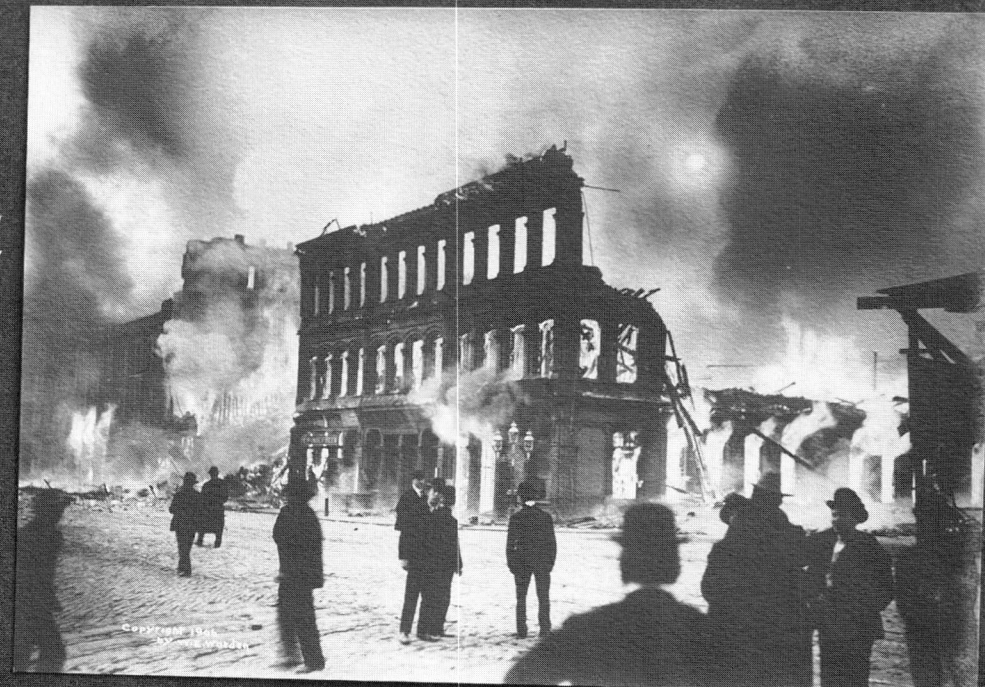

Early morning scene on Market St. S.F. April 18 – 1906 6 a.m.

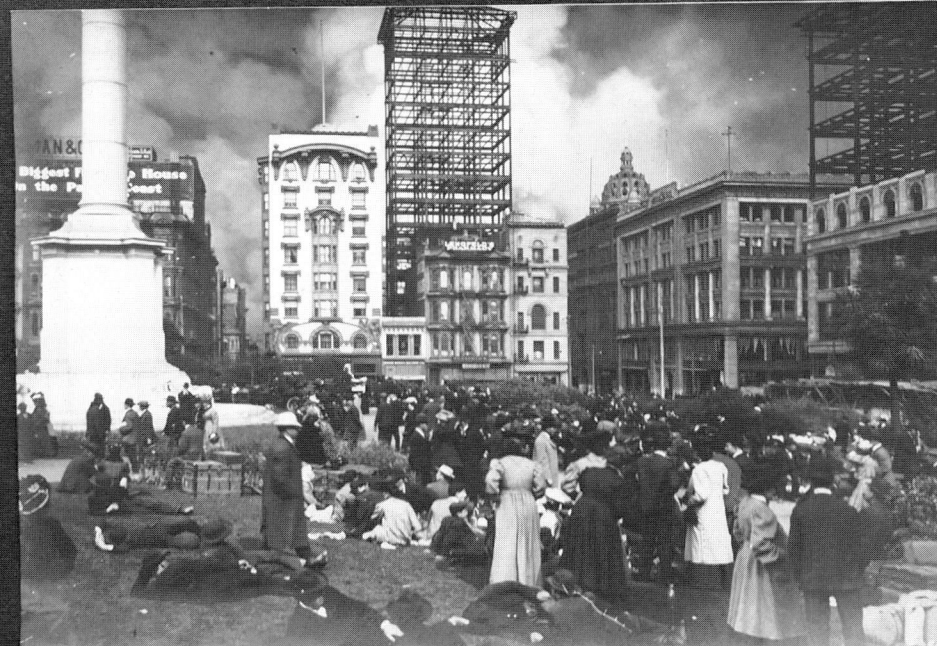

The Homeless Union Square Wednesday, April 18 – '06

Van Ness Ave after fire

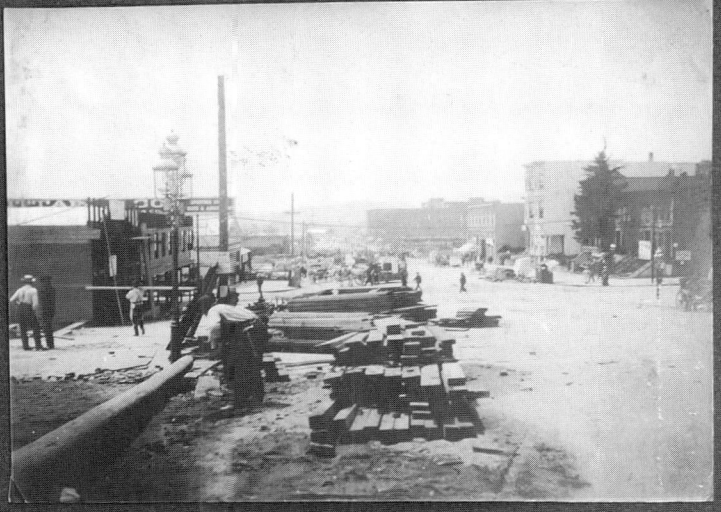

Earthquake destruction at -Butchertown-

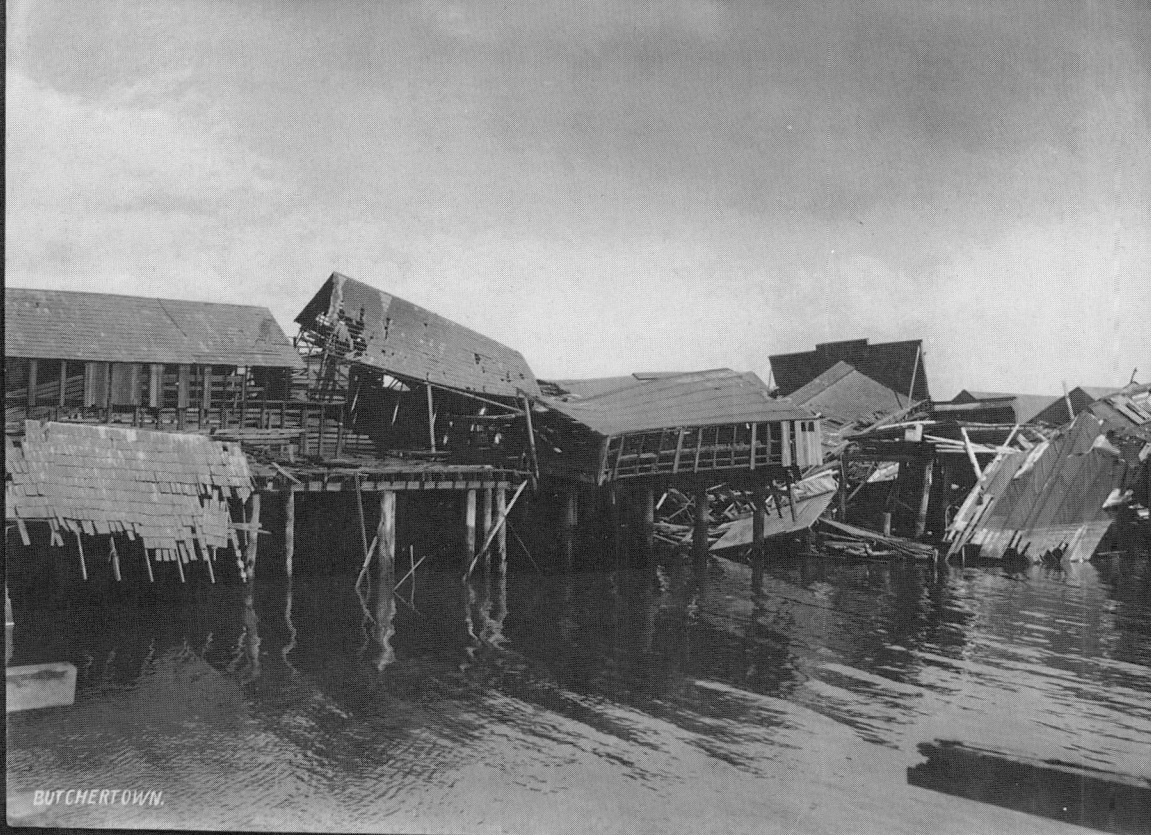

BUTCHERTOWN.

The Album

"Van Ness Ave after fire"
A hazy view showing early reconstruction efforts underway.

"Earthquake destruction at— Butchertown—"
Reserved for all of San Francisco's slaughterhouses after the late 1870s, Butchertown was confined to a portion of today's Bayview section of San Francisco, away from the main commercial areas. Built on fill and with wood, it was badly damaged by the earthquake. (Pillsbury?)

When San Francisco Burned

"View of Van Ness Ave. from Hayes St." Two of the city's more notable ruins are visible here: St. Ignatius to the left and City Hall to the right. (Pillsbury)

"View down Market St. from Turk St." A sweeping view of the fire area east of the Civic Center area. The Call Building can be seen amid the haze, at center. (Pillsbury)

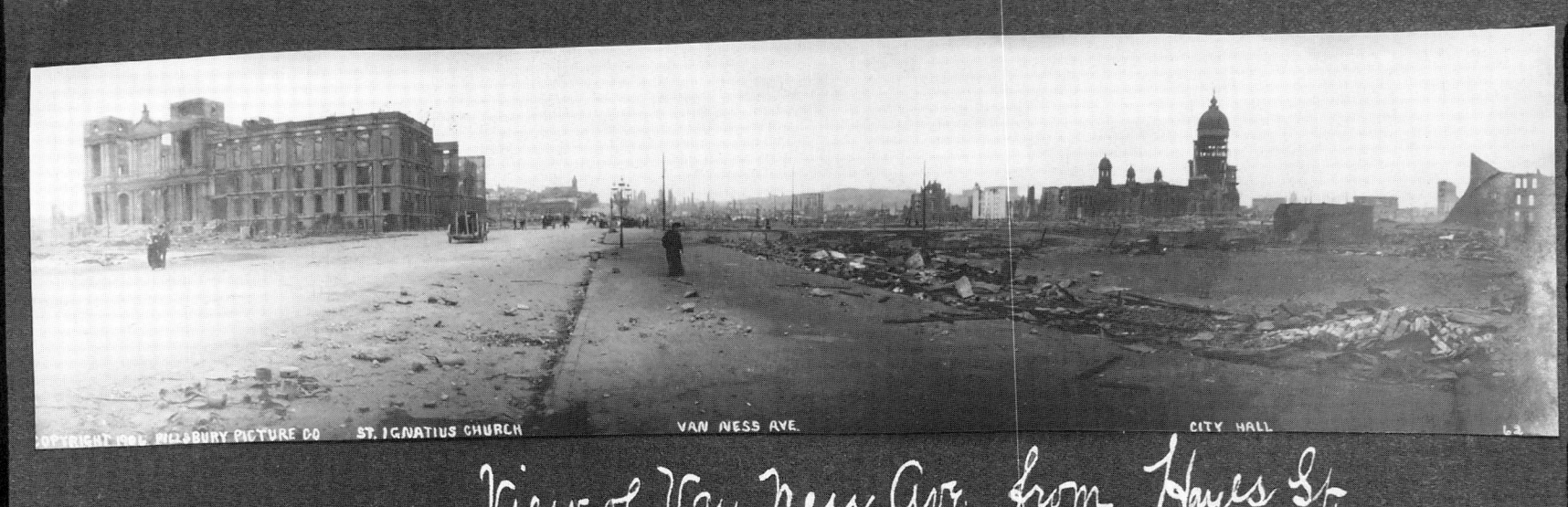

COPYRIGHT 1906 PILLSBURY PICTURE CO   ST. IGNATIUS CHURCH   VAN NESS AVE.   CITY HALL

View of Van Ness Ave from Hayes St.

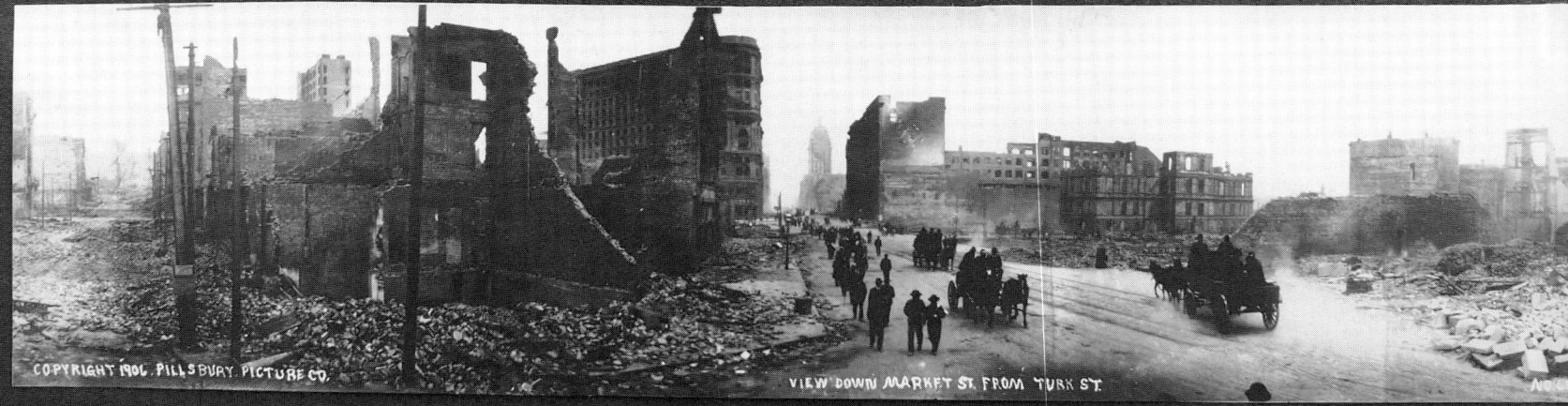

COPYRIGHT 1906 PILLSBURY PICTURE CO.   VIEW DOWN MARKET ST. FROM TURK ST.

View down Market St. from Turk St.

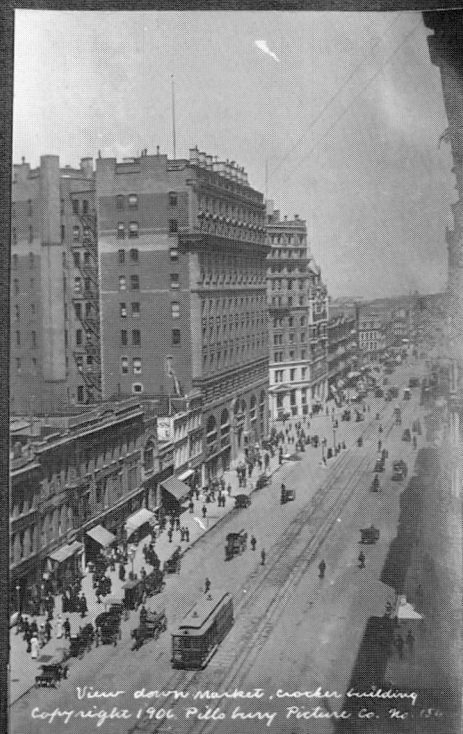

*View down Market St.
Crocker Building*

*View down Market, crocker building
Copyright 1906 Pillsbury Picture Co. No. 134*

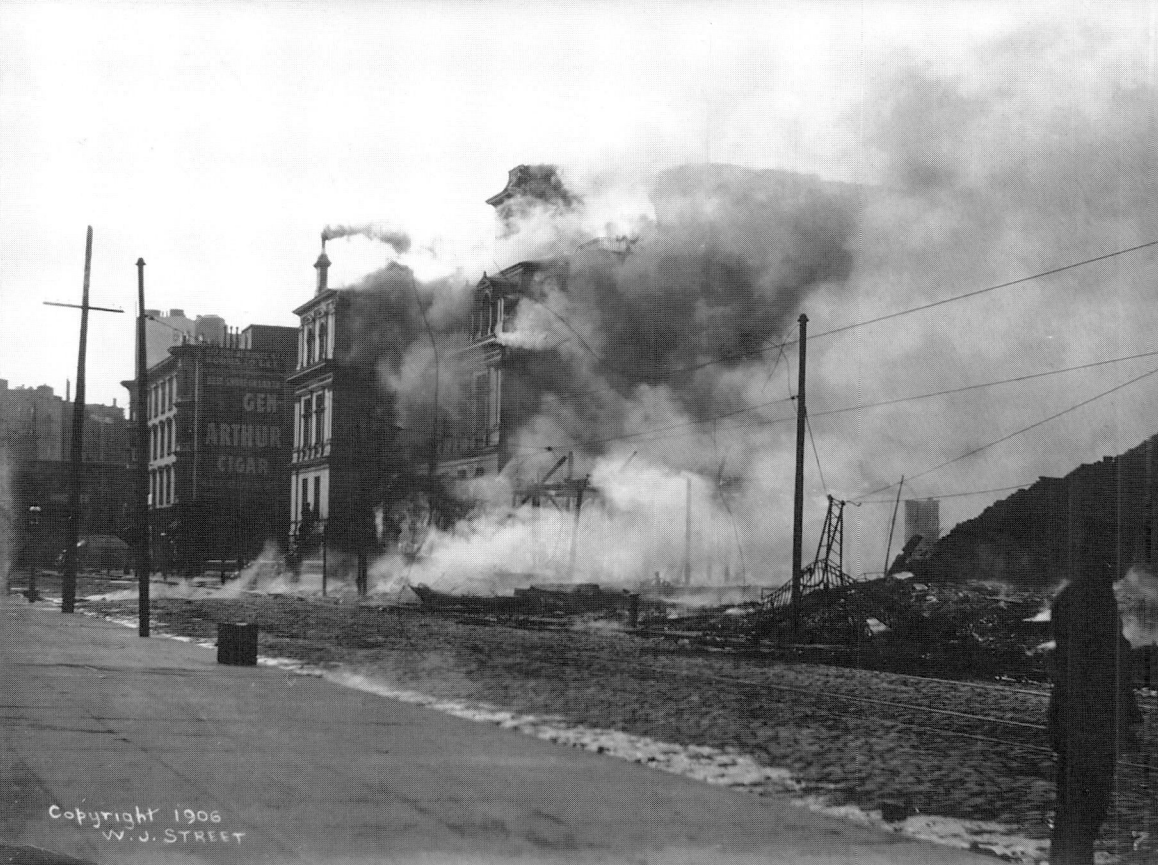

*Burning of the
Metropolitan Temple
&
Lincoln School*

Copyright 1906
W. J. STREET

73

When San Francisco Burned

"Homeless waiting for clothing"
What seems to be an orderly procession, perhaps helped by the presence of two soldiers at far right. (Noel?)

"Bread Line Golden Gate Park"
A soldier and several men standing around find enough time to pose for the camera. By studying the boxes piled next to the building, it can be discerned that this is the same scene recorded above, only from a different angle. (Noel?)

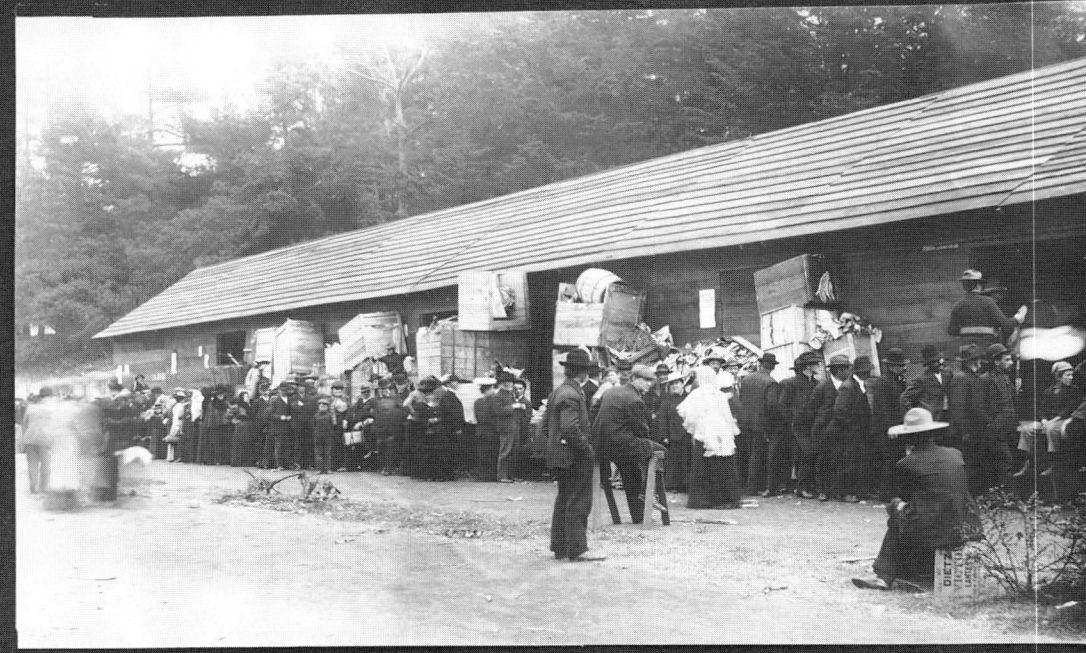

Homeless waiting for Clothing

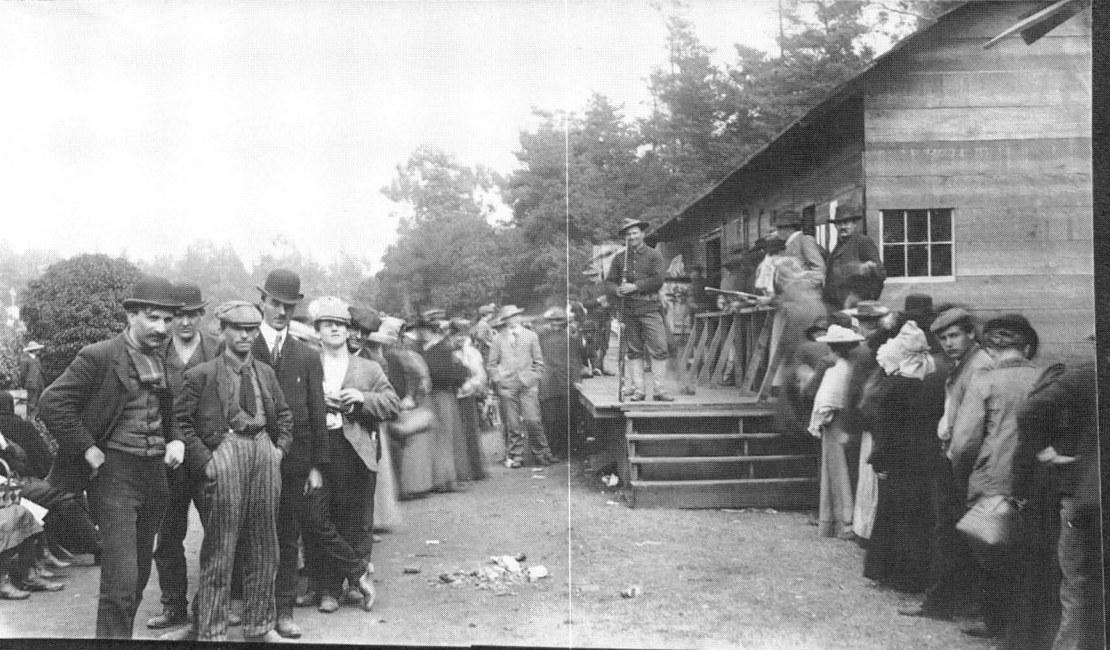

Bread Line Golden Gate Park

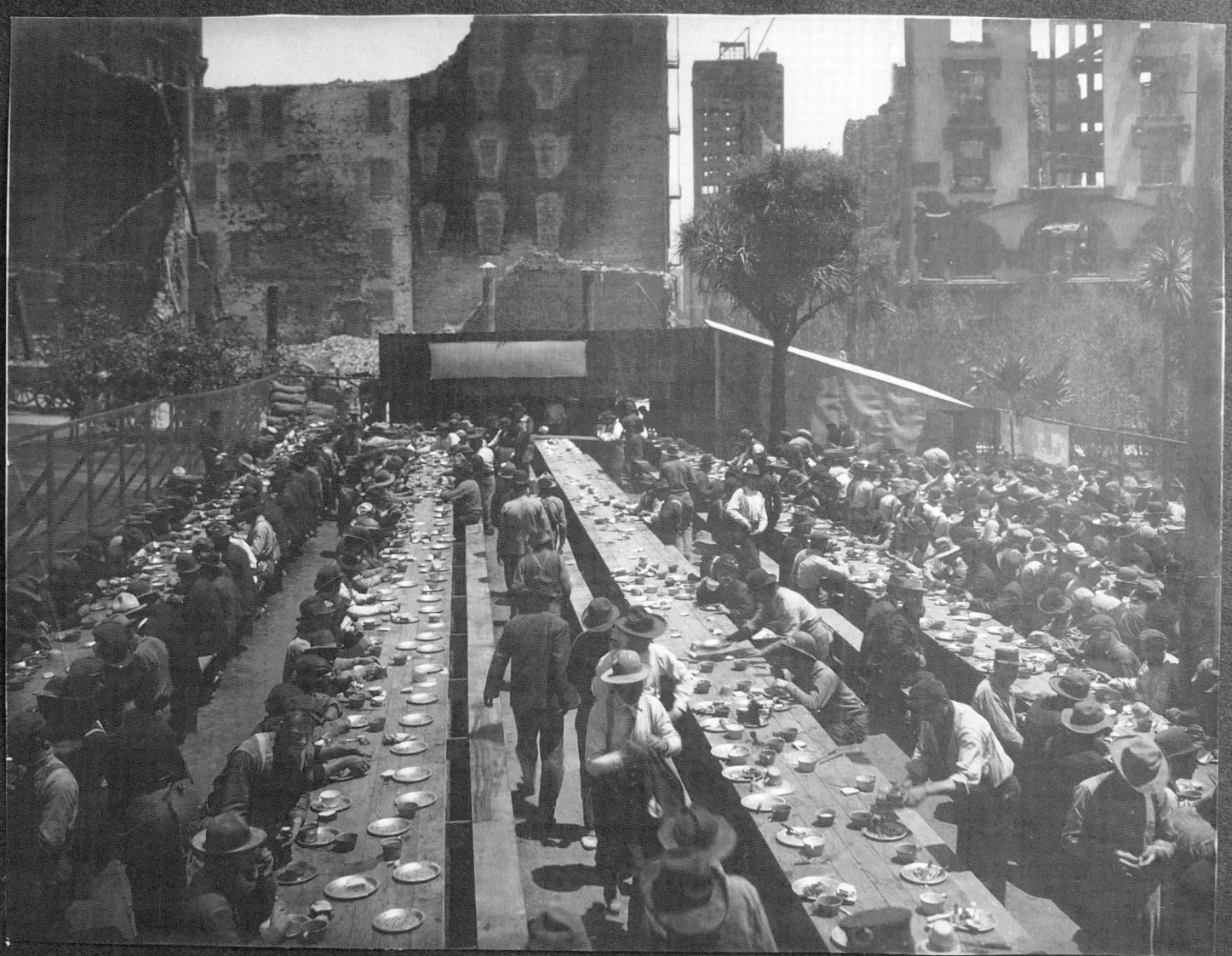

Mrs. Crocker's — Free Lunch Table — Union Square —

"Mrs. Crocker's— Free Lunch Table— Union Square" A post-fire view documenting the prominent Crocker family's generosity. The camera is pointed east, with Geary Street to the far right and the Chronicle Building at center right.

When San Francisco Burned

"'The Hungry' searching the ruins…"
In the disaster's immediate aftermath, food was hard to find and was sought wherever it might be, even underneath the city's smoking ruins.
(Pillsbury)

"'Bread Line' near Golden Gate Park"
Despite the caption, this view was taken down Market, as the Hotel Terminal and Owl Cigar buildings (seen at right) were located on that street.

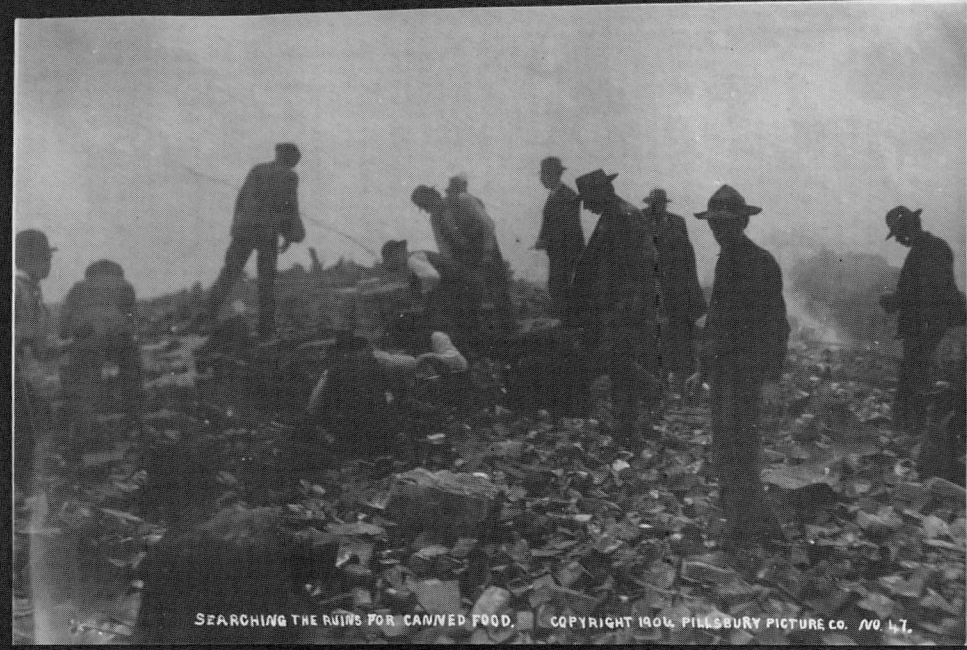

SEARCHING THE RUINS FOR CANNED FOOD.   COPYRIGHT 1904 PILLSBURY PICTURE CO.   NO. 47.

"The Hungry" searching the ruins for canned goods

"Bread Line" near Golden Gate Park

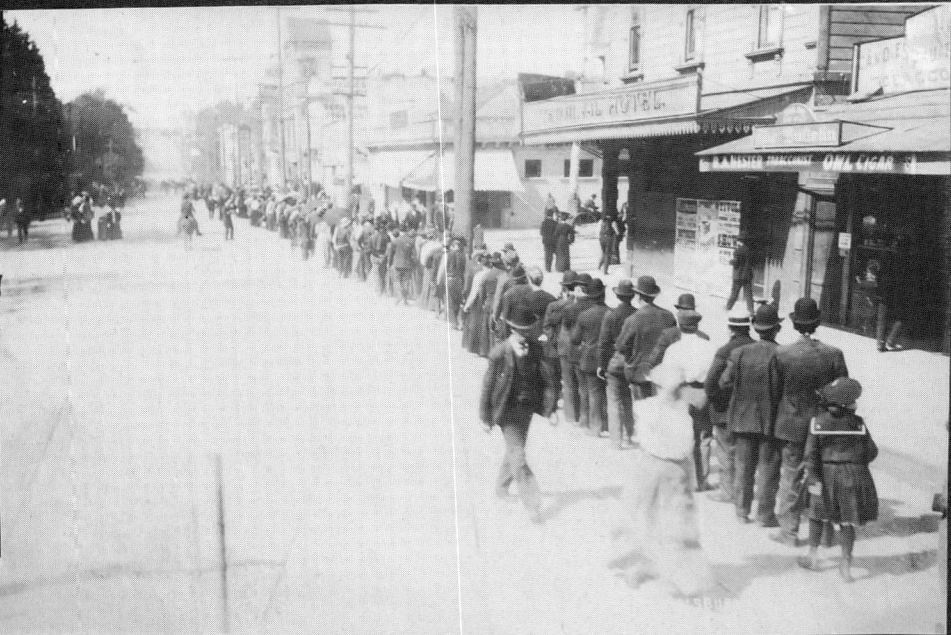

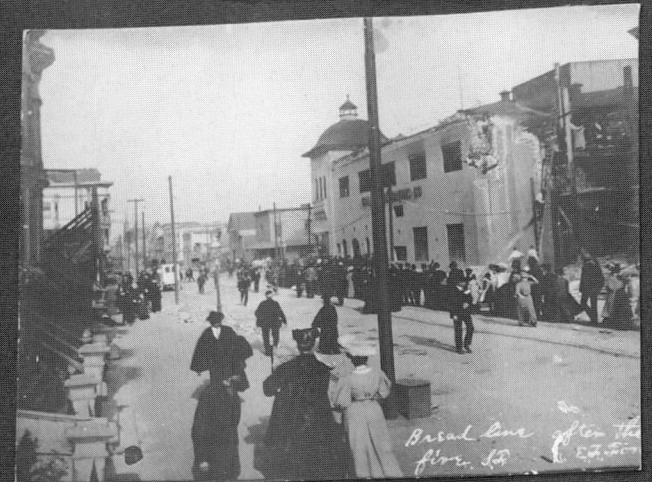

Bread line after the fire, S.F.

Fillmore St - Bread Line - after 5 o'clock

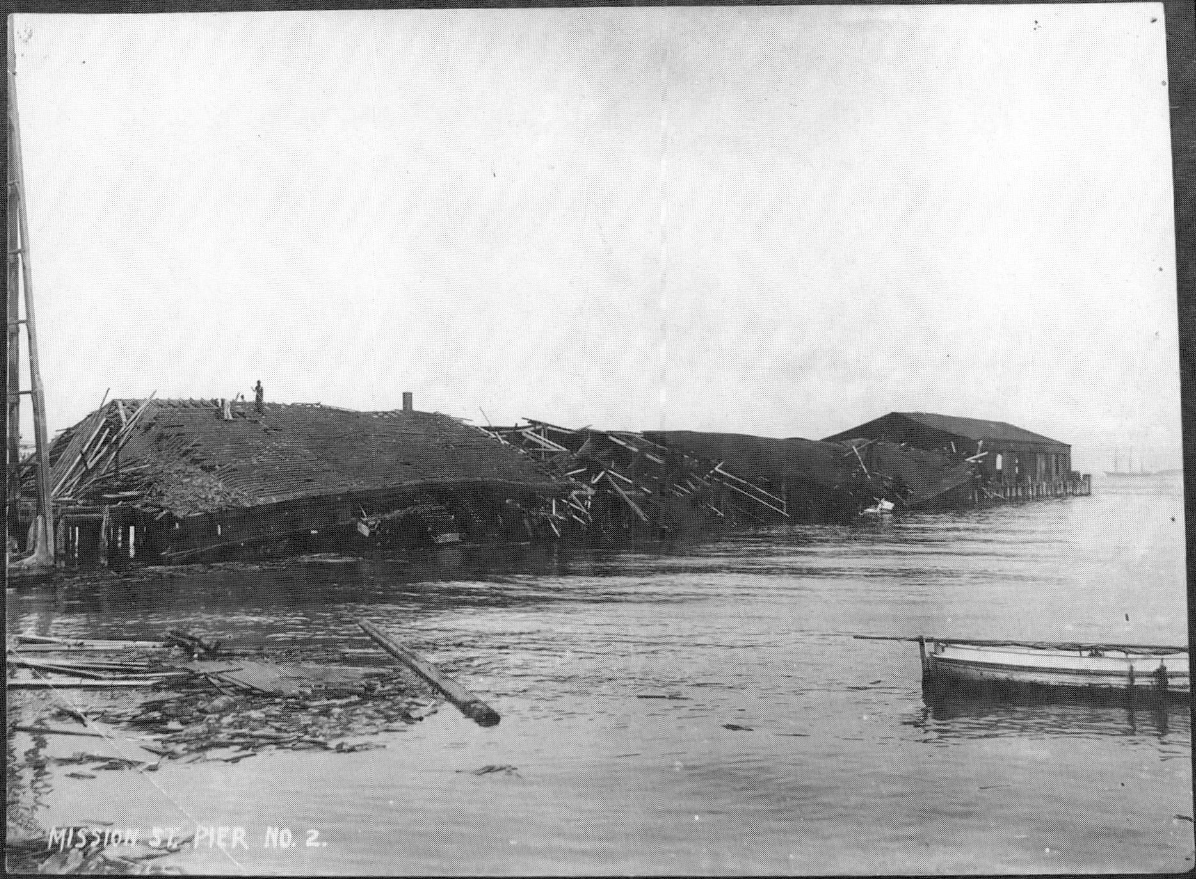

Earthquake destruction at Mission St. Wharf

MISSION ST. PIER NO. 2.

"Fillmore St—Bread Line—after 5 o'clock" This scene is at the California Baking Company's mission-style building, on Fillmore and Eddy streets. Though damaged by the earthquake, it was pressed into service soon afterward. Ultimately, this neighborhood was left unscathed by the fires.

"Earthquake destruction at Mission St. Wharf" A companion view to the photo on page 51. Note men standing on the collapsed roof. (Pillsbury?)

When San Francisco Burned

"Driven from their homes…" The crowd almost looks festive, though it could scarcely have been so.

"San Francisco's closing fire" Water jets labor to put out the omnipresent flames.

"Leaving the City" Near the corner of California and Stockton streets, looking east. Old St. Mary's is at center left. Behind it is the Kohl Building, and to its left is the Merchants' Exchange Building. The dark ruin of Grace Episcopal Church is seen partially at right.

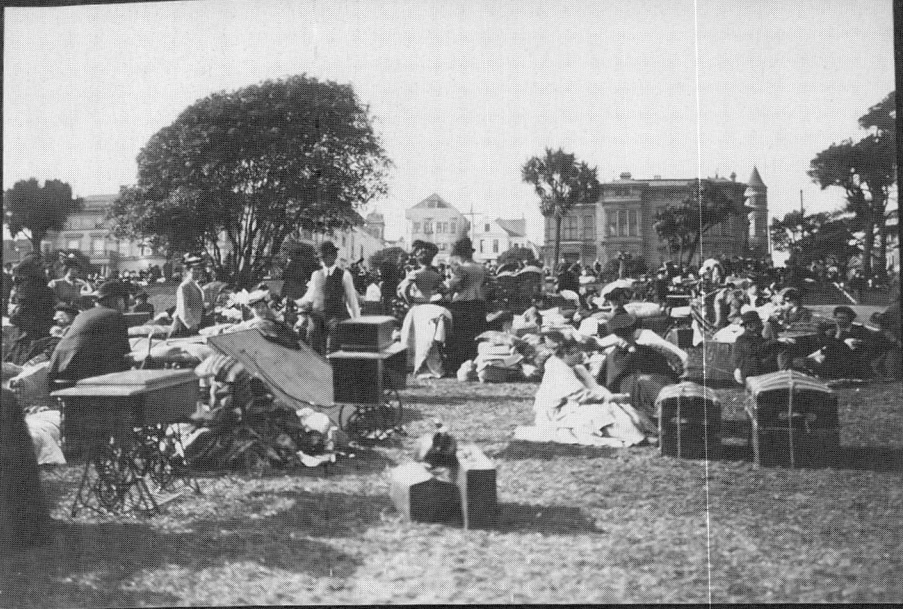

Driven from their homes which the fire is now consuming

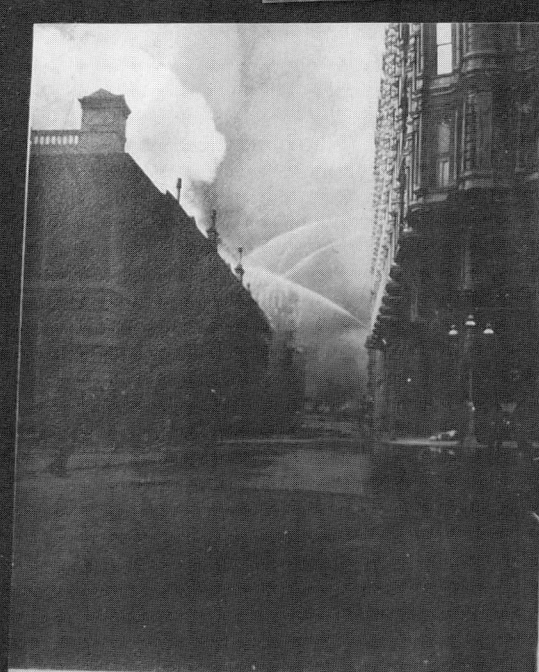

San Francisco's closing fire

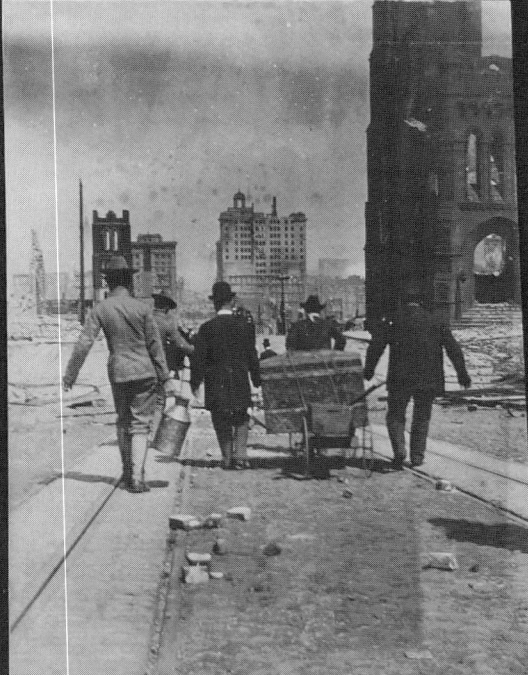

Leaving the City

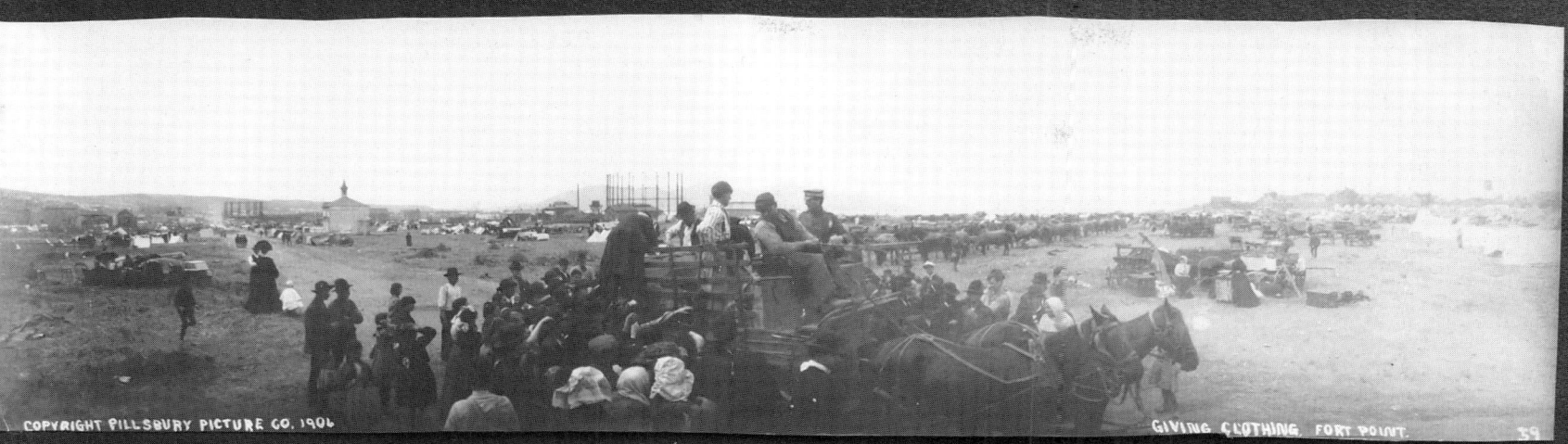

Giving clothing   Fort Point

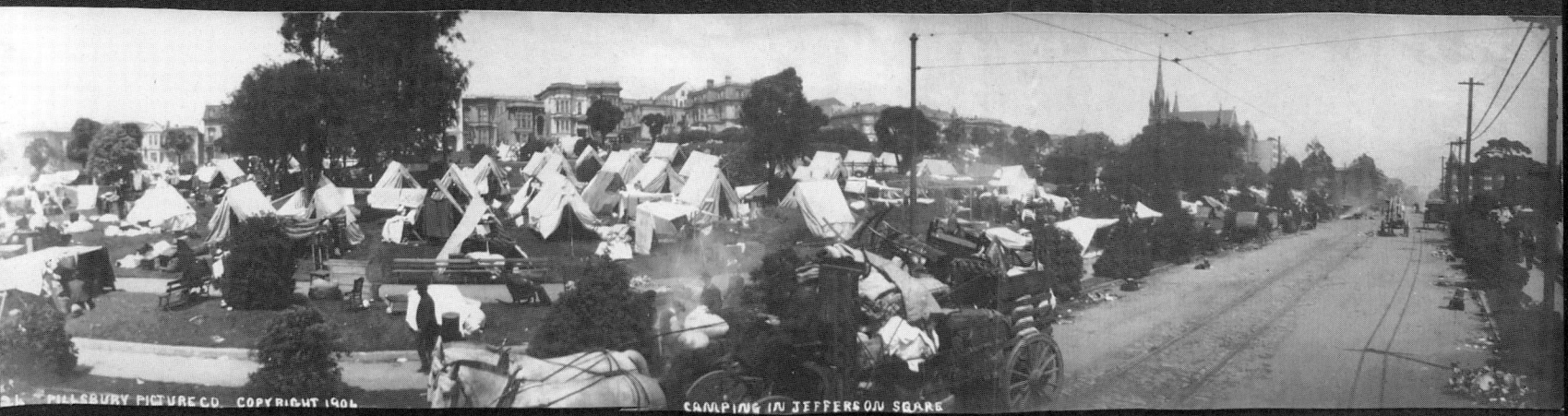

Camping in Jefferson Square

"Giving clothing Fort Point" A scene at the old military installation, immediately after the disasters. The Golden Gate is barely visible at left center. (Pillsbury)

"Camping in Jefferson Square" The tent encampment here is in full swing. Note the overburdened horse-drawn wagon in foreground. (Pillsbury)

When San Francisco Burned

"'Society' Camped in Golden Gate Park" The handsome carriage in fore-ground testifies to the social standing of the people resettled temporarily in this park segment. (Pillsbury)

"Earthquake damage to Union St" An especially notable (and often photographed) example of the earthquake's force and resulting sub-sidence. (Worden)

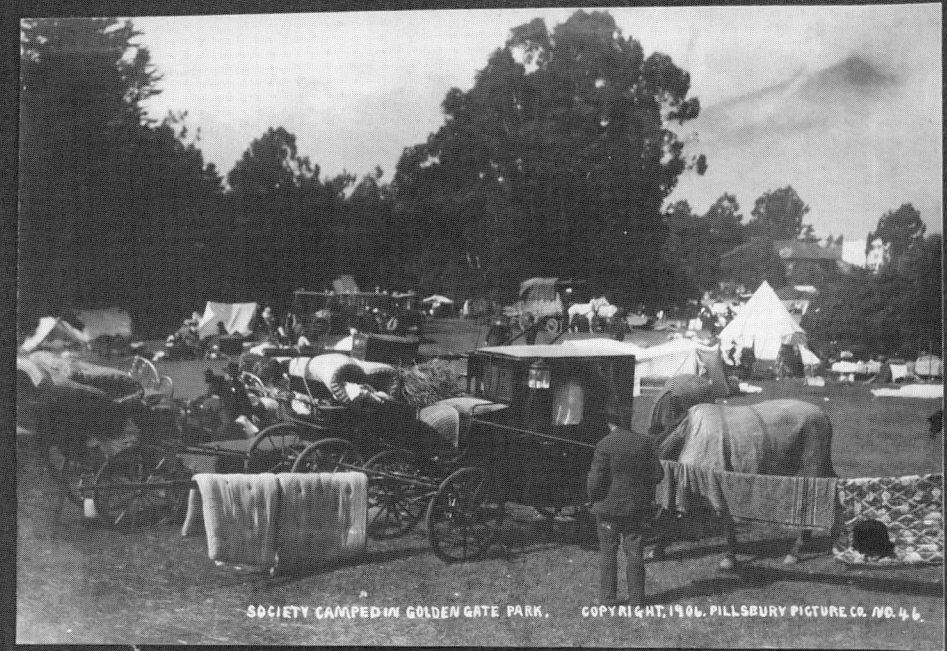

SOCIETY CAMPED IN GOLDEN GATE PARK.   COPYRIGHT, 1906. PILLSBURY PICTURE CO. NO. 46.

"Society" Camped in Golden Gate Park

Earthquake damage to Union St

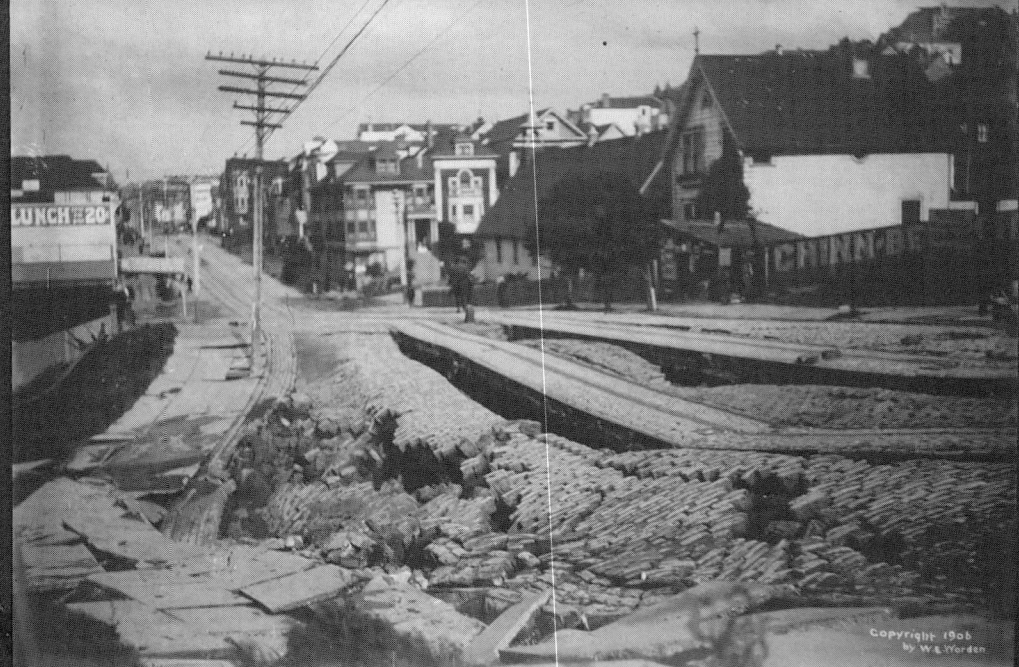

Copyright 1906 by W.E. Worden

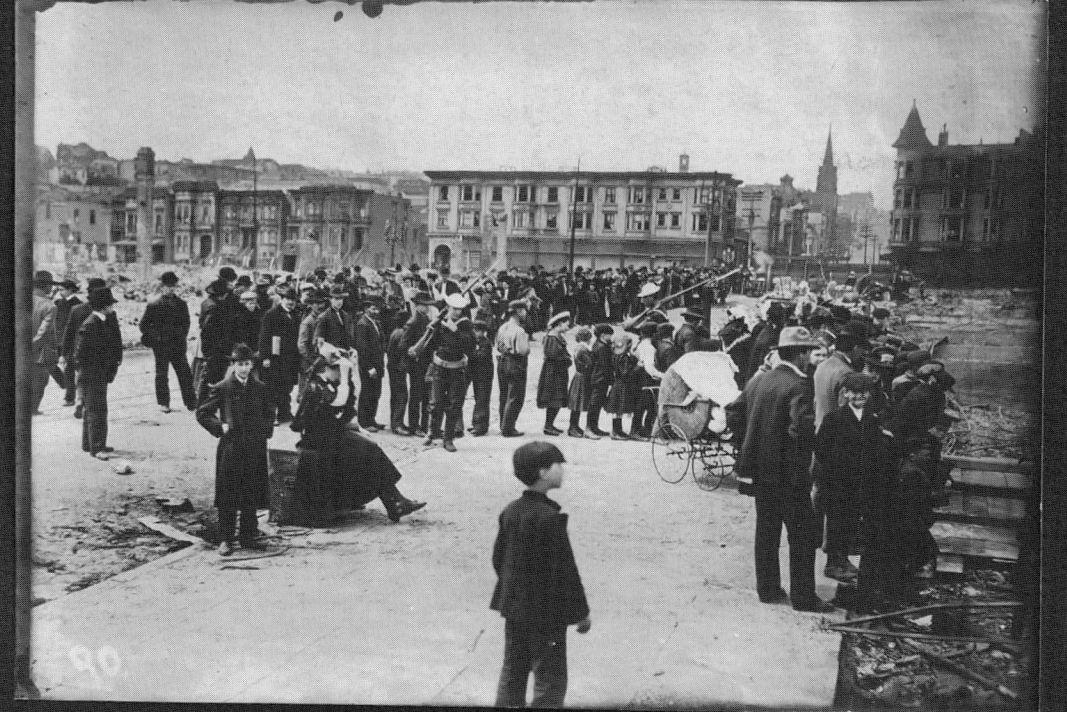

After the fire
Waiting for food —

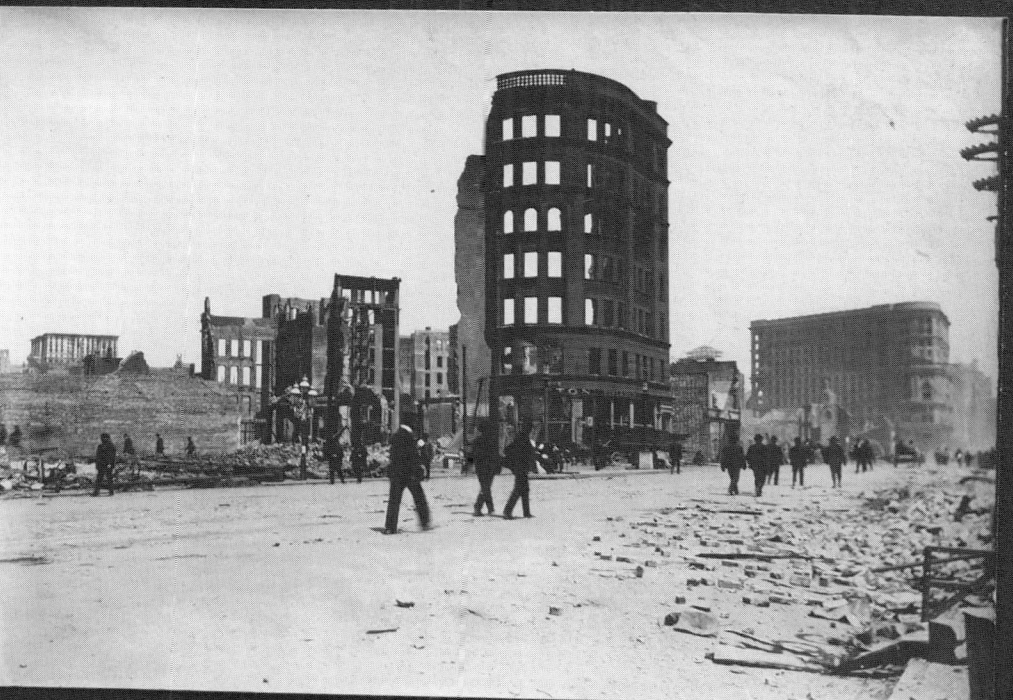

Market St.
from Taylor
after the fire

"After the fire Waiting for food" A common scene in the post-disaster days.

"Market St. from Taylor after the fire" The Fairmont Hotel can be seen at far left, atop Nob Hill. The burned-out Donohue Building, with just its outer walls standing, is in the center, and the Flood Building stands farther down Market at right.

When San Francisco Burned

"California St afire" horse-drawn fire engine stands, presumably useless, to the left. (Worden)

"Crossley Building Burning" Located at Montgomery and Mission streets, this splendid edifice survived the fire, but with only a skeleton of its lower floor left standing.

"Earthquake destruction Howard & 18th" Structures and roadways here suffered tremendous damage, since they were built on landfill.

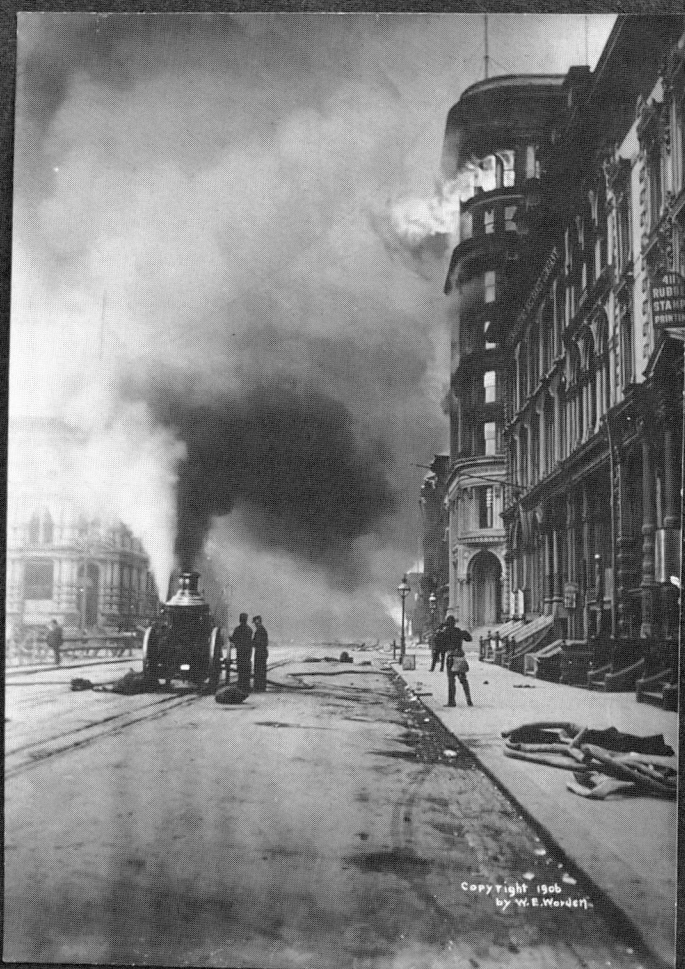

California St afire

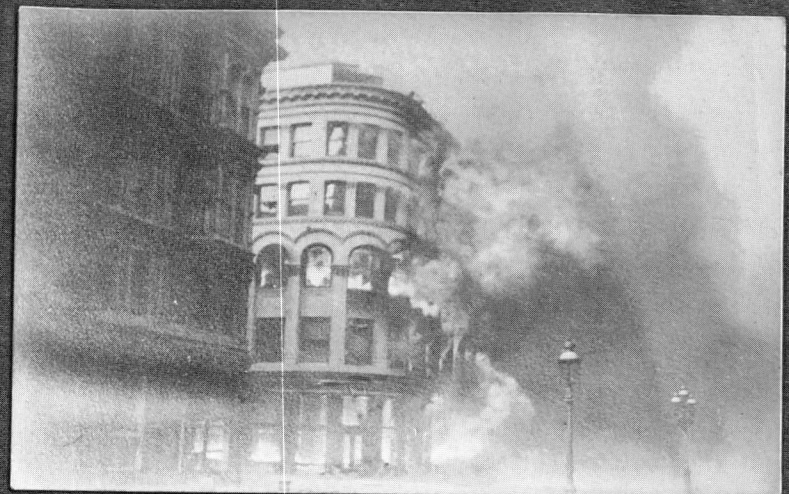

Crossley Building Burning

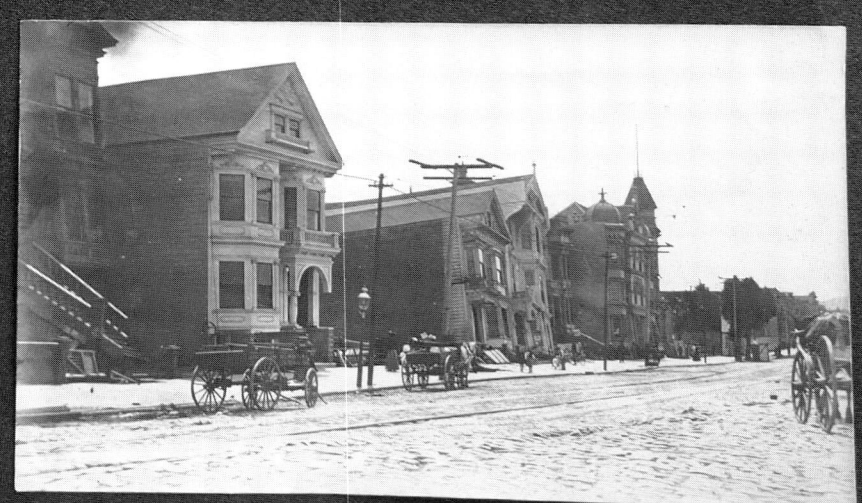

Earthquake destruction Howard + 18th

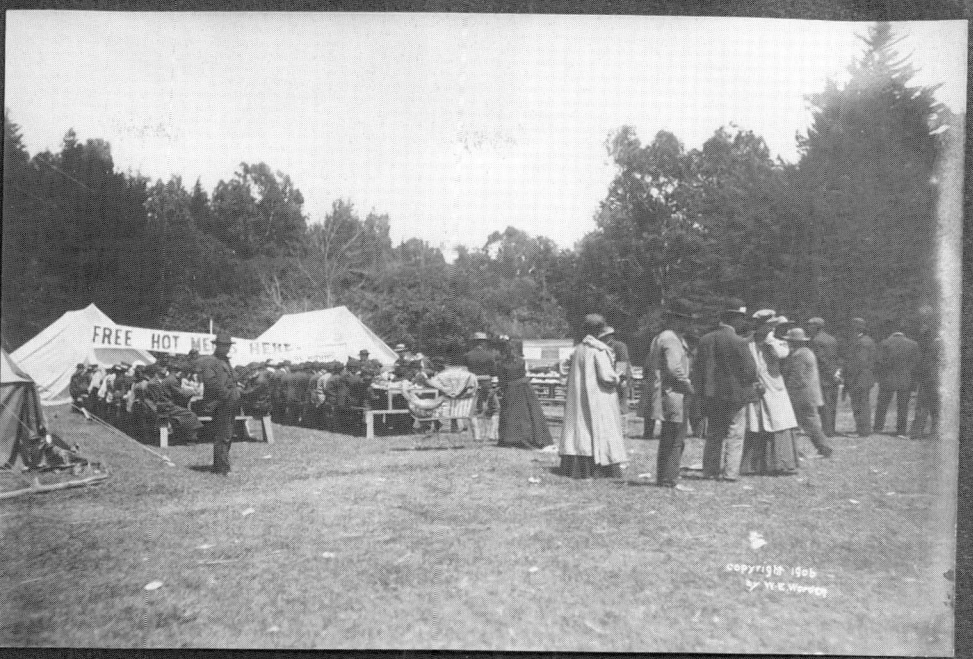

Feeding the Hungry in Golden Gate Park

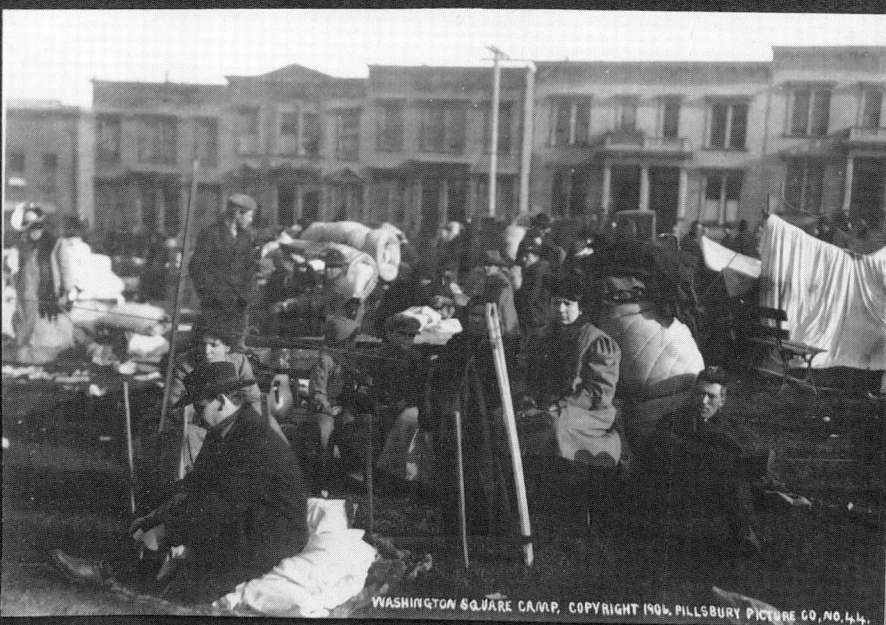

WASHINGTON SQUARE CAMP, COPYRIGHT 1906, PILLSBURY PICTURE CO, NO. 44.

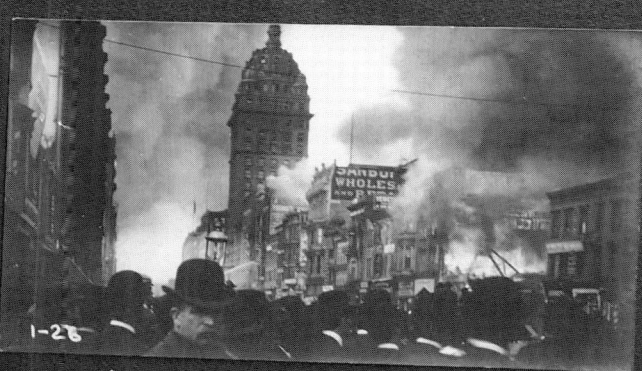

Just before fire reached Call Building.

"Feeding the Hungry in Golden Gate Park" Another of the innumerable bread lines set up in the disaster's wake. (Worden)

"Washington Square Camp" Homeless residents cluster in this space, with all the possessions they could carry, apparently using rope or wire to define their personal spaces. This area eventually fell within the area caught by the fire. (Pillsbury)

"Just before fire reached Call Building" A large segment of Market Street in flames, licking at the imposing skyscraper.

When San Francisco Burned

"Bread Line in the Mission" The J.J. Sullivan store, here being used in relief efforts, was located in San Francisco's Mission District, at the corner of Charles and Chenery streets.

"Relief camp G[olden] G[ate] Park" A companion view to the photos on page 74. (Noel)

"Divisadero St— Bread Line" Located far west of the fire districts, this view shows that some of Divisadero survived the earthquake reasonably intact.

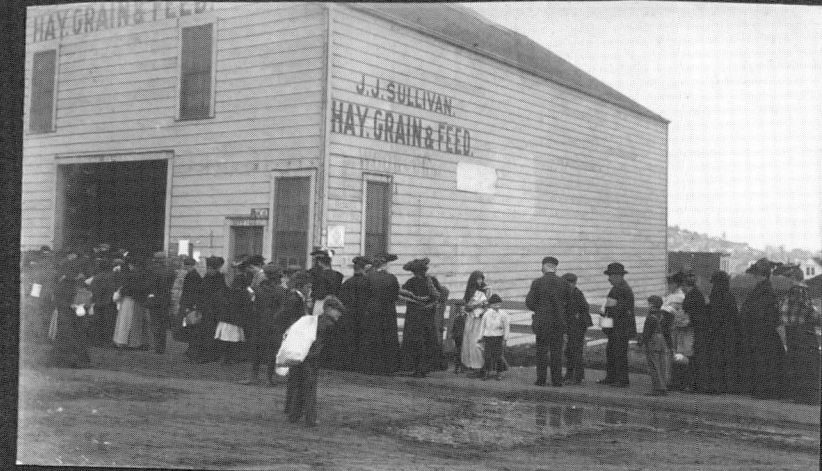

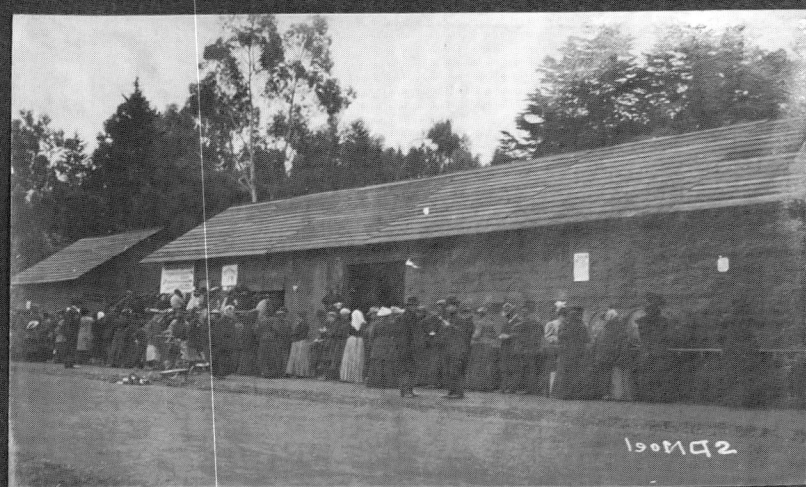

Bread Line in the Mission

Relief Camp G.G. Park

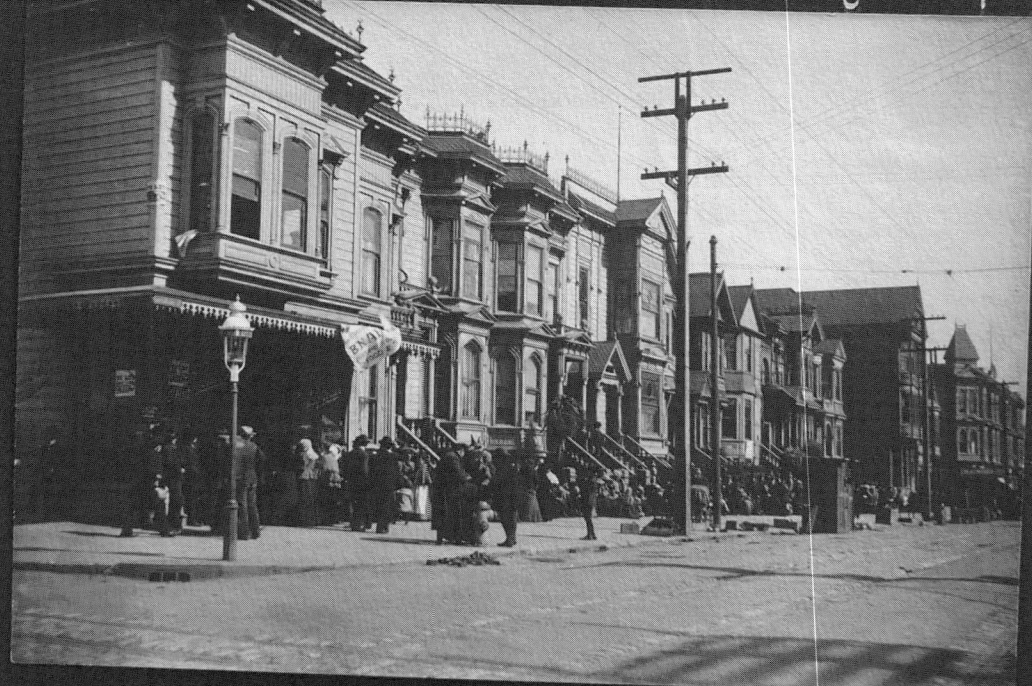

Divisadero St - Bread Line

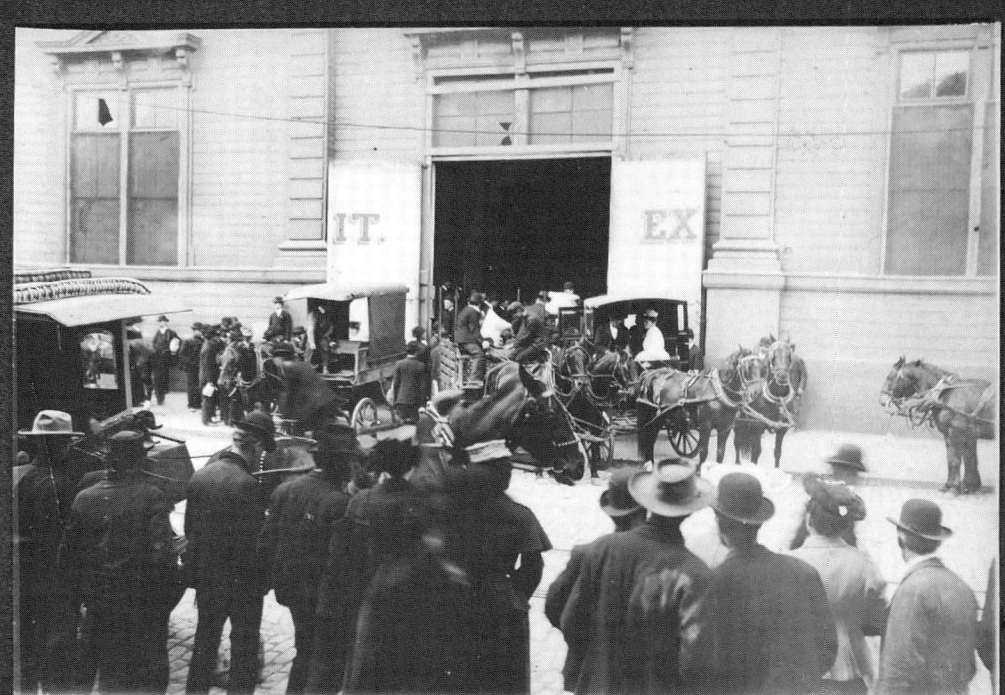

Removing injured from Mechanics Pavilion Hospital fire starting in the rear

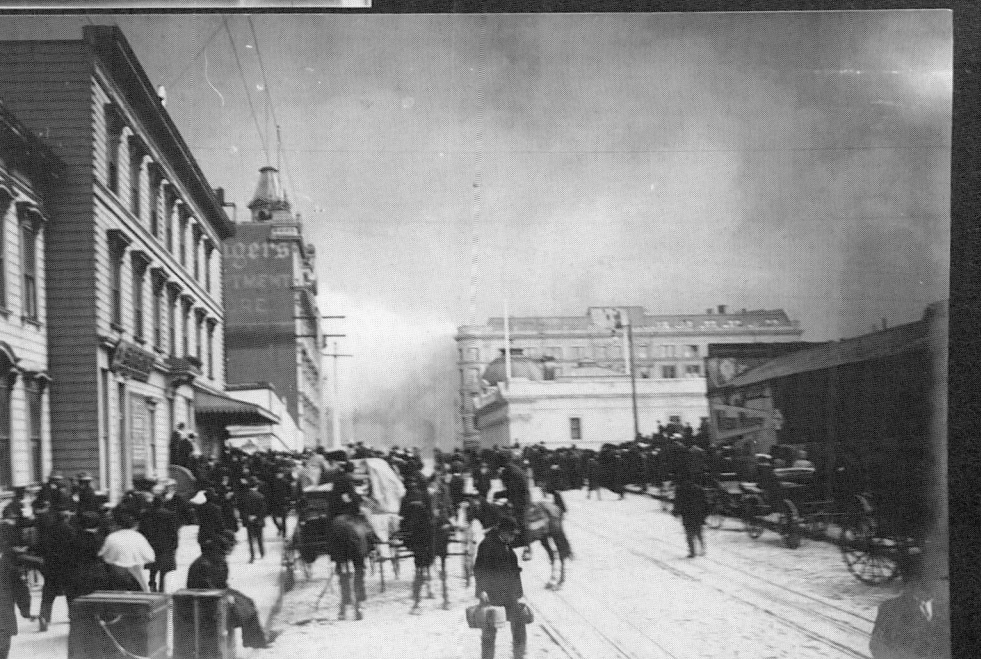

Jones St. Hibernia Bank and Prager's in the distance

"Removing injured from Mechanics Pavilion Hospital…" Built in 1882, the Mechanics' Pavilion at Grove and Larkin was a large indoor arena that hosted various events. Soon after the earthquake, it was transformed into a makeshift hospital and morgue. Ultimately, flames destroyed the pavilion. Today's Bill Graham Civic Auditorium stands on its site.

"Jones St. Hibernia Bank…" This view looks south on Jones toward Market, with Prager's Department Store on the left and the rear of the Hibernia Bank on the right. Residents and business owners are carrying away all the items they can manage.

When San Francisco Burned

"Preparing dinner for the Hungry Refugees" An open-air soup kitchen operating at full tilt, with a horde of refugees on all sides waiting to be fed.

"Valencia Street 'Bread Line'" Apparently taken not long after the disasters, with random debris quite evident in the street.

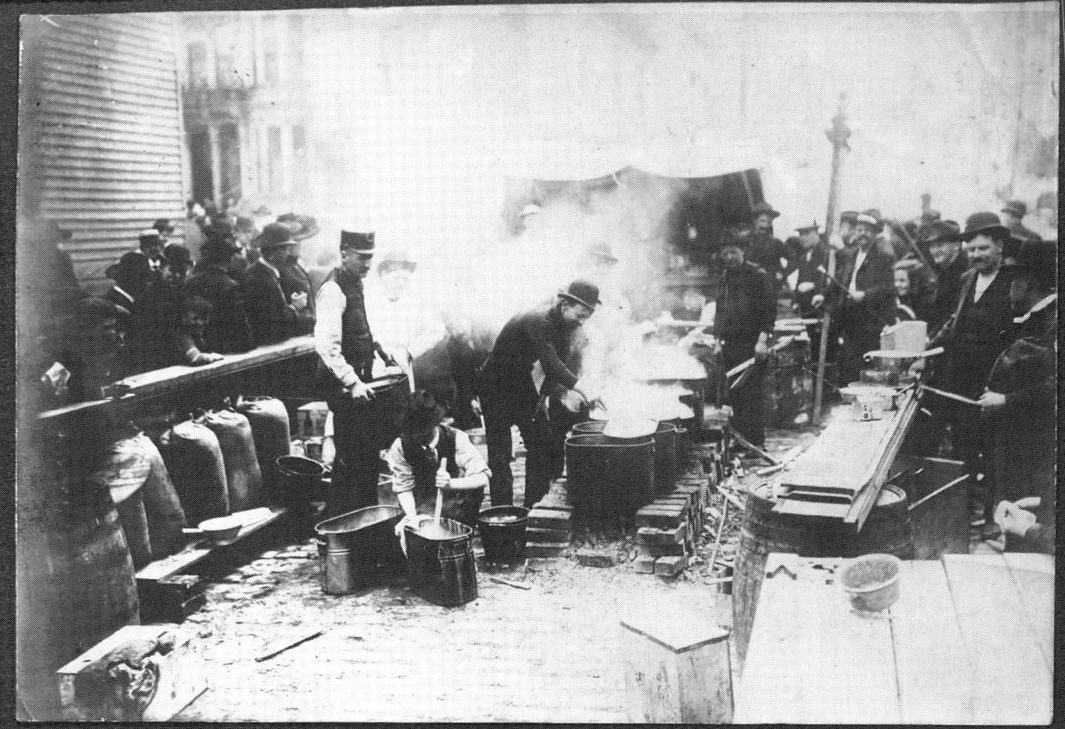

Preparing dinner for the Hungry Refugees

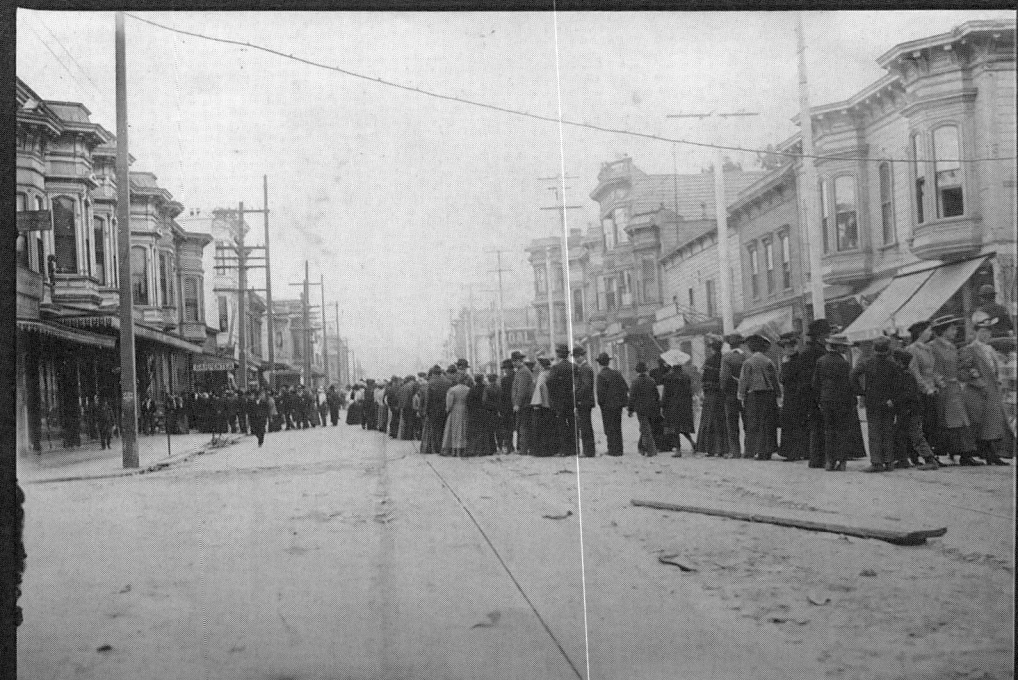

Valencia Street "Bread Line"

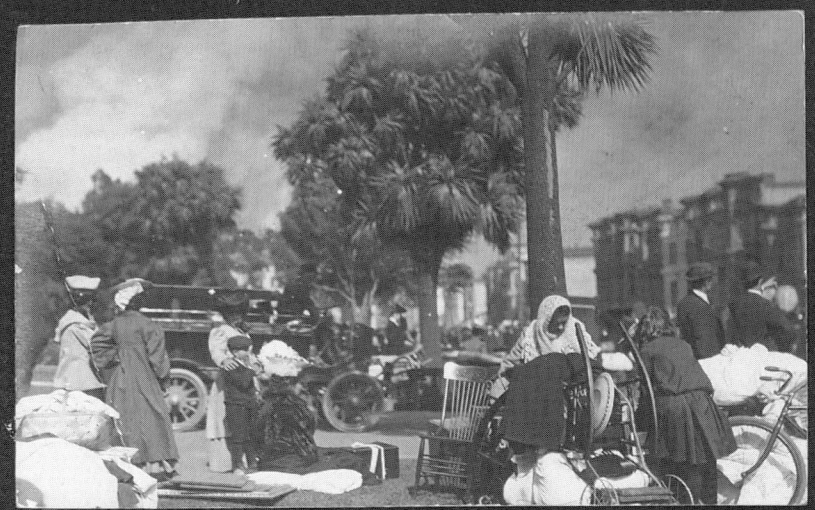

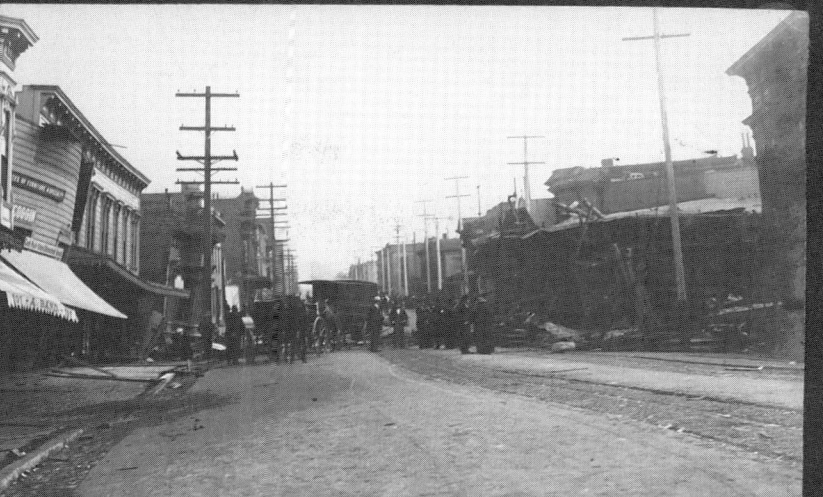

Homeless in Jefferson Square *Valencia Hotel before fire reached it*

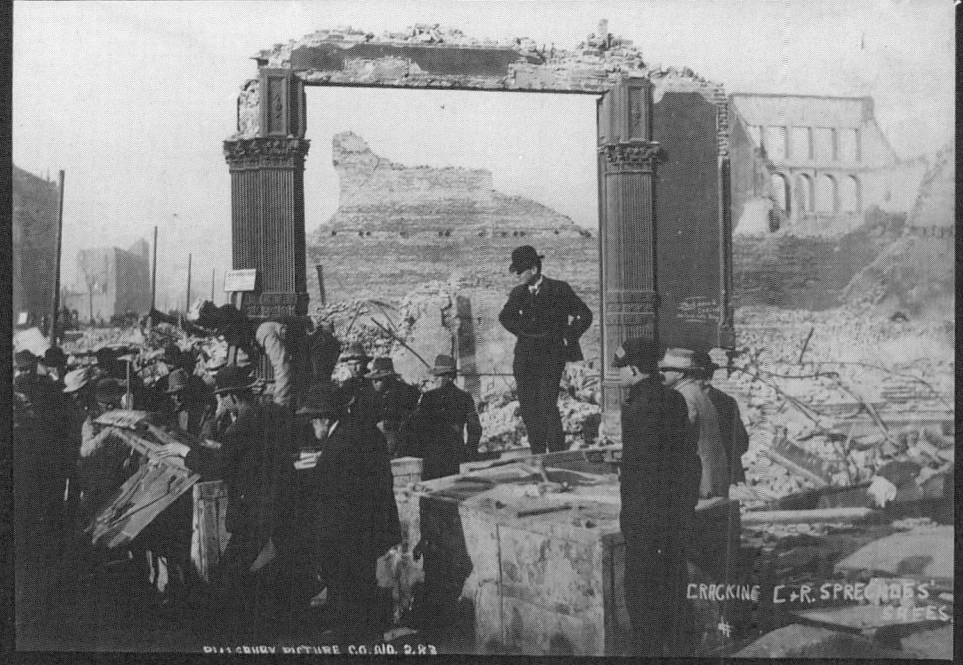

Cracking C & R Spreckels' Safes

"Homeless in Jefferson Square" Another characteristic scene of the homeless, with fire smoke easily visible in the background.

"Valencia Hotel before fire reached it" A more distant view of the scene on page 65. See also pages 61 and 64.

"Cracking C & R Spreckels' Safes" Safes located in the fire zone had to cool down for some time before they could be breached and the contents recovered. Here, the heat has been out for some time as a crew tackles safes owned by prominent San Francisco businessmen Claus and Rudolph Spreckels. (Pillsbury)

When San Francisco Burned

"Waiting for food"
Location uncertain. The "Mount Feed Co." does not appear in period San Francisco directories.

"Earthquake damage to street" Location unknown.

"Market St from Turk" Looking east, with the Flood Building at center and Call Building at right.

"Where Valencia Hotel stood before fire reached it" As opposed to the caption, this appears to be a photo of post-fire devastation, location unknown. (Noel)

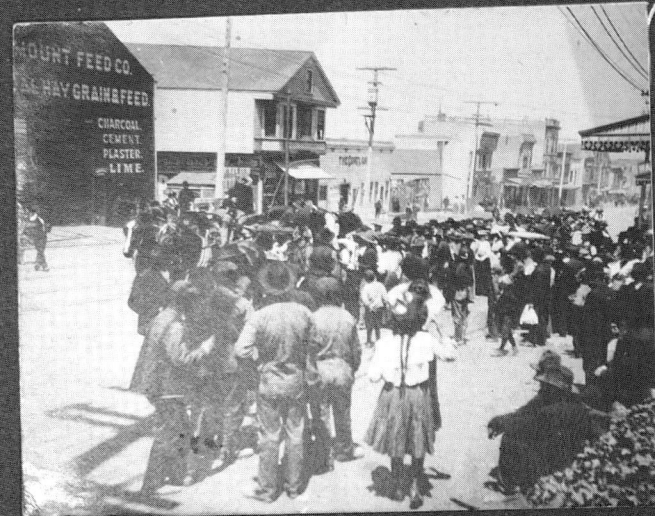

Waiting for food

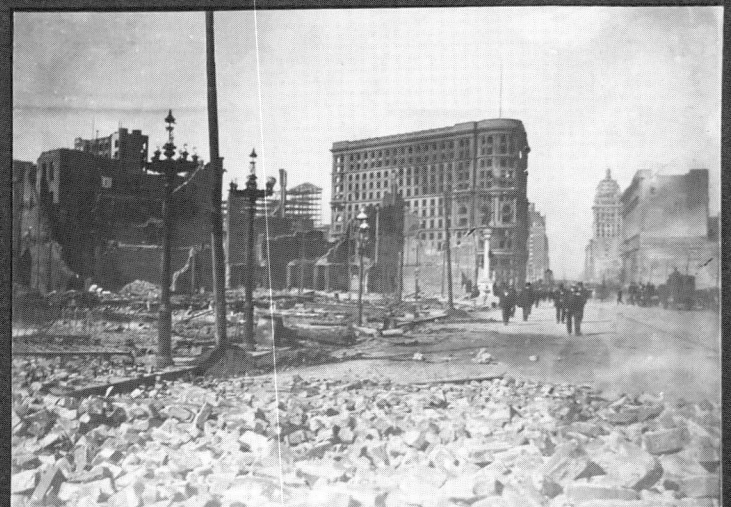

Market St from Turk

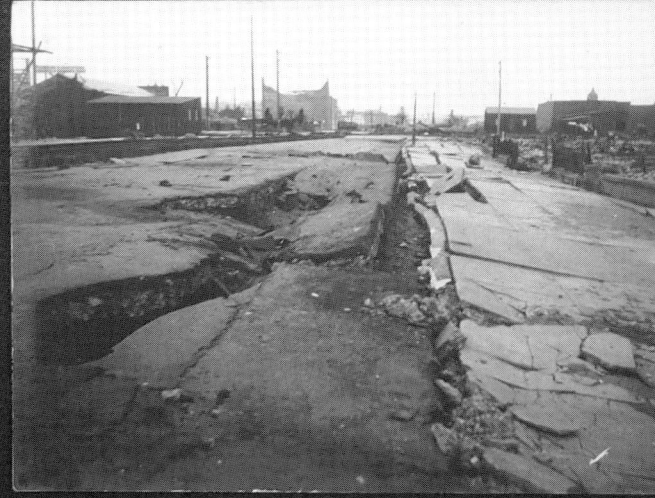

Earthquake damage to street

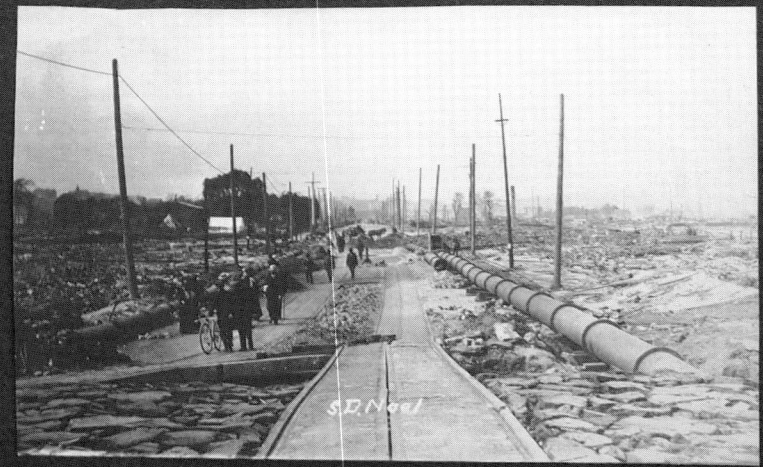

Where Valencia Hotel stood before fire reached it

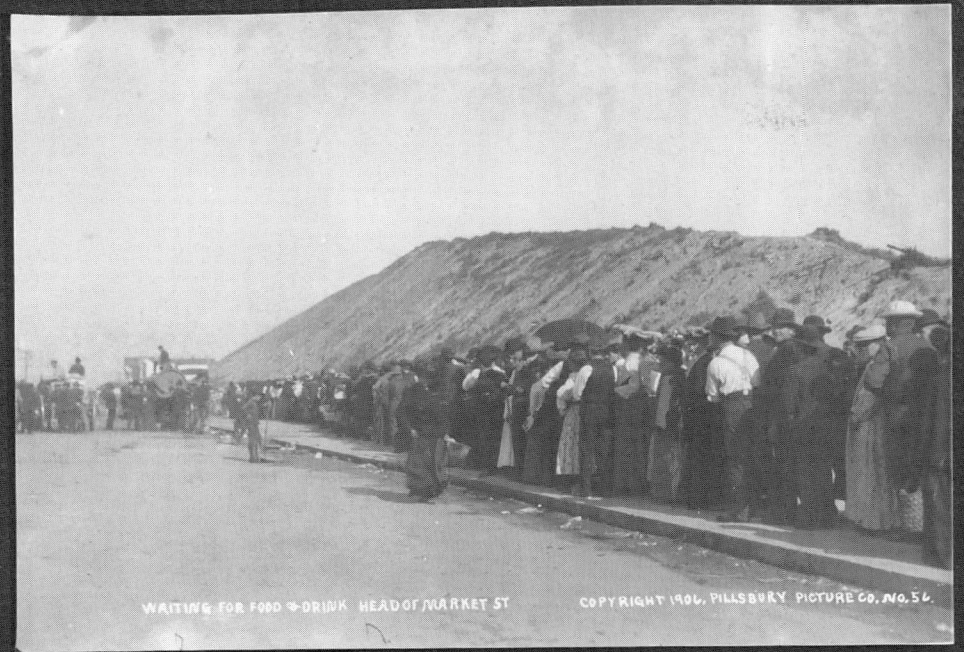

Waiting for food and drink— Head of Market St

WAITING FOR FOOD & DRINK HEAD OF MARKET ST   COPYRIGHT 1906 PILLSBURY PICTURE CO. NO. 56.

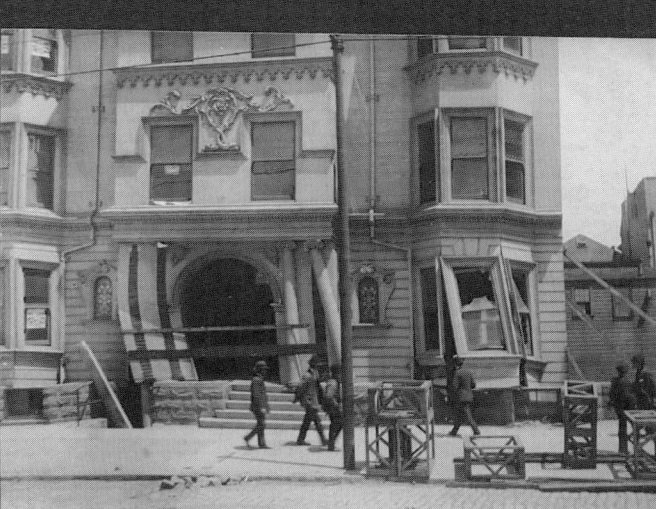

Ellis St Earthquake damage.

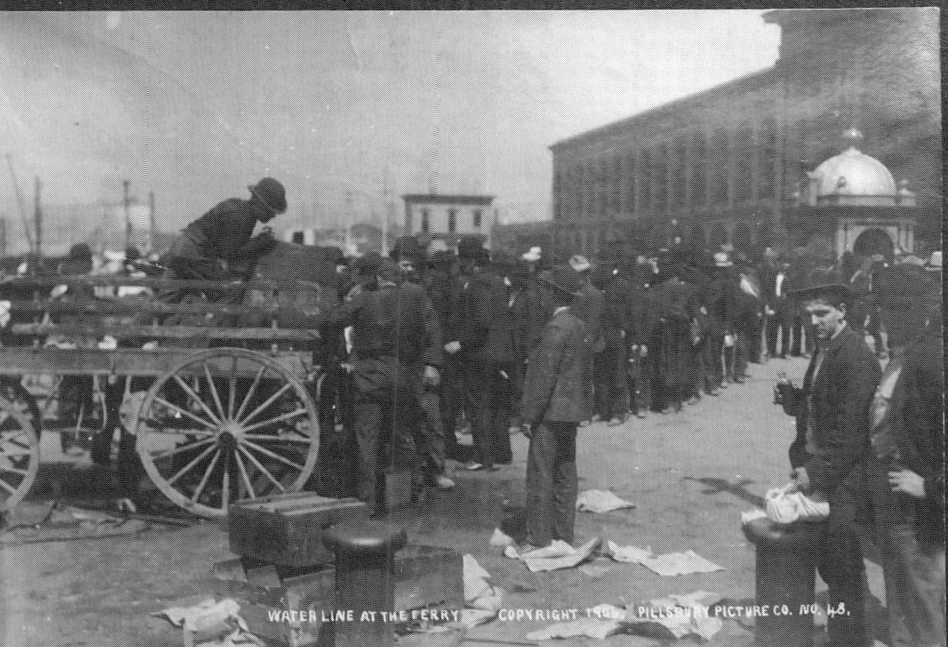

WATER LINE AT THE FERRY   COPYRIGHT 1906 PILLSBURY PICTURE CO. NO. 48.

The Album

"Waiting for food and drink—…" Apparently taken at the far western limit of Market Street. (Pillsbury)

"Ellis St Earthquake damage" A clear depiction of how the earthquake twisted buildings off their foundations, leaving columns and windows askew.

"Waterline at the Ferry" A thirsty crowd clusters for relief, with the Ferry Building visible at right. (Pillsbury)

When San Francisco Burned

"Ruins at North Beach" This area was as hard-hit as downtown San Francisco. Alcatraz Island can be seen in the distance.

"Cooking in the street" The fire hazards created by broken chimneys and exhaust vents made it necessary to cook in the streets. (Pillsbury)

"Bread Line— Mission High School Relief" Called into disaster service, Mission High School would later—and somewhat ironically—burn down in 1922. Rebuilt, it continues to operate at the same location.

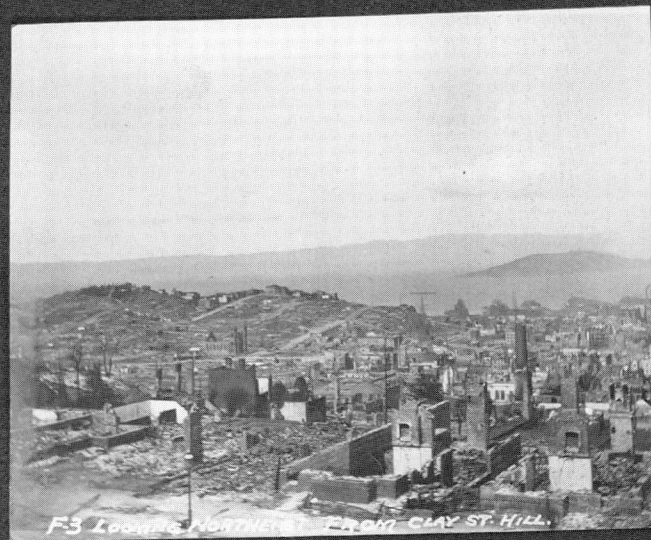

F-3 LOOKING NORTHWEST FROM CLAY ST. HILL.

Ruins at North Beach.

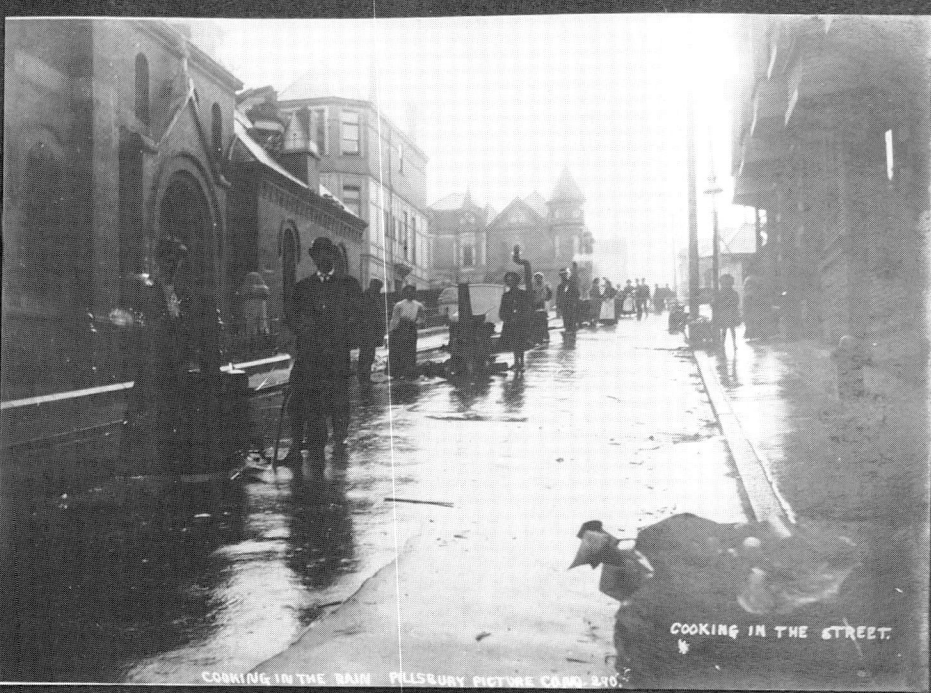

COOKING IN THE RAIN. PILLSBURY PICTURE C. AND SXO.

COOKING IN THE STREET.

Cooking in the Street

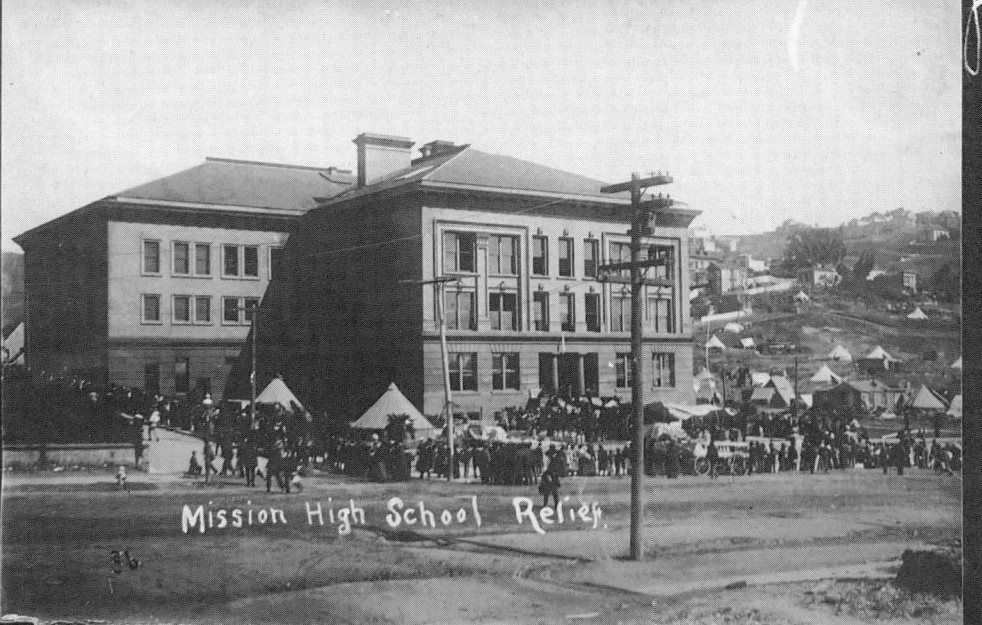

Mission High School Relief.

Bread Line— Mission High School Relief

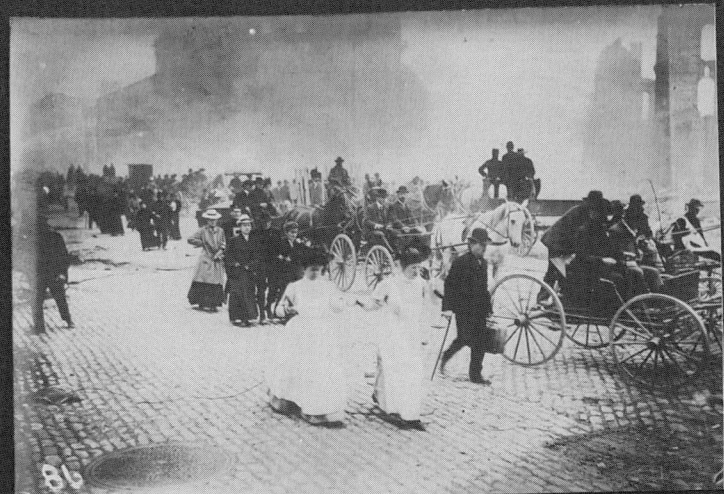

Scene near Ferries, leaving the City.

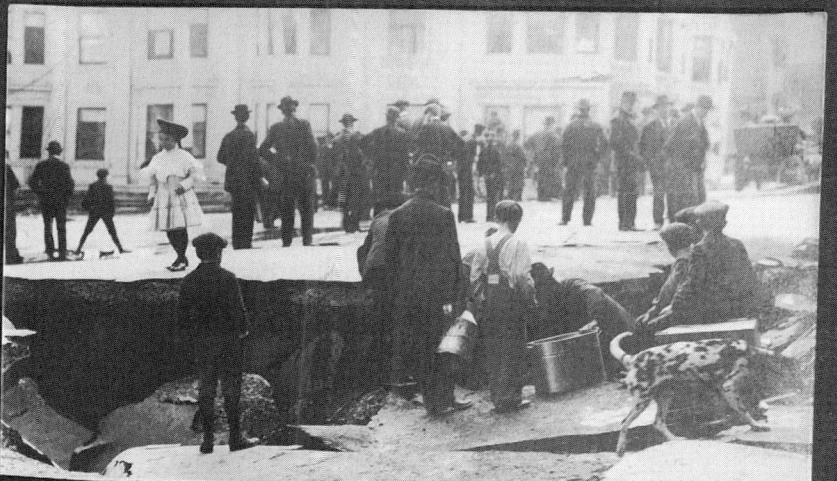

Trying to get drinking water from the broken mains.

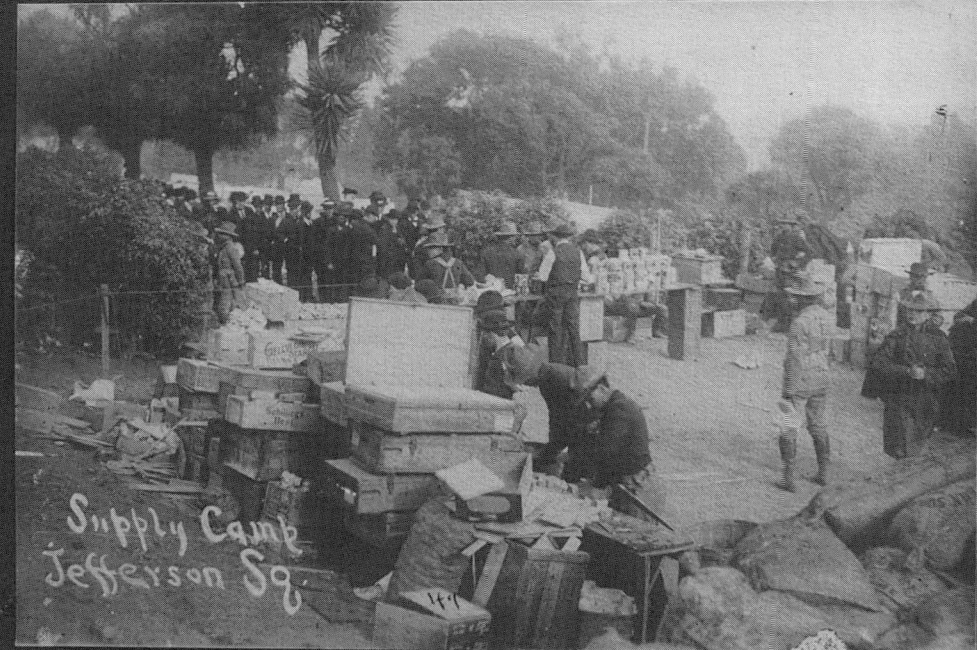

Supply Camp Jefferson Sq.

_ Soldiers distributing food to the Hungry _

"Scene near Ferries, leaving the City"
With the flames all but nipping their heels, the homeless and scared race down a charred Market Street to catch ferries for Oakland and Berkeley.

"Trying to get drinking water…"
In the often-desperate search for water, refugees would climb down into crevices where the water mains broke in hopes of capturing some precious fluid.

"Soldiers distributing food to the Hungry"
Celluloid starch and Schilling seasonings are among the items being handed out here.

When San Francisco Burned

"Cooking lunch—Post near Gough St." In this largely intact neighborhood, residents still had to cook outside. A makeshift kitchen appears to be present at right. (Cohen)

"Bread Line—St. Mary's Cathedral" Not to be confused with Old St. Mary's in Chinatown, this "new" cathedral was on the northwest corner of O'Farrell and Van Ness. It escaped the 1906 fire, only to be burned down in 1962.

"Feeding the Hungry" Another view of the "free lunch" seen on page 75.

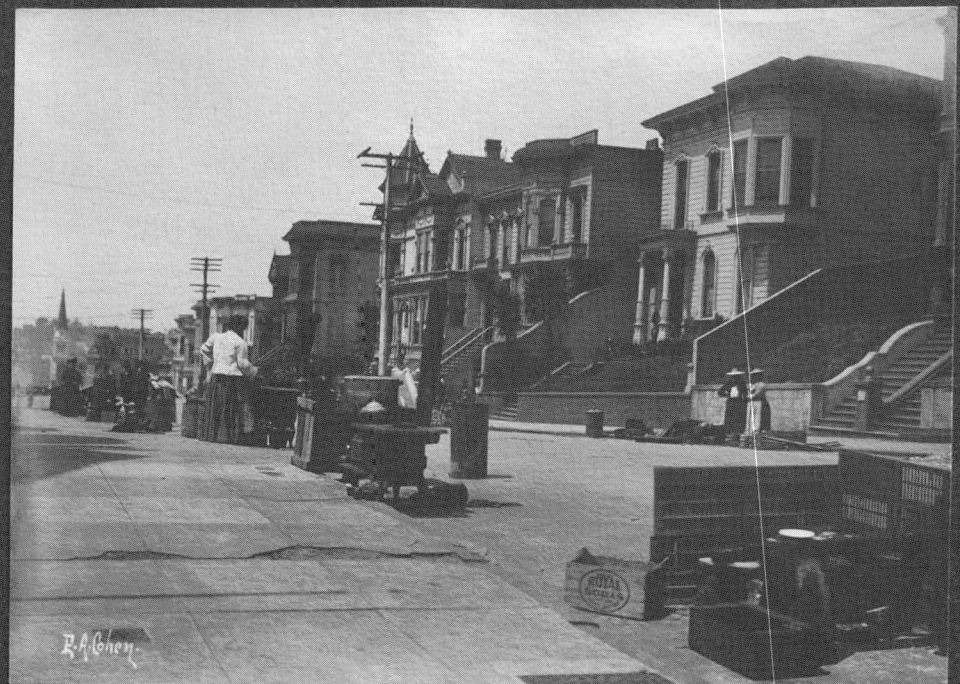

Cooking lunch- Post near Gough St.

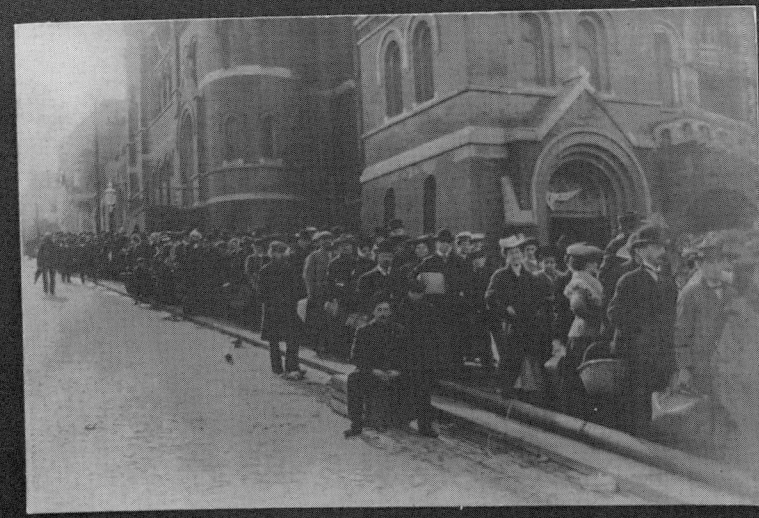

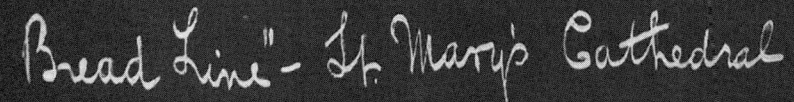

"Bread Line"- St. Mary's Cathedral

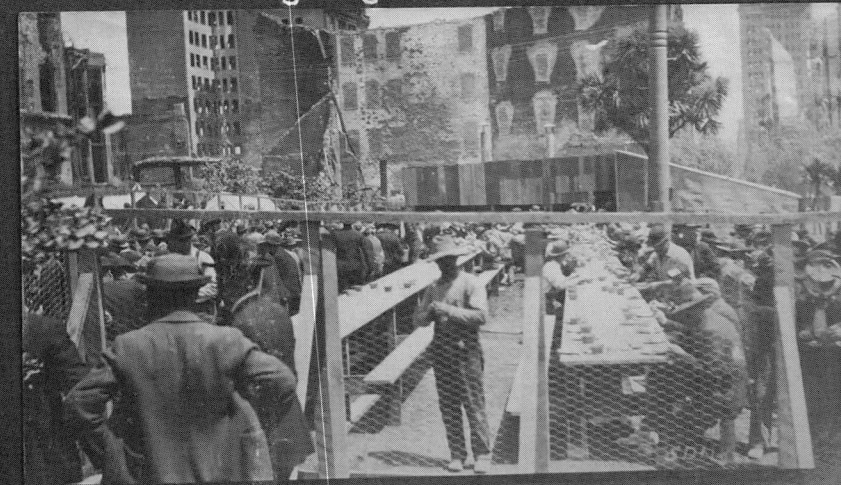

Feeding the Hungry

Refugees leaving the City

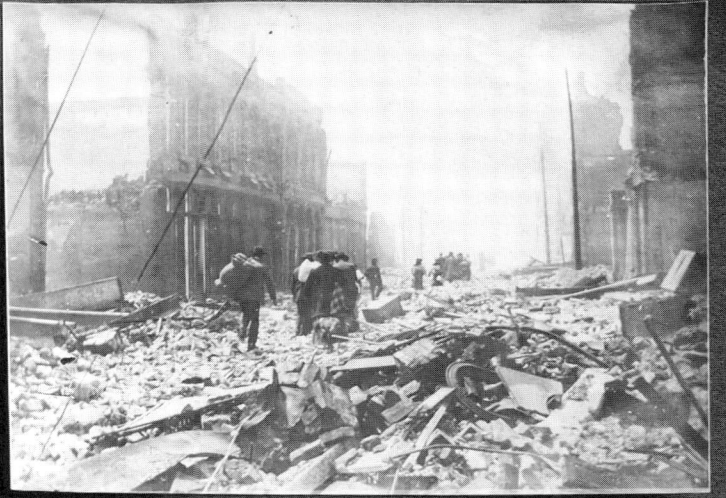

"Refugees leaving the City" The devastation is fresh in this sad image, and smoke still appears to hang in the air.

"Earthquake damage at Vallejo & Van Ness [avenues]" While the structures here seem to have held together fairly well, the many shattered windows testify to the earthquake's strength. (Pillsbury?)

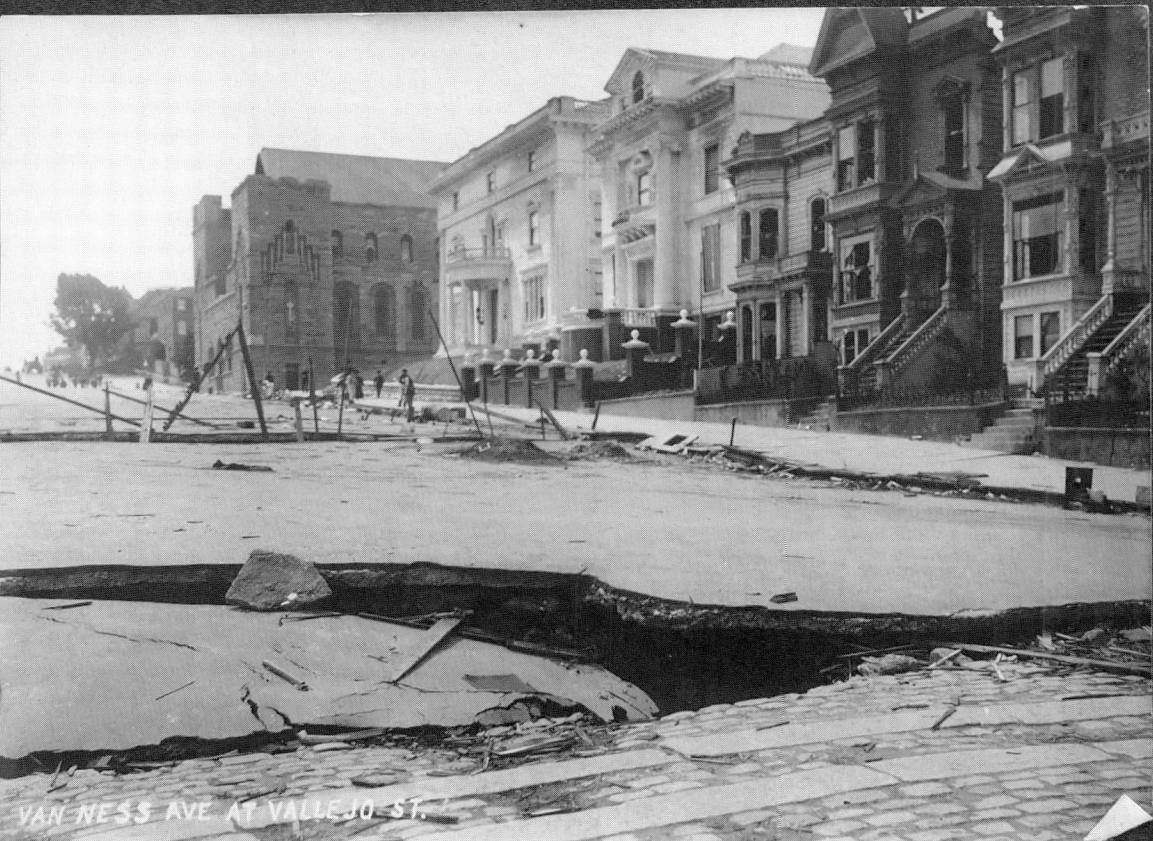

VAN NESS AVE AT VALLEJO ST.

Earthquake damage at Vallejo & Van Ness Ave

When San Francisco Burned

"1st Car run in San Francisco" Trolley service, all-important in the pre-automobile days, returns to San Francisco after the disasters. The car's sign reads "Ferries," suggesting that it was headed to the end of Market and the Ferry Building. (Pillsbury)

"Result of Earthquake Cattle…" This general view of the fires seems to have been mislabeled in haste.

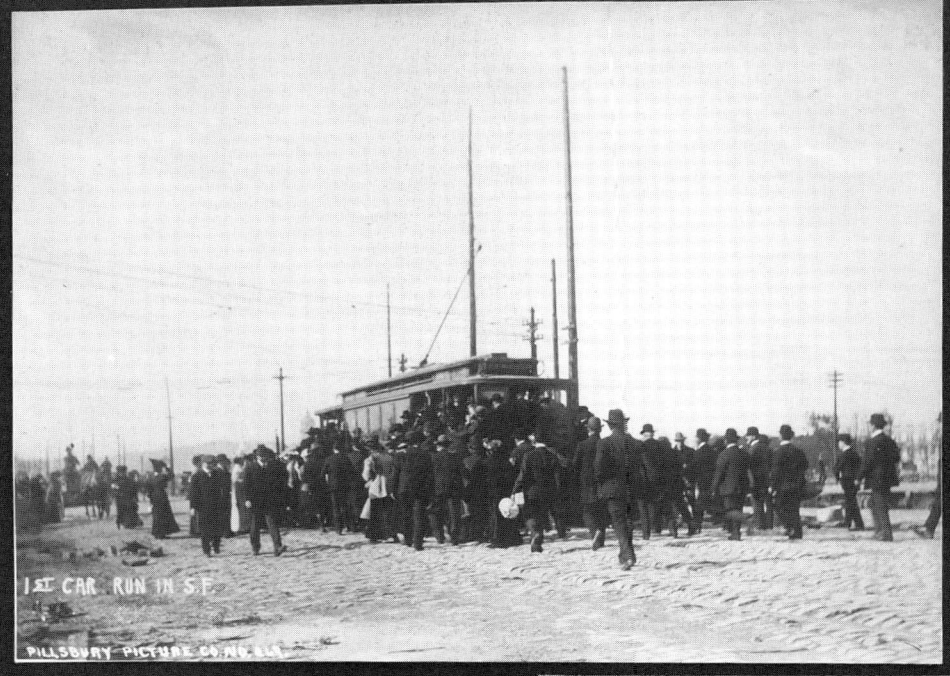

1st Car run in San Francisco

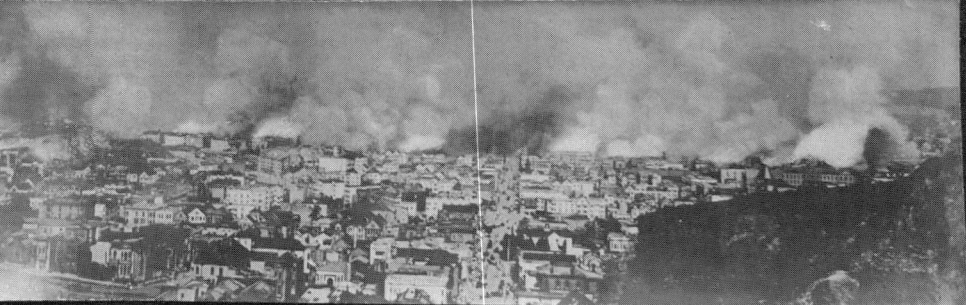

Result of Earthquake Cattle killed by falling walls on Mission St.

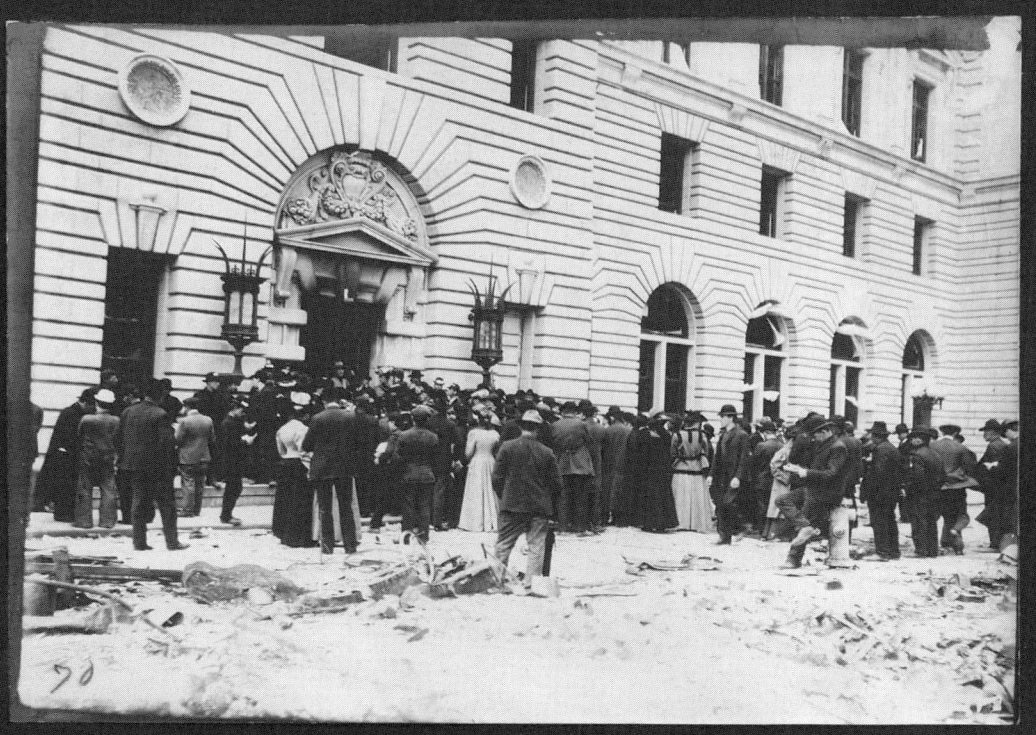

Awaiting mail at
the Post Office
5 days after fire

Earthquake damage
on
Golden Gate Ave

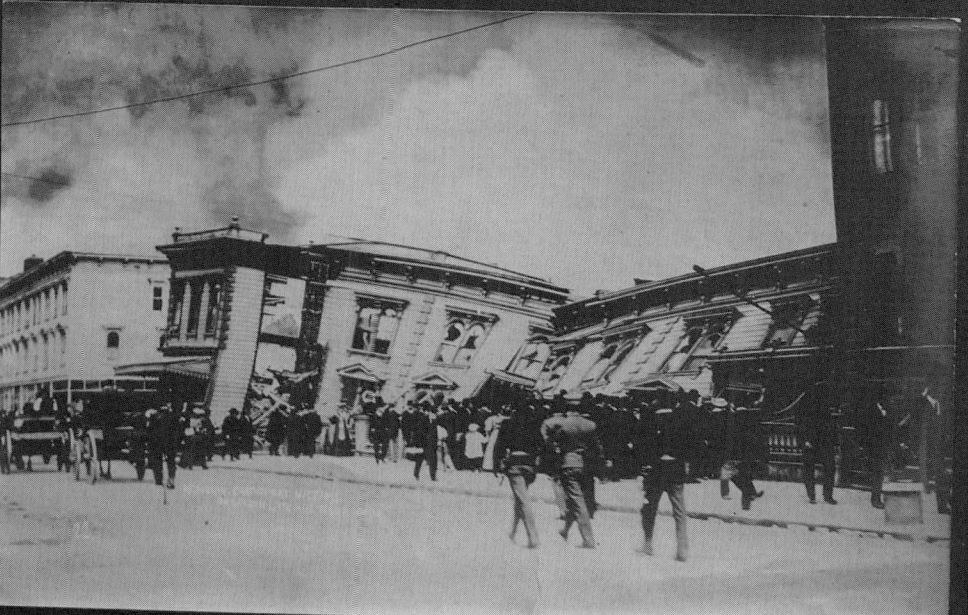

"Awaiting mail at the Post Office…" Amazingly, the San Francisco post office began running again only five days after the fire.

"Earthquake damage on Golden Gate Ave" One of the more spectacular examples of structural collapse produced by the earthquake.

When San Francisco Burned

"Market St 10 days after the Earthquake" This photograph looks west from near California Street. While Market has been badly gutted, the trolleys are running, tents are in place, the streets are full of traffic, and San Francisco is literally rising from its ashes. (Pillsbury?)

"Ruins of the Flood Mansion Nob Hill" Another view of the elegant, though burned-out, home pictured earlier on page 53.

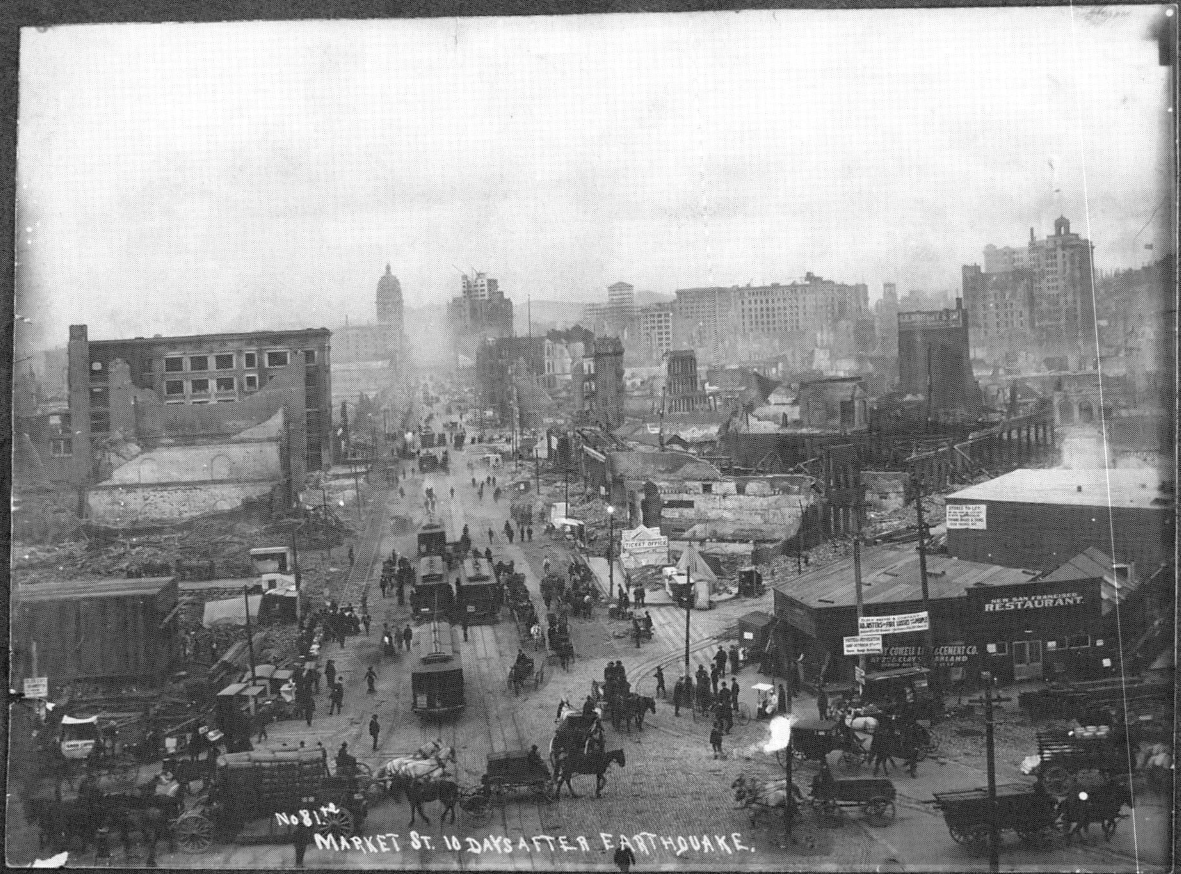

No 81.²
MARKET ST. 10 DAYS AFTER EARTHQUAKE.

Market St
10 day
after the Earthquake

Ruins of the
Flood Mansion
Nob Hill

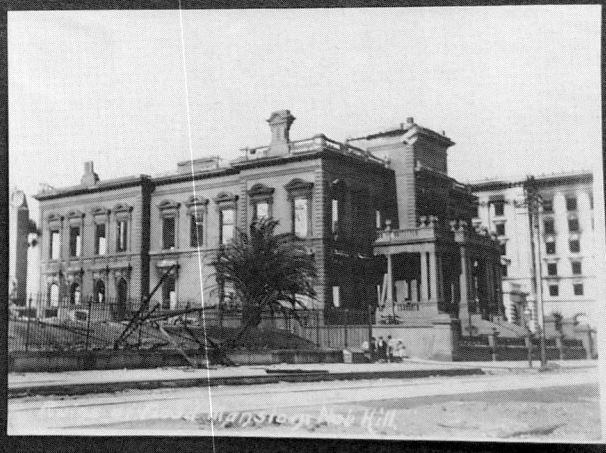

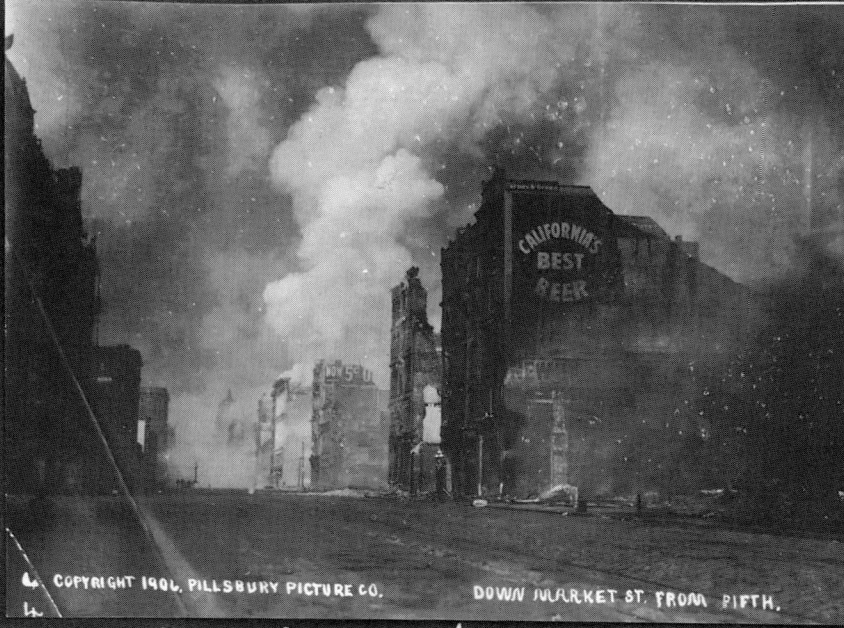

COPYRIGHT 1906, PILLSBURY PICTURE CO.   DOWN MARKET ST. FROM FIFTH.

Down Market St from 5th

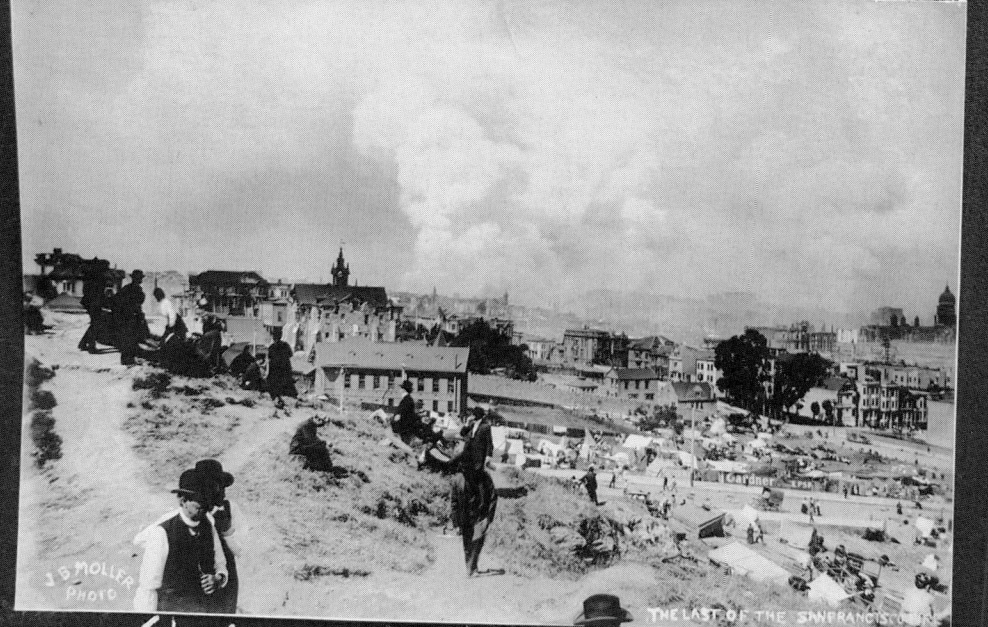

J.B.MOLLER PHOTO   THE LAST OF THE SAN FRANCISCO FIRE

The Last of the San Francisco fire

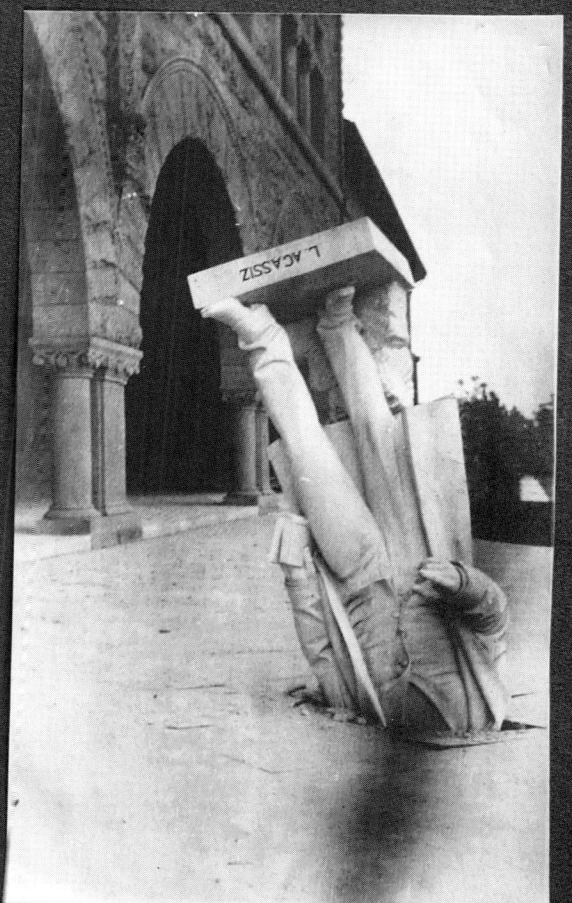

Statue of Agassiz
as it fell — at
Stanford University

The Album

"Down Market
St from 5th"
The street is
indistinguishable
from a war zone.
At center left the
Call Building's
dome can be seen
barely. (Pillsbury)

"The last of the
San Francisco fire"
Homeless San
Franciscans watch
from a hillside as
the last of the fires
burn out. (Moller)

"Statue of
Agassiz as it fell..."
A much-photo-
graphed freak
accident that
occurred on the
Stanford University
campus, when a
statue of the famed
naturalist fell off
a building and
plunged headfirst
into the pavement.

When San Francisco Burned

"San Francisco 4 weeks after the fire"
A view down Market, very similar to that seen on page 96 but from a lower angle.

"Watching the city burn from Lafayette Park"
The park was a temporary homeless refuge until the fire encroached and burned it.

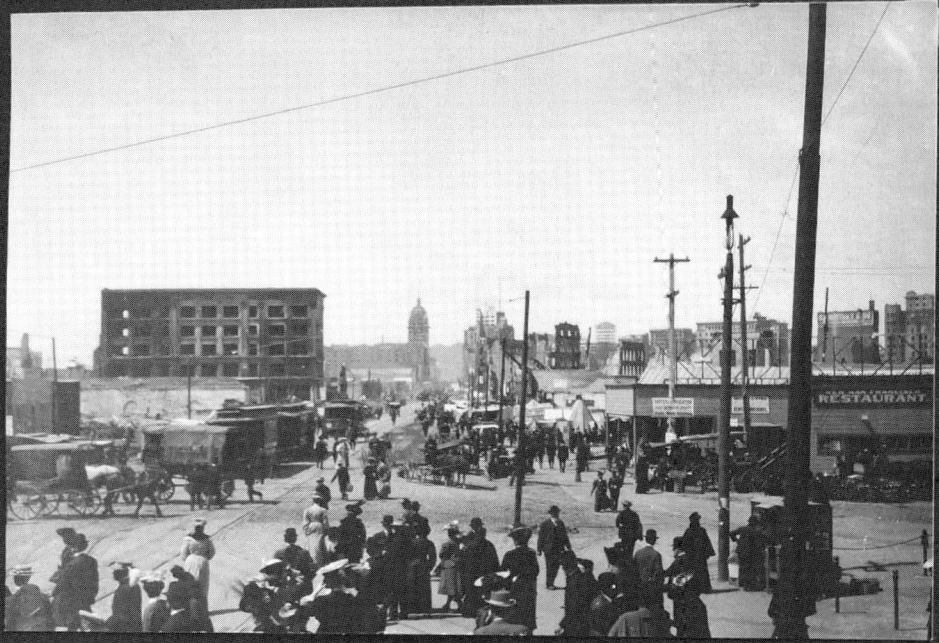

San Francisco 4 weeks after the fire

Watching the city burn from Lafayette Park

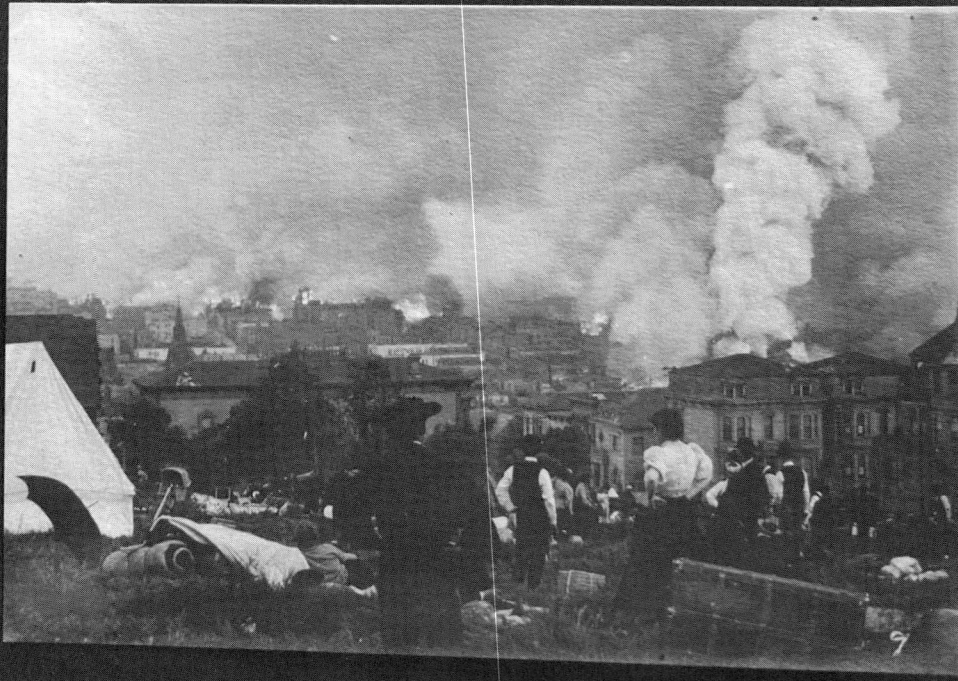

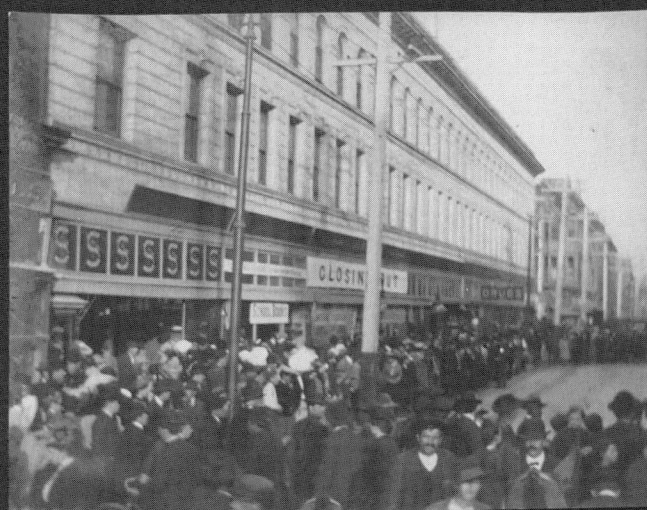

Oakland view 1 hour after Earthquake

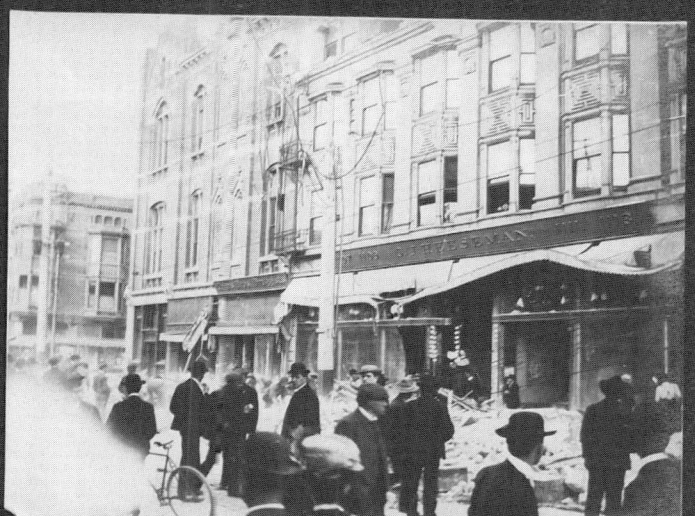

Heeseman's Store Washington St Oakland

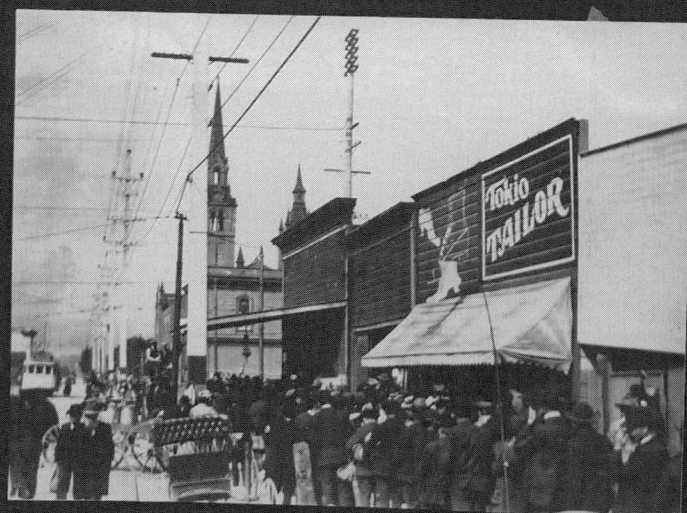

Bread Line – 13th & Franklin Sts Oakland

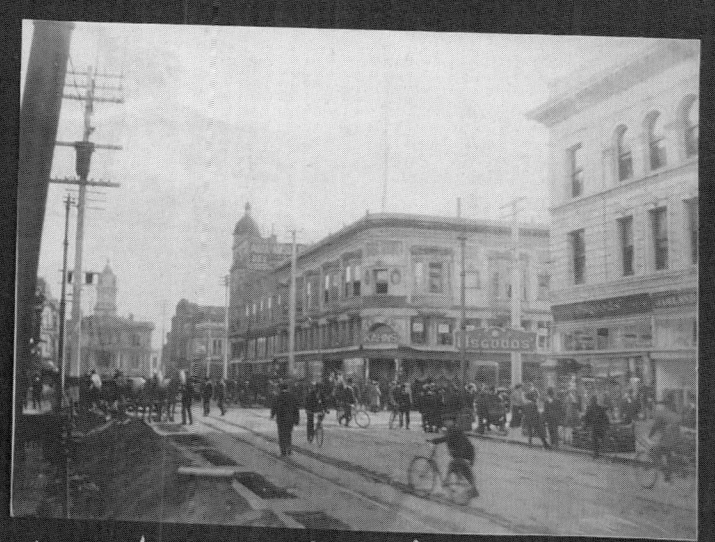

Washington St. 1 hour after Earthquake Oakland

"Oakland view 1 hour after Earthquake" This scene seems to depict more confusion than damage.

"Bread Line—13th and Franklin Sts Oakland" The "Tokio Tailor" appears in no directories of the time. In the background looms the First Presbyterian Church, at 14th and Franklin.

"Heeseman's Store, Washington St Oakland" This men's clothier was located in the 1100 block, fairly close to the Selby Candy Store.

"Washington St. 1 hour after Earthquake Oakland" Little damage present, but much bustle. The Kahn and Osgood stores are visible at right, with Oakland City Hall at far left.

When San Francisco Burned

"First Baptist Church—Jones & Telegraph Ave.— Oakland—" As can be seen here, Oakland's First Baptist Church suffered considerable damage. It was rebuilt minus the steeples, seemingly as a hedge against future damage, and still stands today.

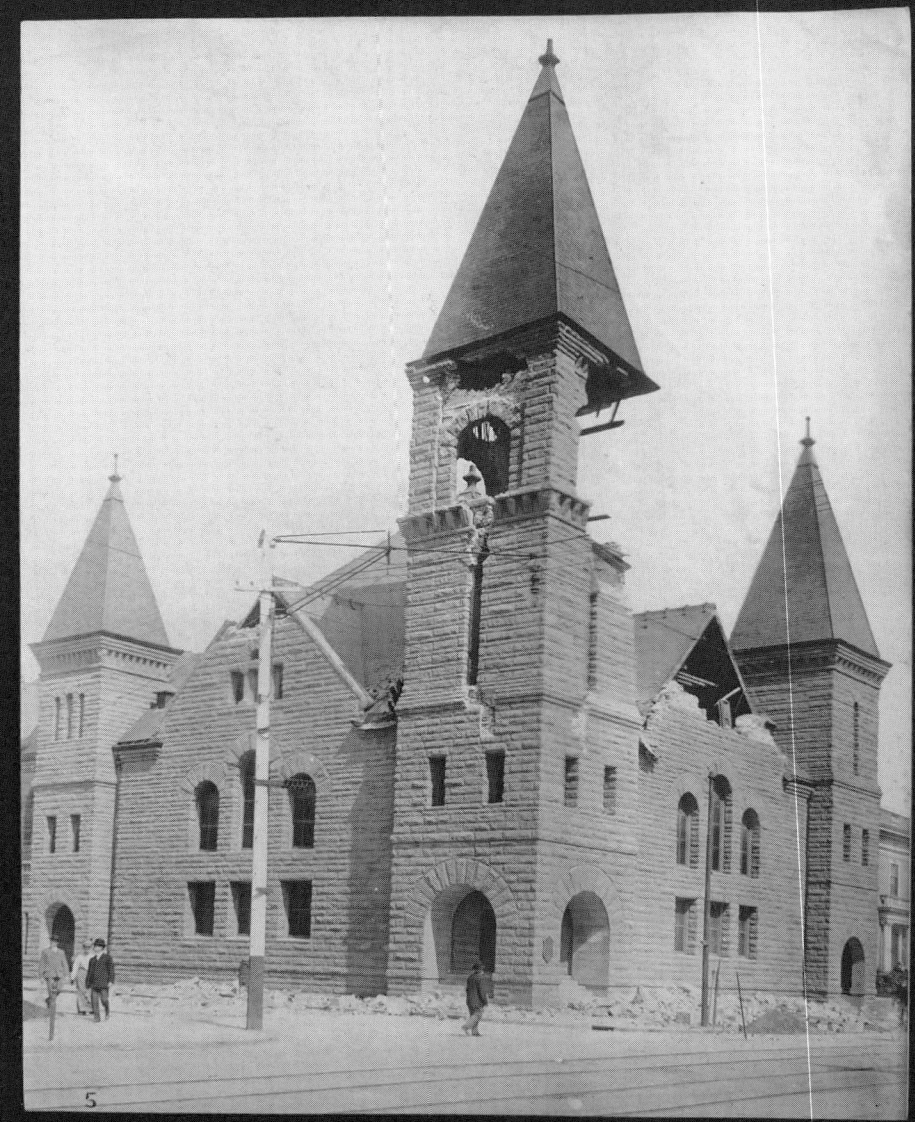

First Baptist Church - Jones & Telegraph Ave. - Oakland -

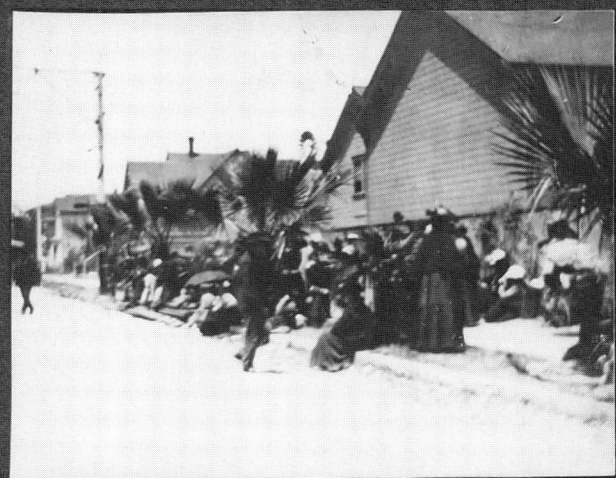

Relief Station Oakland — waiting for clothes

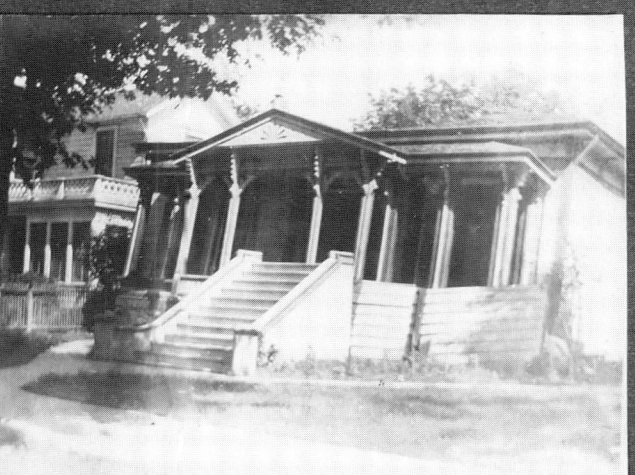

Earthquake damage — Santa Rosa —

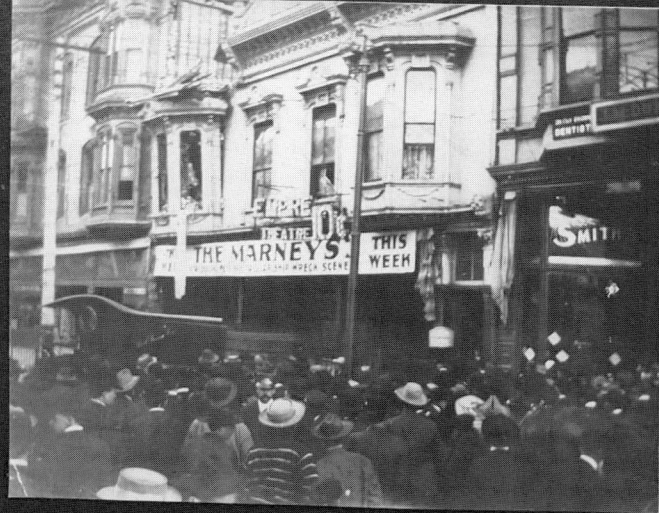

Removing dead Empire Theatre — Oakland —

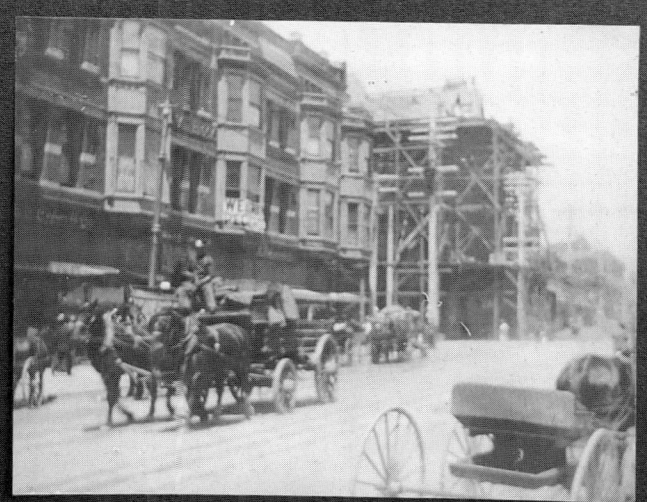

Repairing damage Washington St. — Oakland —

The Album

"Relief Station Oakland…" A blurry, candid shot of relief efforts in the East Bay.

"Removing Dead Empire Theatre— Oakland—" Taken at 466 12th. Louis Selby's caption is doubtlessly accurate, but little of any interest seems to be happening in the scene. Note the badly damaged bay window.

"Earthquake damage— Santa Rosa—" An unidentified home slumps backward on its foundation.

"Repairing damage Washington St.— Oakland—" Reconstruction efforts are seen well underway in this view.

When San Francisco Burned

"Homeless Camping in Golden Gate Park…"
Though this encampment was large, it seems to be relatively clean and orderly.

"Cooking in the Street, Chimneys being unsafe to use"
As seen in previous views on pages 90 and 92.

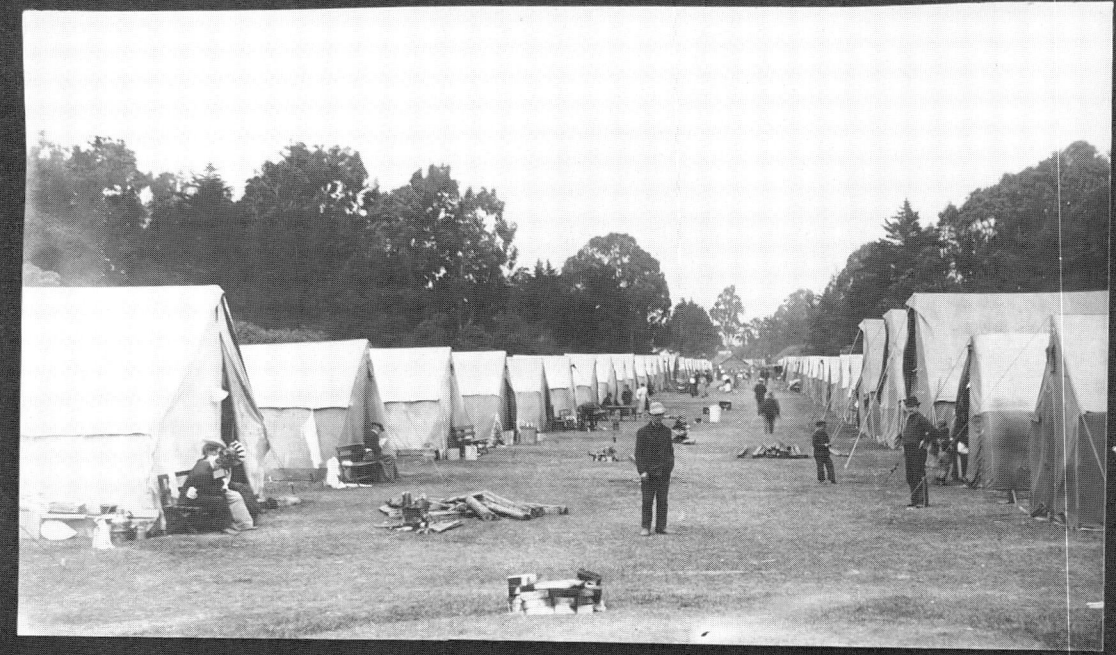

Homeless Camping in Golden Gate Park two months after disaster.

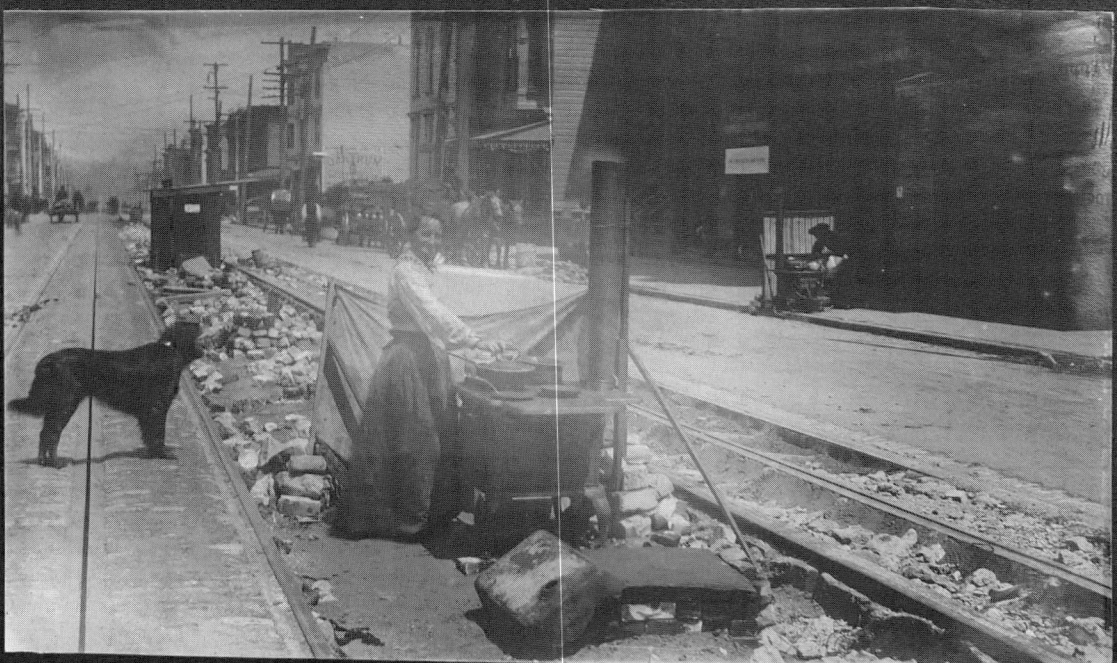

Cooking in the Street Chimneys being Unsafe to use

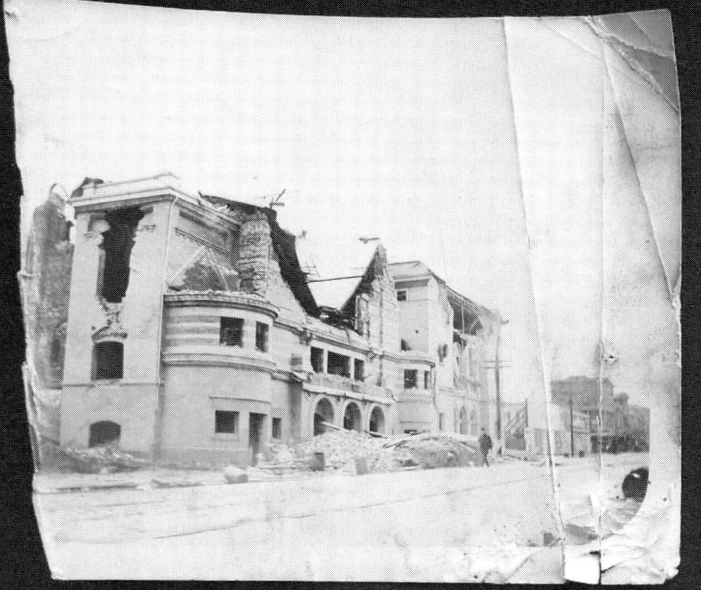

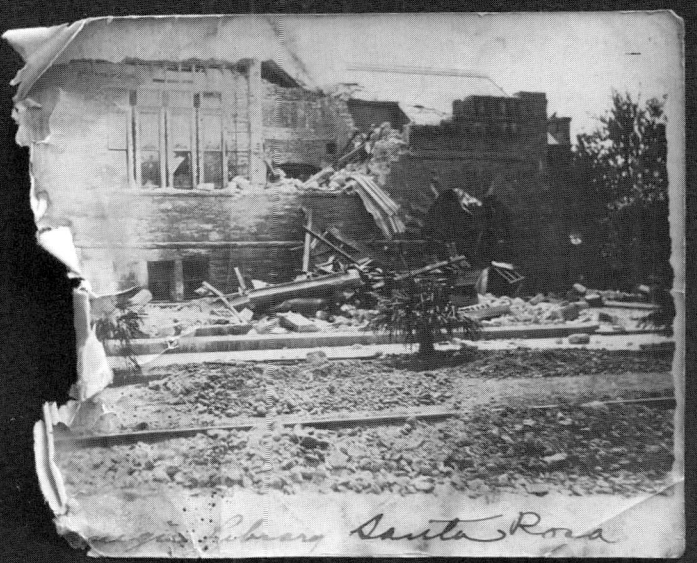

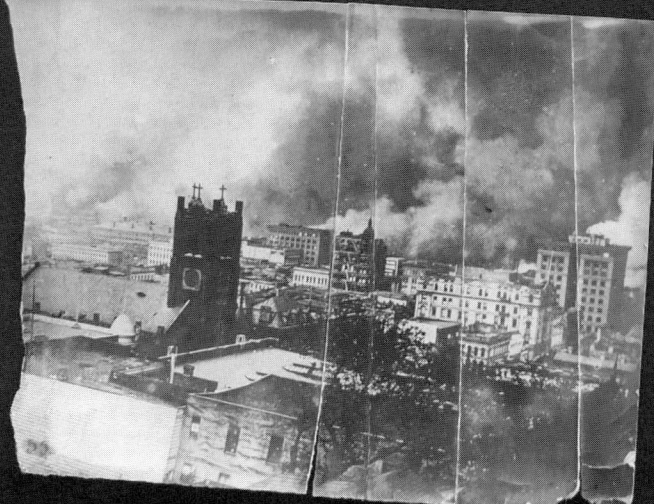

Carnegie Library, Santa Rosa

The Album

Three views left uncaptioned by Louis Selby. The one at top left shows Temple Beth Israel on Geary, seen previously on pages 15 and 46. Below it is a San Francisco fire view, with Old St. Mary's at left, the Kohl Building at right, and California Street in the middle ground. The last shot shows Santa Rosa's shattered Carnegie Library, which was rebuilt and served the public until its 1964 demolition.

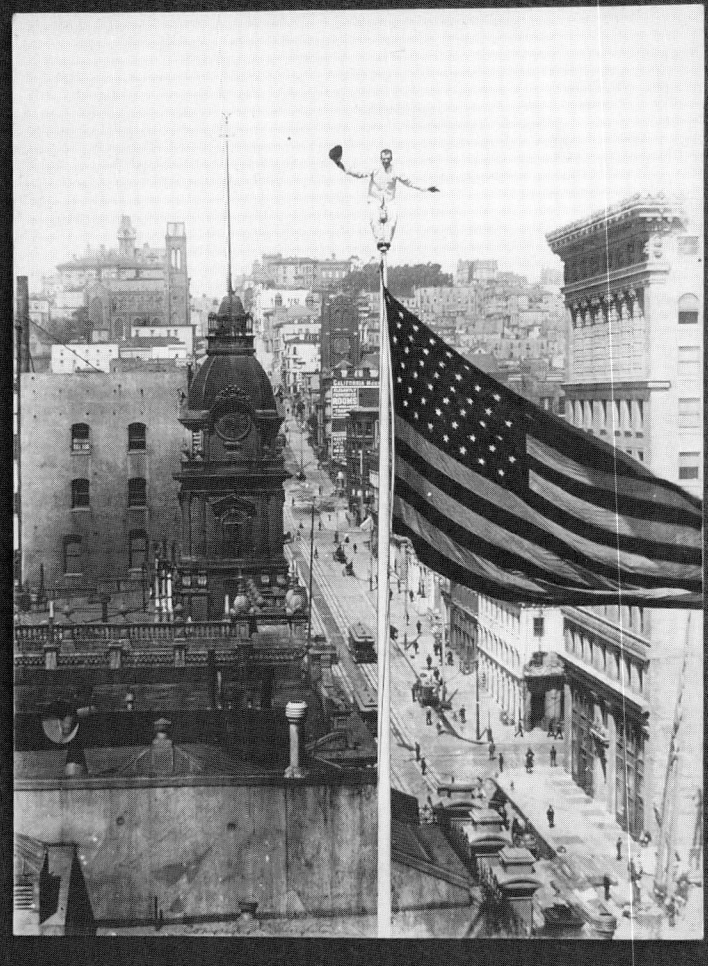

San Francisco Street Scene
before the fire".

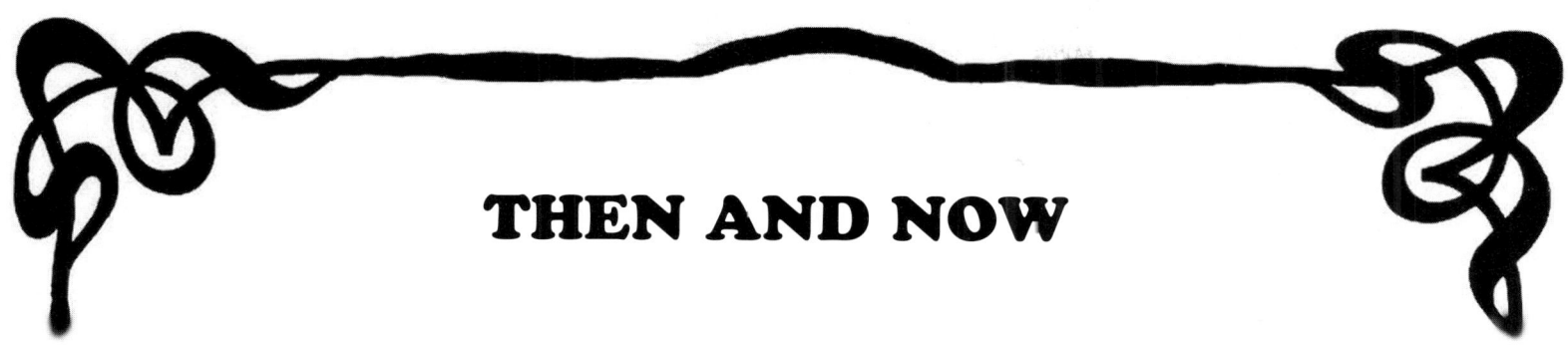

THEN AND NOW

As I planned this book over the past few years, I always envisioned blending photographs from the past with those of today's San Francisco so readers could walk backward into 1906 and visualize the disaster scenes. To that end, in January 2005, I took a trip back to the city with my daughter. While Megan attended a conference, I climbed the hills and jumped on an occasional cable car to try to combine old and new photography.

As one might imagine, it was often difficult to line up precise locations, given the traffic and growth in the city. In many cases, buildings now loom above where period photos were taken. Still, I managed to match numerous locations. In a few cases, buildings and features survived the disaster to be seen again, one hundred years afterward.

For those familiar with San Francisco, this should be a fascinating exercise. Those with less knowledge of the streetscapes should still enjoy these images, mingling yesterday with today.

The image on the following page repeats the one seen on page 57, taken by San Francisco photographer Willard Worden, who captured the Ferry Building framed in smoke just as the fires were dying down. While the Ferry Building remains, the skyscrapers framing it have dramatically changed the scene during the past century.

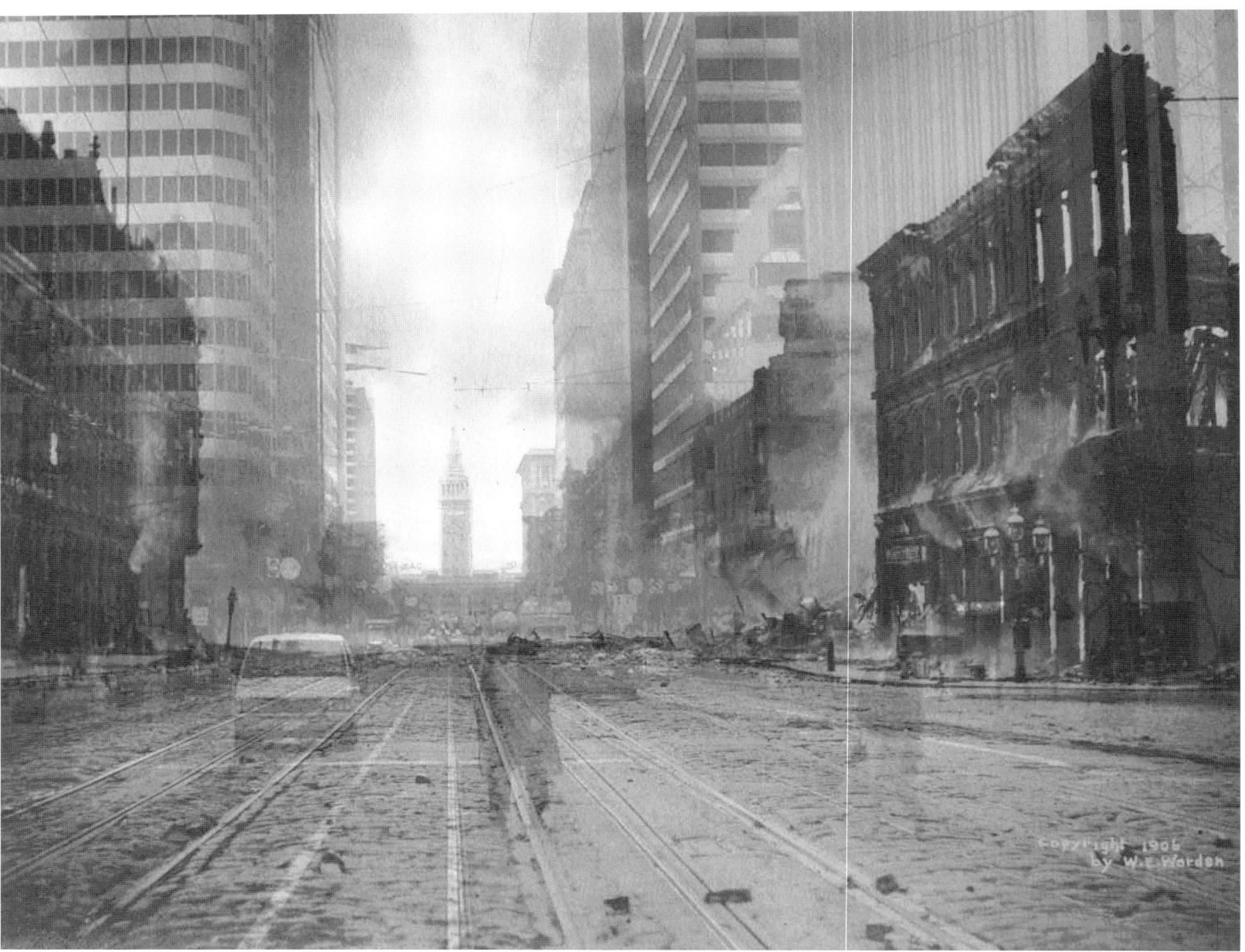

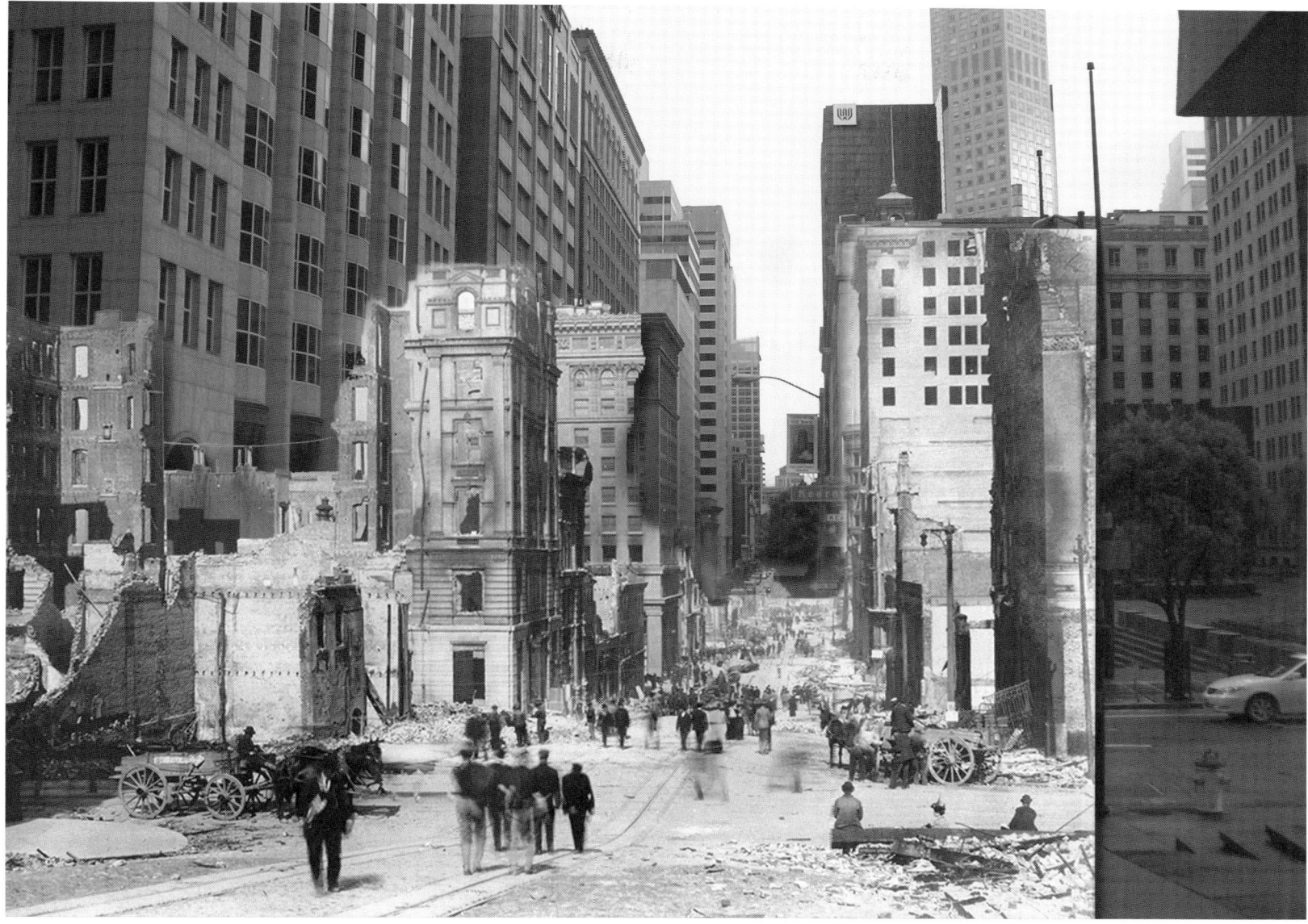

The image above shows the ruins around California and Kearney streets. Only a few of these buildings still stand, one of them being 476 California (on the street's left side and shadowed by other buildings). See also page 67.

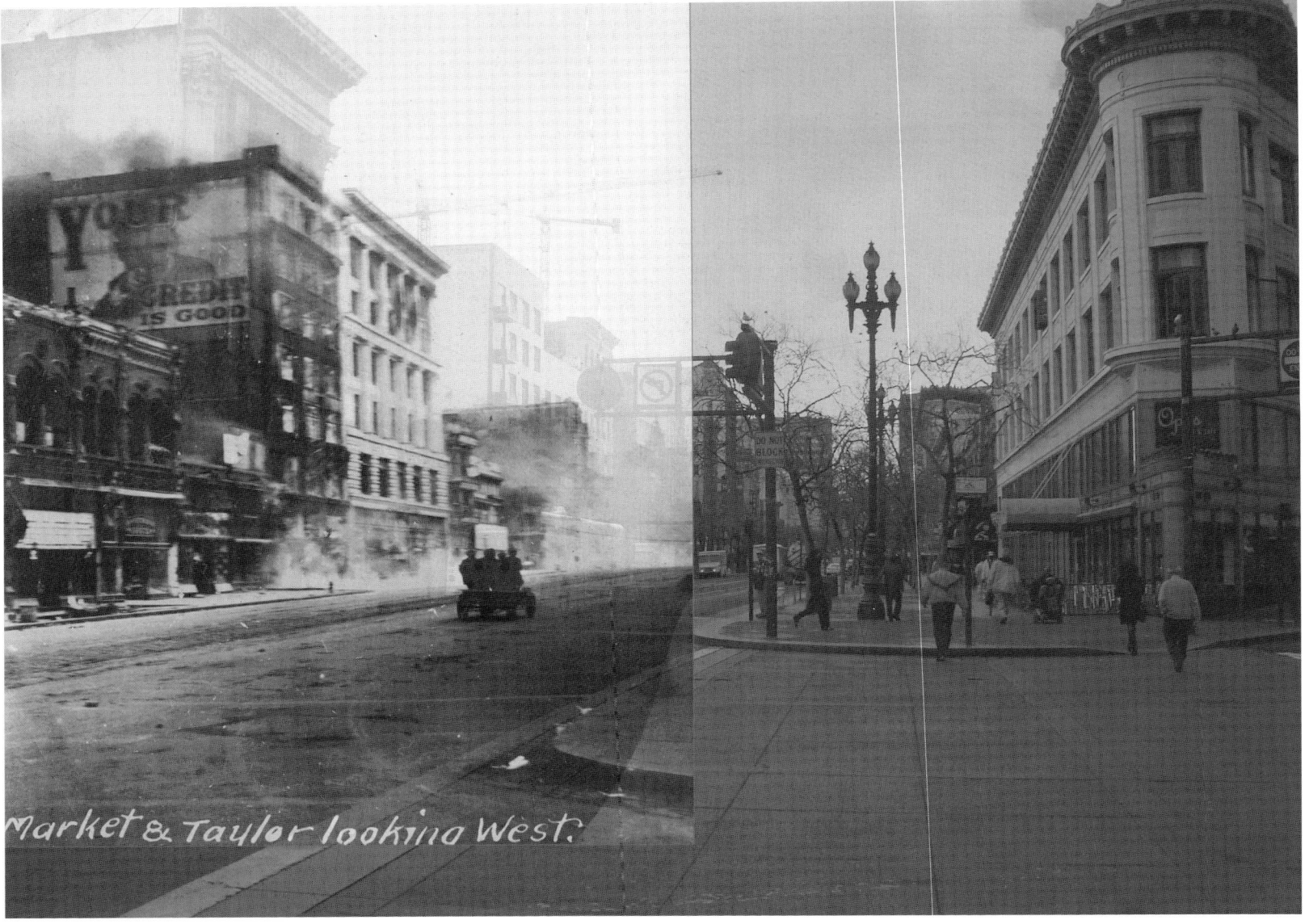

Market & Taylor looking West.

Here the Market and Taylor intersection is seen, with the left hand of the street on fire and modern-day pedestrians visible at right. See also page 33.

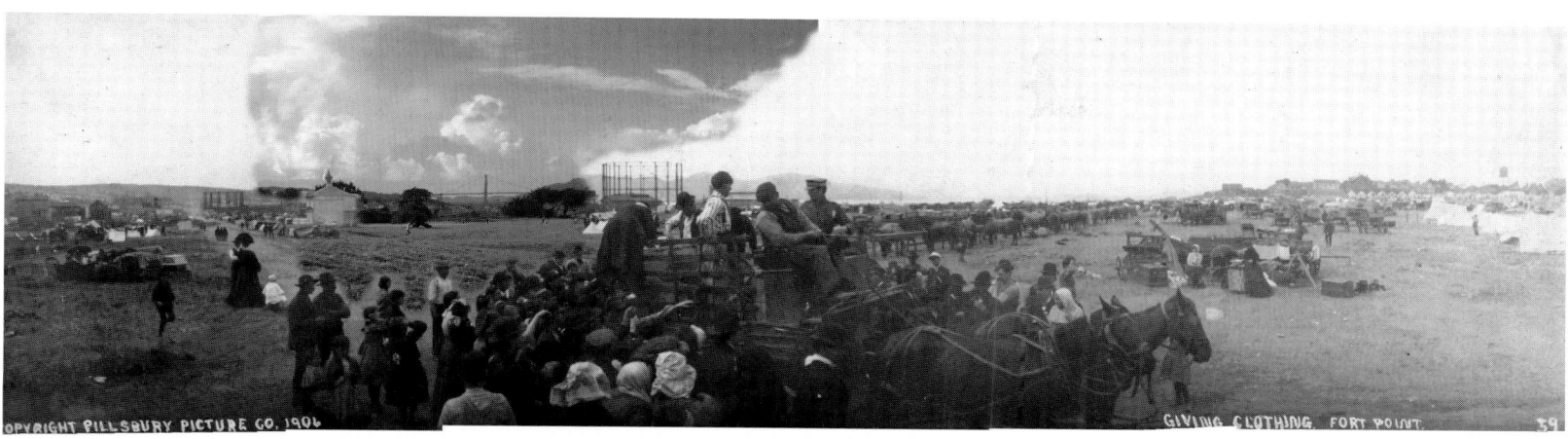

Above is the wonderful panoramic photograph seen earlier on page 79, showing soldiers handing out clothing at Fort Point. This land remains open space and now offers a great view of the Golden Gate Bridge, still only a dream in 1906.

The image at right combines 1906 and 2005 photos of the Market and Fifth intersection. The Emporium is the dark building at right, and the Call Building is seen dimly at center. See also page 7.

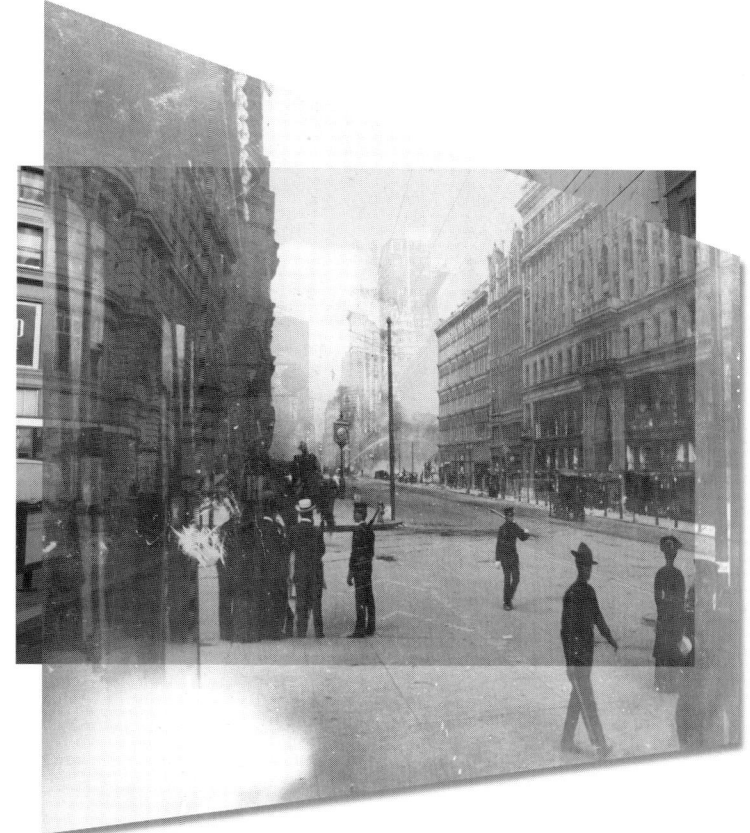

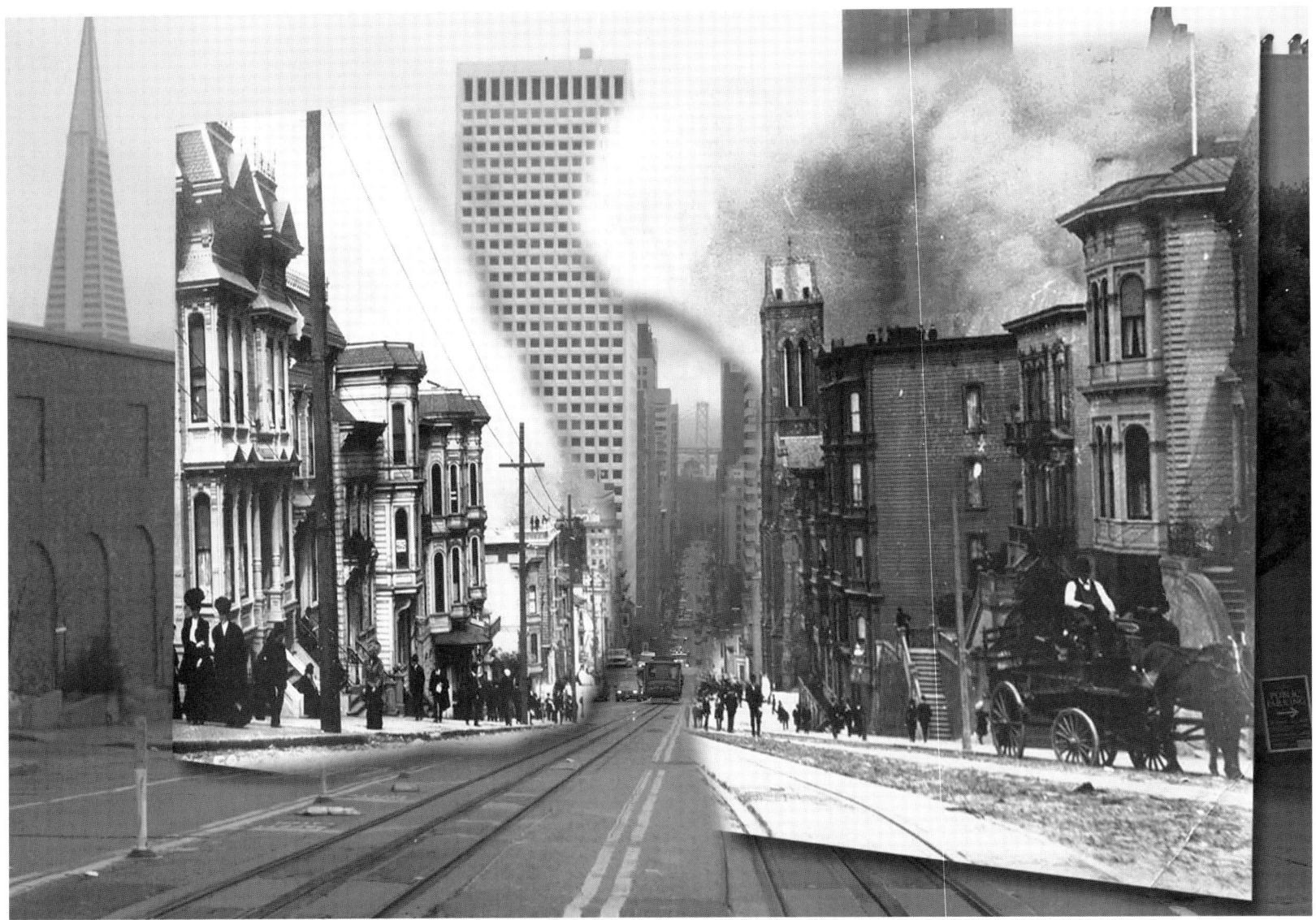

The image at right was taken at California and Powell streets, looking into downtown San Francisco. The 1906 photograph shows the city on fire as her citizens climb the hill to safety. Today, the Bay Bridge is barely visible in the far center, with the Transamerica Pyramid at left. See also page 56.

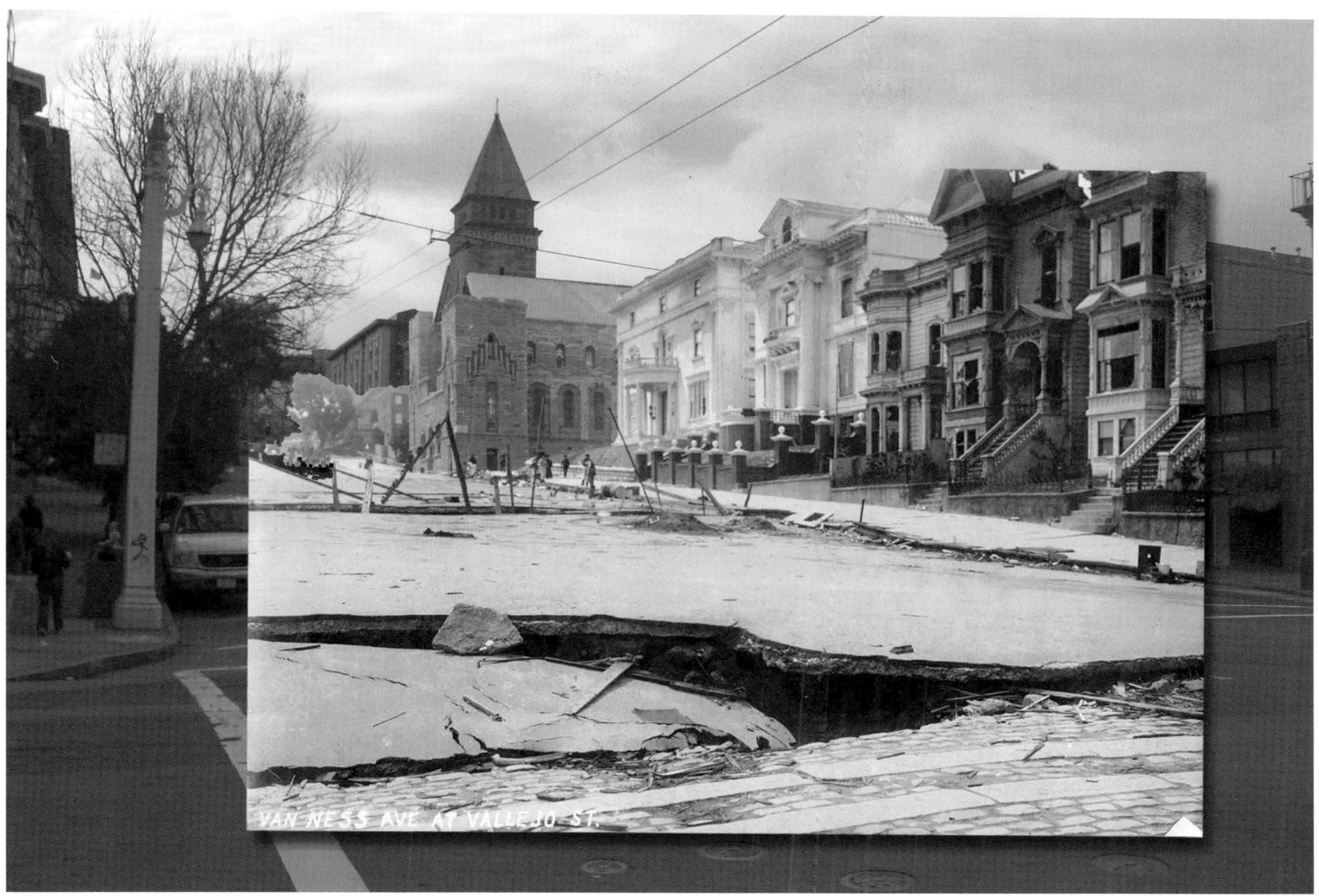

The photographs above were taken at Van Ness and Vallejo, looking toward St. Brigid's Catholic Church and the intersection with Broadway. One was taken in 1906 and the other ninety-nine years later. The remaining buildings are the same, with some changed elements due to past damage or remodeling. This area suffered severe ground disruption from the earthquake. See also page 93.

111

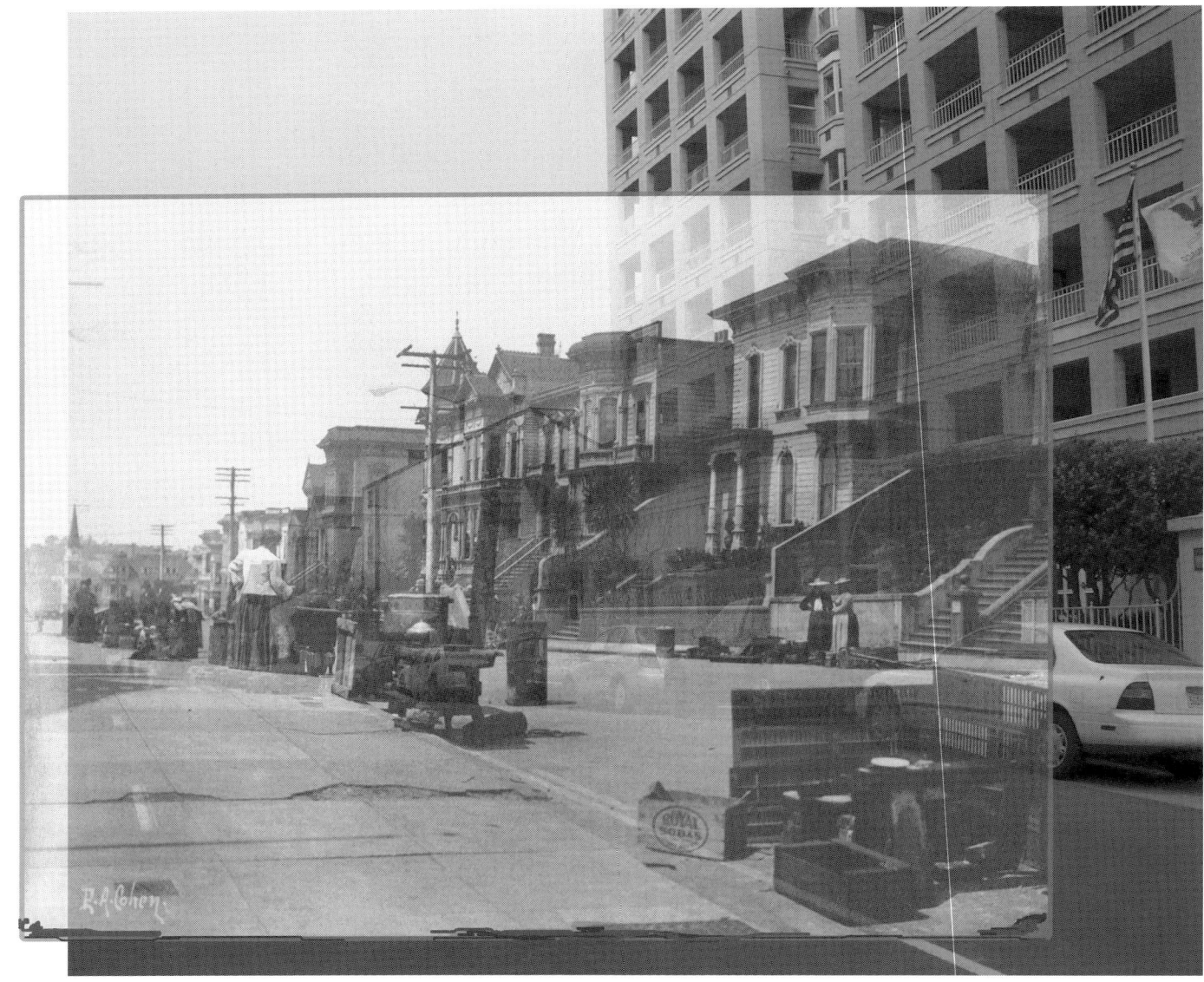

The photo above was taken on Post Street near Gough. All of the 1906 buildings are now gone, replaced by modern apartment buildings and other structures. The earlier photo shows a lineup of cooking stoves placed in the street for safety. See also page 92.

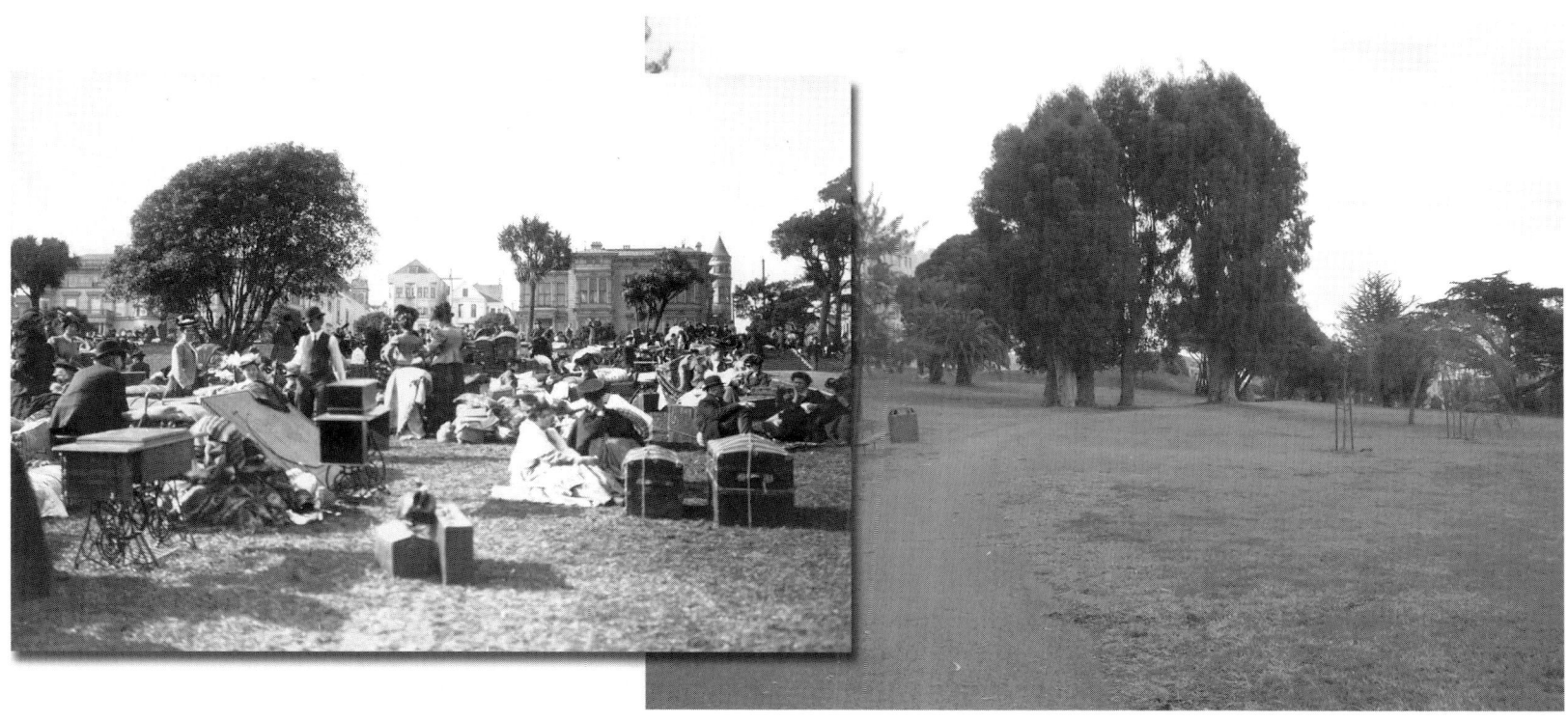

Above, Jefferson Square is seen with the 1906 homeless on the left, and today's peaceful scenery at right. See also page 78.

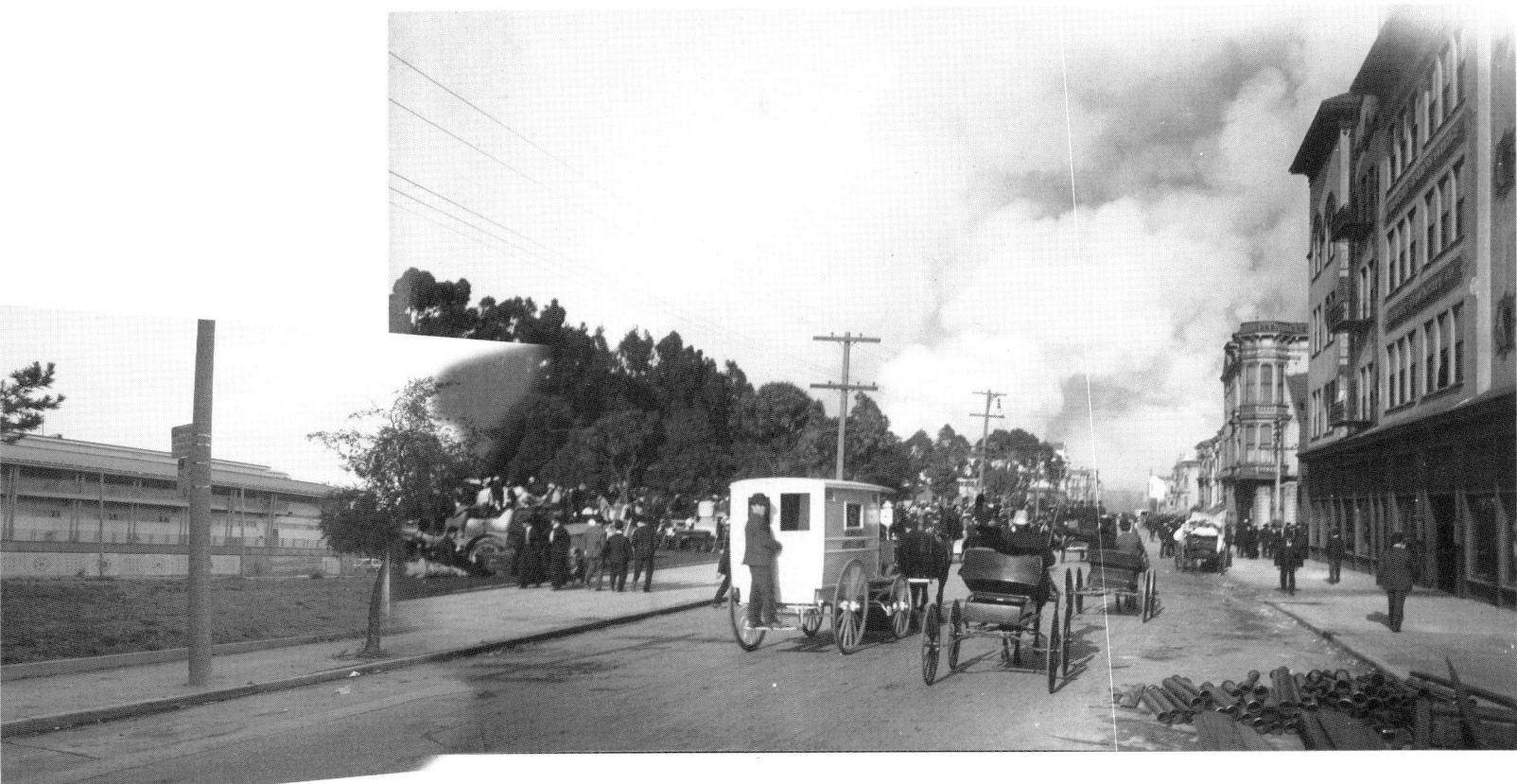

The photo above shows a horse-drawn ambulance heading east on Golden Gate Avenue toward Gough Street. See also page 23.

TIMELINE

You will find a timeline of events for the disaster on the next several pages. This timeline was prepared through exhaustive research by Gladys Hansen, a San Francisco historian and avid researcher. Mrs. Hansen co-authored the book *Denial of Disaster* with retired San Francisco Fire Chief Emmet Condon in 1989. Both of these historians have made substantial contributions to documenting San Francisco's history, leaving a wonderful legacy. Chief Condon passed away in 2007 and Gladys Hansen in 2011. *Denial of Disaster* was published by Cameron and Company of San Francisco is 1989. Our use of this timeline is provided with the publisher's permission.

APRIL 18, 1906

San Francisco was wrecked by a great earthquake at 5:13 a.m., and then destroyed by the great fire that burned for four days. Hundreds, perhaps thousands of trapped persons died when south-of-Market Street tenements collapsed as the ground liquefied beneath them. Most of those buildings immediately caught fire, and trapped victims could not be rescued. Reevaluation of the 1906 data during the 1980s placed the total earthquake death toll at more than 3,000 from all causes. Damage was estimated at $500,000,000 in 1906 dollars.

Fire Chief Engineer Dennis T. Sullivan was mortally wounded when the dome of the California Theatre and hotel crashed through the fire station in which he was living at 410-412 Bush St. Acting Chief Engineer John Dougherty commanded fire operations.

The earthquake shock was felt from Coos Bay, Oregon, to Los Angeles, and as far east as central Nevada, an area of about 375,000 square miles, approximately half of which was in the Pacific Ocean. The region of destructive effect extended from the southern part of Fresno County to Eureka, about 400 miles, and for a distance of twenty-five to thirty miles on either side of the fault zone. The distribution of intensity within the region of destruction was uneven. Of course, all structures standing on or crossing the rift were destroyed or badly damaged. Many trees standing near the fault were either uprooted or broken off. Perhaps the most marked destruction of trees was near Loma Prieta in Santa Cruz County, where, according to Dr. John C.

Branner of Stanford University, "The forest looked as though a swath had been cut through it two hundred feet in width." In little less than a mile, he counted 345 earthquake cracks running in all directions.

The U.S. Post Office at Seventh and Mission Streets was dreadfully damaged by the earthquake. Assistant to the Postmaster Burke said, "walls had been thrown into the middle of various rooms, destroying furniture and covering everything with dust. In the main corridors the marble was split and cracked, while the mosaics were shattered and had come rattling down upon the floor. Chandeliers were rent and twisted by falling arches and ceilings."

Fireman James O'Neill, drawing water for the horses in Fire Station No. 4 on Howard Street opposite Hawthorne, was killed when a wall of the American Hotel collapsed onto the fire station.

Police officer Max Fenner was mortally wounded when a wall at 138 Mason Street collapsed on him.

All telephone and telegraph communications stopped within the city, although some commercial telegraph circuits to New York and to India, via the Pacific cable at the Ocean Beach, remained in temporary operation.

A messenger arrived at Fort Mason at 6:30 a.m. with orders from Gen. Funston to send all available troops to the Hall of Justice.

First army troops from Fort Mason reported to Mayor Schmitz at the Hall of Justice around 7 a.m.

At 8 a.m., the 10th, 29th, 38th, 66th, 67th, 70th, and 105th companies of Coast Artillery, Troops I and K of the 14th Cavalry, and the First, Ninth, and 24th batteries of field artillery arrived downtown to take up patrol.

Seventy-five soldiers from companies C and D, Engineer Corps, were assigned to the Financial District at 8 a.m., and another 75 along Market from Third Street to the City Hall at Grove and Larkin streets.

A major aftershock struck at 8:14 a.m., and caused the collapse of many damaged buildings.

The second day session of the Grand Chapter of the Royal Arch Masons of the state of California's fifty-second annual convocation was held. The group met after the earthquake but evacuated before the temple at Montgomery and Post streets was destroyed by fire. The Masons listed the date as April 18, A.I. 2436, A.D.

At 10 a.m., Headquarters and First Battalion 22nd Infantry, were brought from Fort McDowell by boat, and were held for a time in reserve at O'Farrell Street. They were later utilized as patrols and to assist the fire department.

At about 10:05 a.m., the DeForest Wireless Telegraph Station at San Diego radioed press reports of the disaster at San Francisco to the USS *Chicago*. Admiral Caspar Goodrich immediately ordered fires started under all boilers, and after a confirmation message from the mayor of San Diego, the *Chicago* steamed full speed for San Francisco. It was the first time wireless telegraphy was used in a major natural disaster.

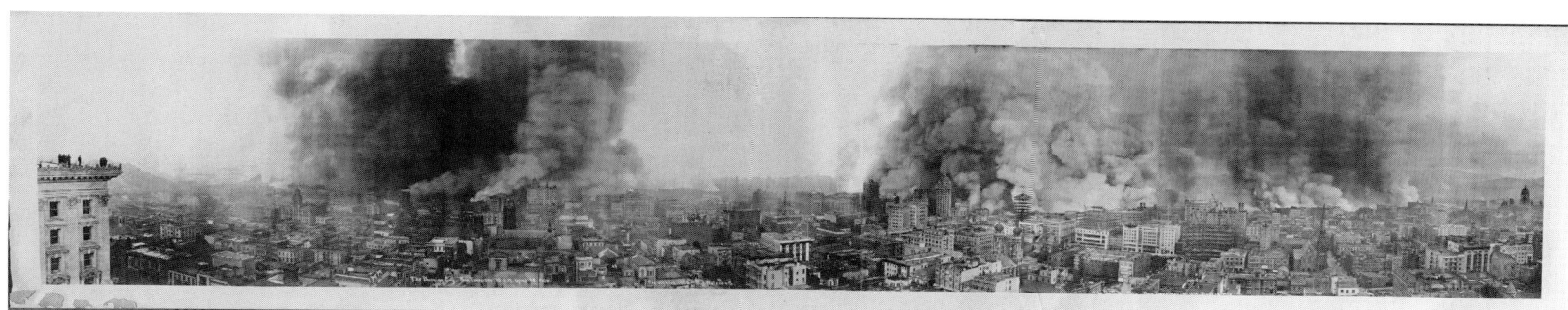

Above: The fire panorama seen above the Selby family desk on page xviii. Below: A post-fire aerial image of San Francisco, looking west from the Ferry Building and with a perspective similar to the bird's-eye view at the end of this section.

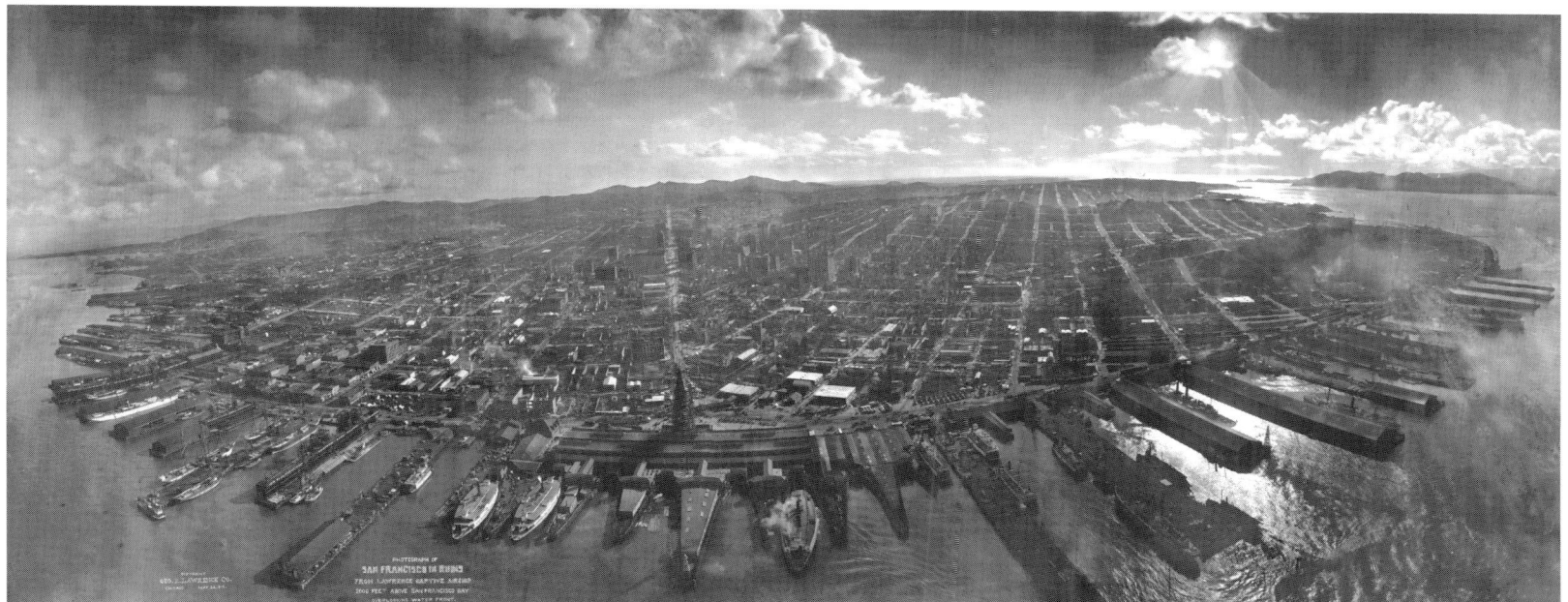

At 10:30 a.m., the USS *Preble* from Mare Island, under the command of Lt. Frederick Newton Freeman, landed a hospital shore party at the foot of Howard Street to help the wounded and dying who sought help at Harbor Emergency Hospital.

Another fire broke out at 395 Hayes Street, on the southwest corner of Hayes and Gough. It would become known as the "Ham and Egg" fire, and would destroy part of the Western Addition, the Mechanics' Pavilion, and City Hall, and then jump Market Street at Ninth.

General Funston's staff abandoned the Department of California's headquarters in the Phelan Building, across from the Palace Hotel, at 11 a.m. They did manage to save valuable records.

Winchester Hotel caught fire at Third and Stevenson streets and collapsed at 11 a.m.

Fort Miley troops, the 25th and 64th companies Coast Artillery, arrived at 11:30 a.m.

Two earthquakes occur in Los Angeles just before noon, about ten minutes apart. The quaking began as crowds gathered around bulletin boards to read the latest telegraphic dispatches from San Francisco. Thousands ran in panic when the earthquakes struck.

The Hearst Building at Third and Market streets caught fire at noon.

Evacuation of the injured from Mechanics' Pavilion, Grove and Larkin, began at noon because of the spreading "Ham and Egg" fire. The wounded were taken to Golden Gate Park, Children's Hospital, and the Presidio.

Mechanics' Pavilion took fire at 1 p.m.

St. Mary's Hospital at First and Bryant streets was abandoned to the fire at 1 p.m. Patients were loaded aboard the ferryboat *Modoc* and taken to Oakland.

Entire area in the Financial District, behind the Hall of Justice, was on fire by 1 p.m.

Fires so threatened the Portsmouth Square area by 1 p.m. that General Manager Hewitt of the Department of Electricity decided to abandon the Central Fire Alarm Station at 15 Brenham Place in Chinatown.

Restaurant atop the Call, or Claus Spreckels Building, at Third and Market streets, took fire at 2 p.m.

Postal Telegraph operators transmitted their last message to the outside world as army troops ordered them from the building at 534 Market St., opposite Second St., at 2:20 p.m. because of the approaching fire.

Latest casualty count: 750 people seriously injured people were being treated at various hospitals at 2:30 p.m.

Dynamiting of buildings around the U.S. Mint at Fifth and Mission streets began at 2:30 p.m.

U.S. Army Signal Corps established Ferry Building telegraph operations at 3 p.m.

Mayor Schmitz appointed the Committee of Fifty at 3 p.m. at the Hall of Justice. The mayor also said: "Let it be given out that three men have already been shot down without mercy for looting. Let it also be understood that the order has been given to all soldiers and policemen to do likewise without hesitation in the cases of any and all miscreants who may seek to take advantage of the city's awful misfortune."

The Mayor appointed ex-Mayor James Phelan to head the Relief Committee.

Fifty or more corpses had been buried by the police in Portsmouth Square by 5 p.m because the morgue and police pistol range could hold no more bodies.

Mayor Schmitz, at 8 p.m., was still confident that a good part of downtown could be saved.

Unfortunately, a possible arsonist set fire to the Delmonico Restaurant in the Alcazar Theatre Building on O'Farrell near Stockton, and that blaze burned into Downtown and to Nob Hill.

War Department received a telegram from Gen. Funston at 8:40 p.m., Pacific Coast time, that asked for thousands of tents and all available rations. Funston placed the death toll at 1,000.

Firefighters attempted to make a stand at 9 p.m. along Powell St. between Sutter and Pine, but it was unsuccessful in keeping the fire from sweeping up Nob Hill.

Crocker-Woolworth Bank Building at Post and Market took fire at 9 p.m.

APRIL 19, 1906

Governor Pardee arrived in Oakland at 2 a.m. He was supposed to arrive three hours earlier, but his train was stalled because of sinking of the track in the Susuin marshes. St. Francis Hotel at Union Square caught fire at 2:30 a.m.

Mayor Schmitz and Capt. Thomas Magner of Engine No. 3 found a cistern at the Hopkins Mansion, Mason and California streets, at 4 a.m., and attempted to keep the fire from burning the structure. They were not successful.

Secretary of War Taft at 4 a.m. ordered 200,000 rations sent to San Francisco from the Vancouver Barracks.

Secretary Taft ordered all hospital, wall, and conical tents sent to San Francisco from forts Douglas, Logan, Snelling, Sheridan, and Russell, and from army posts at Vancouver, San Antonio, and the Presidio of Monterey.

Secretary Taft wired Gen. Funston at 4:55 a.m. that all tents in the U.S. Army were en route to San Francisco.

The San Francisco *Call*, *Chronicle*, and *Examiner* newspapers printed a combined newspaper on the presses of the *Oakland Herald*.

176 prisoners moved from city prison to Alcatraz.

U.S.S. *Chicago* arrived in San Francisco Bay at 6 p.m.

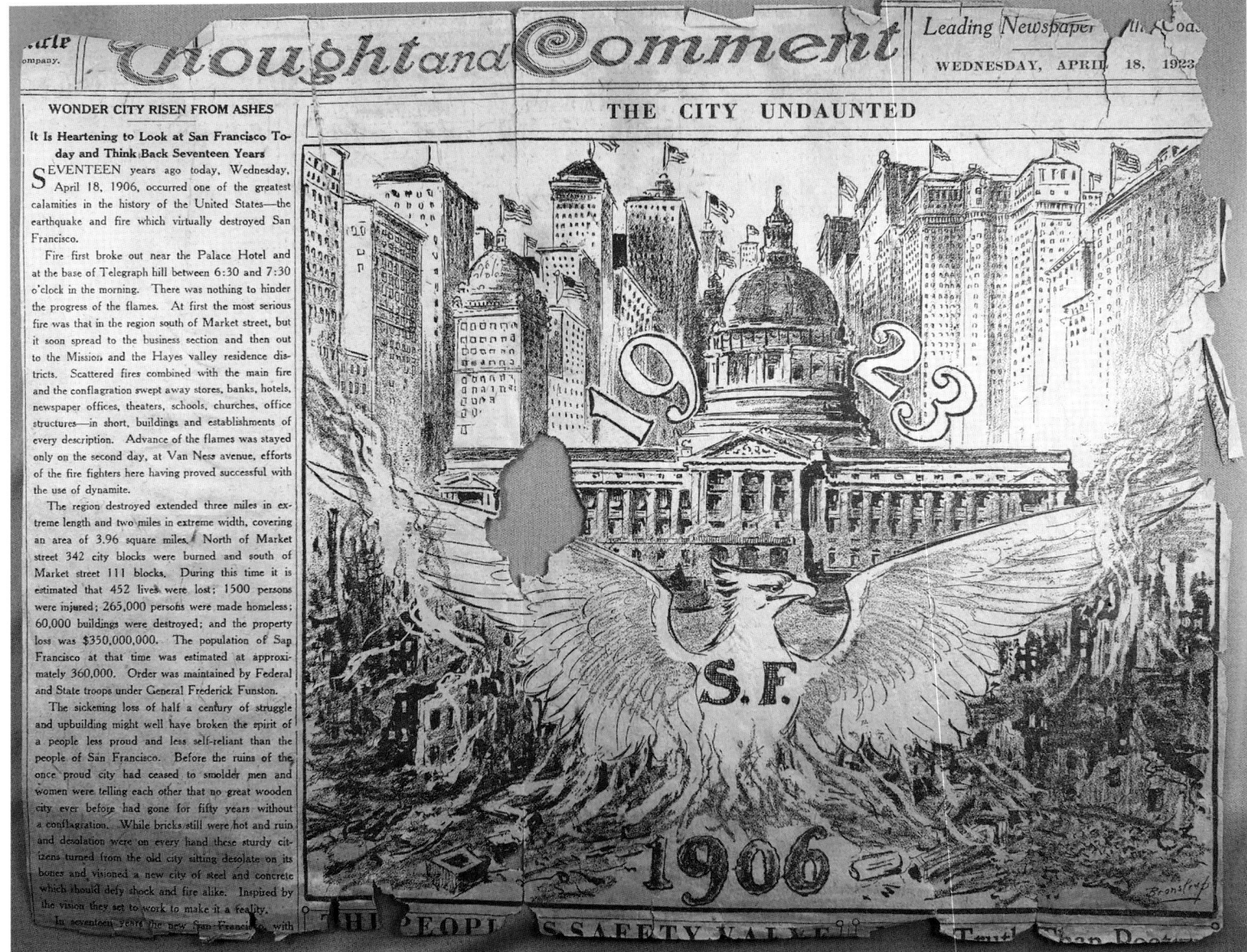

A tattered clipping from the Selby album demonstrates how the indominable spirit of San Francisco remained intact seventeen years after the twin disasters.

Fire reached Van Ness Avenue during the evening. The army dynamited mansions along the street in an attempt to build a firebreak. Demolition to stop the fire was ordered by Col. Charles Morris of the Artillery Corps.

APRIL 20, 1906
The fire burned as far as Franklin Street by 5 a.m., then attempted to circle south.

At the foot of Van Ness Avenue, sixteen enlisted men and two officers from the U.S.S. *Chicago* supervised the rescue of 20,000 refugees fleeing the fire. It was the largest evacuation by sea in history and was probably as large as the evacuation of Dunkirk during World War II.

Fire approached the Appraisers' Building for a second time at 3 p.m. Lt. Freeman attempted to pump saltwater from the bay but found that his hose connections would not fit those of the fire department, so the effort was abandoned.

Gen. Funston issued General Order No. 37, which placed Lt. Col. George Torney of the Medical Department in full control of sanitation in San Francisco.

Gen. Funston wired the War Department at 8:30 p.m. to report on the fire. He advised that Fort Mason has been saved, and some looters have been shot. His telegram said most casualties are in the poorer districts, south of Market; not many had been killed in better portions of the city.

APRIL 21, 1906

Haig Patigian's statue of President McKinley, commissioned for the city of Arcata, was found in the rubble of a local foundry and saved by several artisans who carried it into the street.

The fire that swept the Mission District was stopped at 20th and Dolores streets by three thousand volunteers and a few firemen who fought the blaze with knapsacks, brooms, and a little water from an operating hydrant at 20th and Church.

APRIL 22, 1906
Fire Chief Engineer Dennis T. Sullivan died at the Army General Hospital at the Presidio at 1 a.m.

Major-General Adolphus W. Greely, commander of the army's Pacific Division, returned to San Francisco.

United Railroad crews began stringing temporary overhead trolley wires on Market Street, but did not repair the cable traction system in the street.

APRIL 23, 1906
Governor Pardee told a newspaper reporter: "The work of rebuilding San Francisco has commenced, and I expect to see the great metropolis replaced on a much grander scale than ever before."

Imperial decree on the 30th Day of the Third Moon from Empress Dowager of China to send a personal contribution to the relief of the San Francisco sufferers. President Theodore Roosevelt declined the offer, as well as donations from other foreign governments.

BIRD'S EYE VIEW OF SAN FRANCISCO.

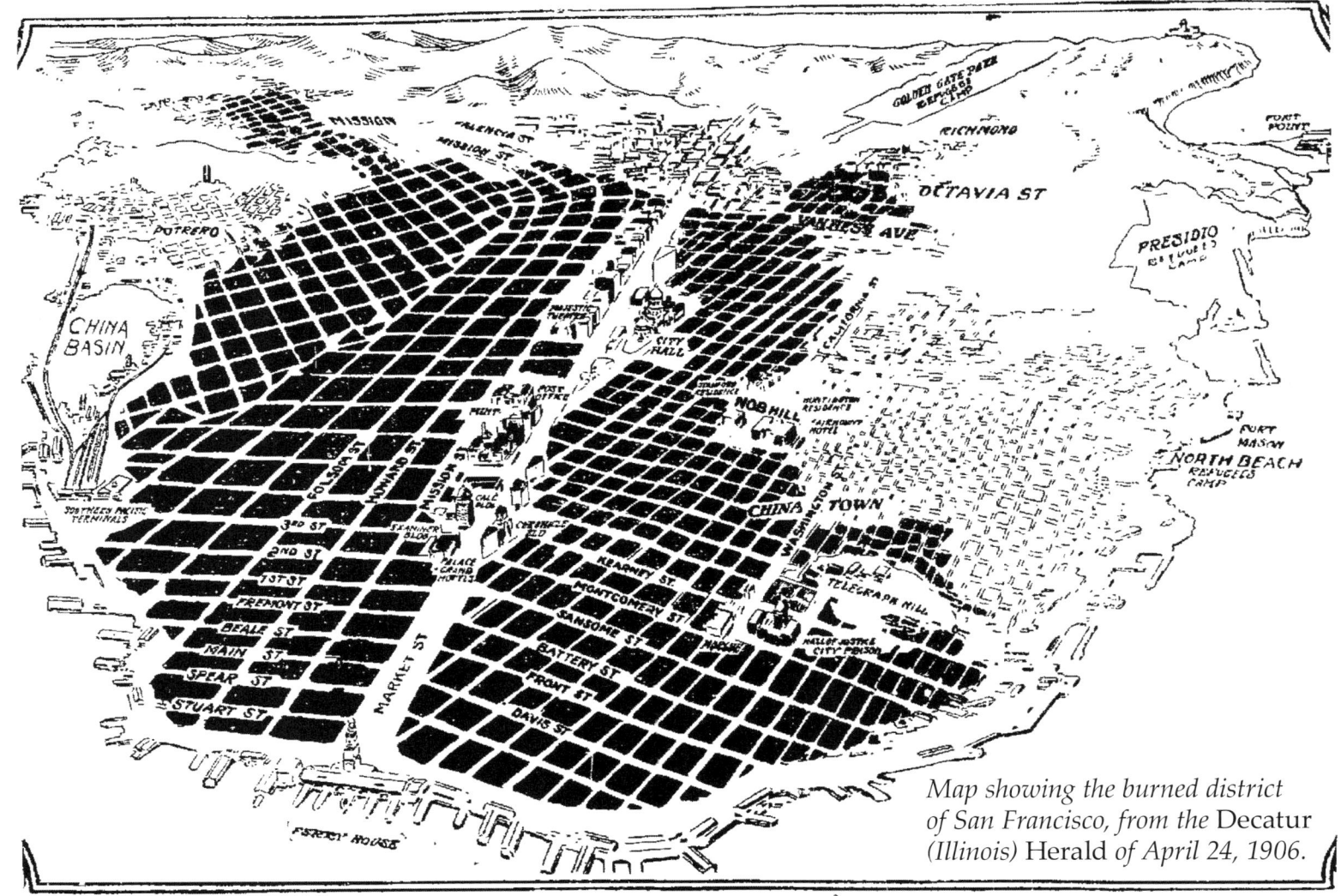

Map showing the burned district of San Francisco, from the Decatur (Illinois) Herald *of April 24, 1906.*

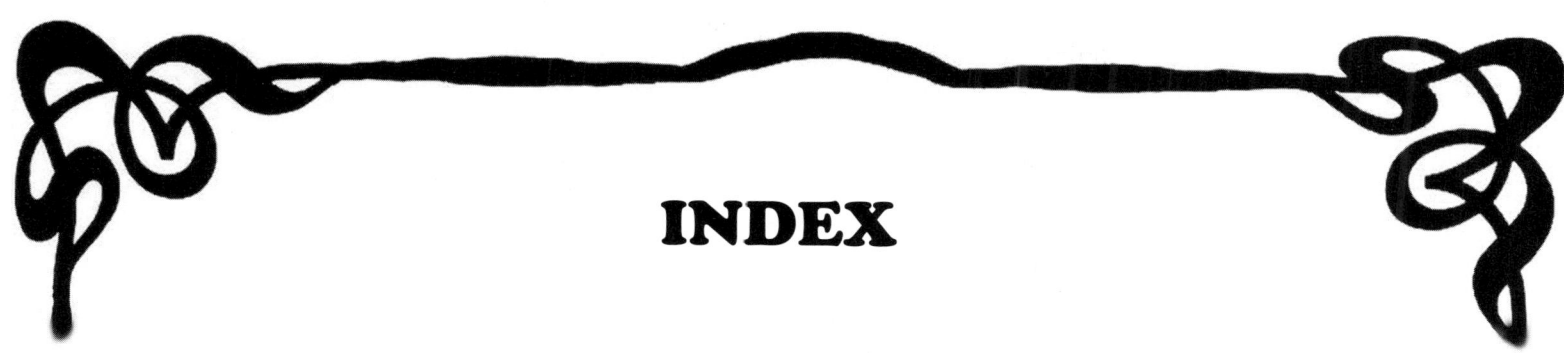

INDEX

More Great Books Celebrating California History and Culture

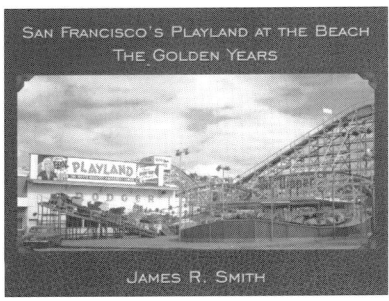
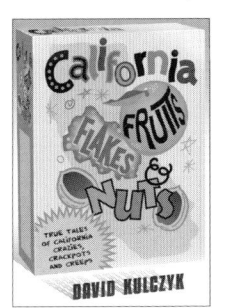
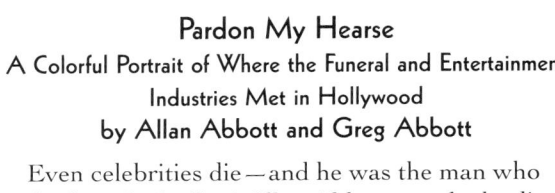
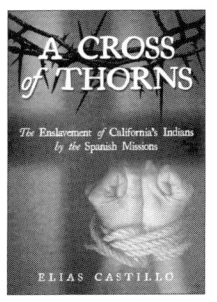
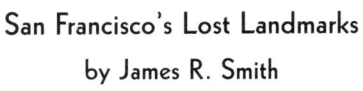
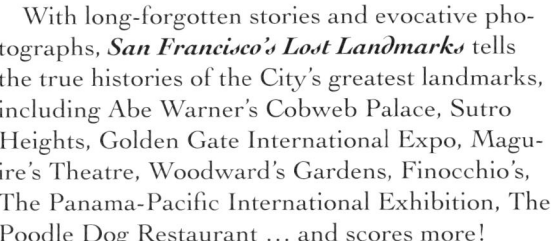